THE CONSTITUTION OF THE ~~~~
FEDERATION

cur-
tion
sia's
and
tion
ebi-
t as
ent;
rm-
the
the
for
s on
:on-
1tial
ving
the

Constitutional Systems of the World
General Editors: Peter Leyland and Andrew Harding
Associate Editors: Benjamin L Berger and Alexander Fischer

In the era of globalisation, issues of constitutional law and good governance are being seen increasingly as vital issues in all types of society. Since the end of the Cold War, there have been dramatic developments in democratic and legal reform, and post-conflict societies are also in the throes of reconstructing their governance systems. Even societies already firmly based on constitutional governance and the rule of law have undergone constitutional change and experimentation with new forms of governance; and their constitutional systems are increasingly subjected to comparative analysis and transplantation. Constitutional texts for practically every country in the world are now easily available on the Internet. However, texts which enable one to understand the true context, purposes, interpretation and incidents of a constitutional system are much harder to locate, and are often extremely detailed and descriptive. This series seeks to provide scholars and students with accessible introductions to the constitutional systems of the world, supplying both a road map for the novice and, at the same time, a deeper understanding of the key historical, political and legal events which have shaped the constitutional landscape of each country. Each book in this series deals with a single country, and each author is an expert in their field.

Published volumes

The Constitution of the United Kingdom
The Constitution of the United States
The Constitution of Vietnam
The Constitution of South Africa
The Constitution of Japan
The Constitution of Germany
The Constitution of Finland
The Constitution of Australia
The Constitution System of Thailand
The Constitution of the Republic of Austria

Forthcoming titles in this series

The Constitution of France
Sophie Boyron

The Constitution of Ireland
Colm O'Cinneide

Link to series website

http://www.hartpub.co.uk/series/csw

The Constitution of the Russian Federation

A Contextual Analysis

Jane Henderson

·HART·
PUBLISHING

OXFORD AND PORTLAND, OREGON

2011

Published in the United Kingdom by Hart Publishing Ltd
16C Worcester Place, Oxford, OX1 2JW
Telephone: +44 (0)1865 517530
Fax: +44 (0)1865 510710
E-mail: mail@hartpub.co.uk

Website: http://www.hartpub.co.uk
Published in North America (US and Canada) by
Hart Publishing
c/o International Specialized Book Services
920 NE 58th Avenue, Suite 300
Portland, OR 97213-3786
USA
Tel: +1 503 287 3093 or toll-free: (1) 800 944 6190
Fax: +1 503 280 8832
E-mail: orders@isbs.com
Website: http://www.isbs.com

British Library Cataloguing in Publication Data

Data Available

ISBN: 978-1-84113-784-1

Typeset by Hope Services Ltd, Abingdon
Printed and bound in Great Britain by
TJ International Ltd, Padstow, Cornwall

Acknowledgements

I owe a debt of gratitude to the series editors, Professors Andrew Harding and Peter Leyland, and the publishers, for their patience and support, and to Nong Leyland for her exciting and appropriate front cover. Warmest thanks are also due to Professor Bill Bowring, who not only fielded occasional queries but was kind enough to read chapters four and six in draft and make extremely helpful suggestions. Similarly, Professor Gene Huskey read an earlier version of chapter four and gave valuable pointers. Dr Devin Giddings gave useful feedback on early drafts of chapters one, two and three, and James F and James M Henderson reviewed some sections. I am responsible for all remaining errors. Those named, the rest of my family, my friends and students have given unfailing encouragement, for which I am indebted. Regular intake of Montezuma chocolate also played its part in bringing this work to fruition.

This book aims to state the law as at October 2010

Transliteration

Cyrillic has been transliterated according to the American Library Association-Library of Congress convention, including soft sign and hard sign, apart from some commonly-spelt words such as Chechnya. References to Russian materials have been kept to a minimum. Russian readers are likely to know sources for original language texts of relevant legislation, including the invaluable archive of federal law on the presidential website.[1]

---

[1] '*Bank Documentov*' at <http://kremlin.ru/acts>, accessed 28 August 2010.

Summary Contents

Contents

Table of Legislation

RUSSIA

Table of Conventions, Treaties, etc

Documents From The Communist Party of The Soviet Union

1

The State of Russia

Introduction – Conclusion – Further Reading

I. INTRODUCTION

A. Russia's struggle for constitutionality

THE CURRENT RUSSIAN Constitution dates from 12 December 1993. It is the first Constitution adopted in a Russian State with universal adult franchise and multiple political parties. It is also the first Russian Constitution to be directly applicable and not subject to an overriding veto, either *de jure* by a pre-revolutionary autocrat or *de facto* by the one political party which ruled during the Soviet era, the Communist Party of the Soviet Union (CPSU), 'the Party'.[1]

The Constitution makes the claim that Russia is a democratic federated rule-of-law State with a republican form of government. Its section on human rights compares favourably with international human rights law. However, both the Constitution and its application remain problematic. It was created during a time of troubles and is not a balanced document, being weighted heavily in favour of presidential authority. It does stipulate a separation of powers, but without an effective check-and-balance system. Its form of federalism also allows for substantial

---

[1] The Party went through a series of names: originally the Bolshevik wing of the Russian Social Democratic Labour Party, it took the name of Russian Communist Party (Bolsheviks) on 8 March 1918. On 31 December 1925 it became the All-Union Communist Party (Bolsheviks). On 13 October 1952 at the XIX Party Congress, Stalin declared that as there were no more Mensheviks, the name Bolshevik should be dropped so it was renamed the Communist Party of the Soviet Union.

asymmetry despite a claim of equality for the different entities which constitute Russia's federation. Nevertheless, the 1993 Constitution is a landmark document – the first in Russia to be taken seriously as a legal document – to which public figures try to conform.

This book will explore the background to the Constitution in chapters two and three, and important characteristics of the three branches of State power – executive, legislative and judicial – in chapters four, five and six, before a conclusionary chapter seven. The current chapter will give an overview of Russia and the place of law in her culture.

B.   Russia's place in the world

Russia is the largest country in the world. In her current form she spreads nearly halfway round the globe, from longitude 20 degrees east to 169 degrees west, covering 17 million square kilometres (6.5 million square miles) and spanning nine time zones (reduced from 11 in 2010). She has two alternative official names: Russia and the Russian Federation. These were adopted on 25 December 1991, shortly before the dissolution by the end of that year of the Union of Soviet Socialist Republics (USSR, also known as the Soviet Union). Russia, in the form of the Russian Soviet Federated Socialist Republic (RSFSR, Soviet Russia), was the largest of the socialist republics, also known as Union Republics, which made up the USSR.[2]

Russia is a country of contrasts. She works on a different scale from practically all other States because of her physical extent and diverse population. Even her climate runs to extremes, of hot dry summers and very cold winters. She spans two continents, Europe and Asia. At different stages of her history for different reasons has she weathered isolation from neighbouring cultures.

---

[2] In its developed form from 1956, the USSR comprised 15 Socialist Republics: Armenian, Azerbaijan, Belorussian, Estonian, Georgian, Kazakh, Kirghiz, Latvian, Lithuanian, Moldavian, Russian Soviet Federated, Tajik, Turkmen, Ukrainian and Uzbek. Initially Russia was known as the Russian Socialist Federated Soviet Republic, but the order was changed to indicate the victory of socialism; see GP van den Berg, 'Power-sharing Compacts under Russian Constitutional Law' in R Sharlet and FJM Feldbrugge (eds), *Public Policy and Law in Russia: in Search of a Unified Legal and Political Space* (Leiden, Nijhoff, 2005) 43, fn 5.

In the second half of the 20th century, the Cold War created a legacy of alienation and mistrust between the USSR, including Soviet Russia, and Western States. The division of the world between socialist and capitalist during the Soviet period created an ideological rift. The USSR and Russia were presented by most western media and politicians as the enemy, irrespective of the fact that the USSR was one of the Allies successful against the Axis forces in World War II (known to Russians as the Great Patriotic War). Despite the passage of time since the dissolution of the USSR at the end of December 1991, this heritage of a polarised world still influences commentators, making it difficult for them to be balanced in their reportage. There is ready condemnation by Western analysts of Russian practices in relation to, for example, human rights or criminal procedure, when comparatively little adverse comment is made of other States with equally problematic practices.

C. The federal dimension

As noted, Russia is a federation. At time of writing she is composed of 83 federal subjects (*sub"ekty Rossiiskoi Federatsii*). There are 21 republics (*respubliki* – singular *respublika*), nine territories (*kraia* – singular *krai*), 46 regions (*oblasti* – singular *oblast'*, sometimes translated as 'province'), two cities of federal status, one autonomous region (*avtomnaia oblast'*), and four autonomous areas (*avtomnye okruga* – singular *avtomnyi okrug*, sometimes translated as 'district').[3] Voluntary amalgamations reduced the number from the 89 listed in Article 54 in the 1993 Constitution.[4]

---

[3] (In Cyrillic alphabetical order) *Republics*: Adygeia, Altai, Bashkortostan, Buriatiia, Dagestan, Ingushetia, Kabardino-Balkariia, Kalmykiia, Karachaevo-Cherkesskaia, Karelia, Komi, Marii El, Mordoviia, Sakha (Iakutiia), Northern Osetia-Alaniia, Tatarstan, Tyva, Udmurt, Khakasiia, Chechnia, Chuvashia; *Territories*: Altai, Zabaikal, Kamchat, Krasnodar, Krasnoiar, Perm, Maritime (Primorskii), Stavropol, Khabarov; *Regions*: Amur, Arkhangel, Astrakhan, Belgorod, Briansk, Vladimir, Volgograd, Vologda, Voronezh, Ivanovo, Irkutsk, Kaliningrad, Kaluga, Kemerovo, Kirov, Kostroma, Kurgan, Kursk, Leningrad, Lipetsk, Magadan, Moscow, Murmansk, Nizhegorod, Novgorod, Novosibirsk, Omsk, Orenburg, Orlovsk, Penza, Pskov, Rostov, Riazan, Samara, Saratov, Sakhalin, Sverdlovsk, Smolensk Region, Tambov, Tver, Tomsk, Tula, Tiumen, Ul'ianovsk, Cheliabinsk, Iaroslavl; *Cities of federal significance*: Moscow, St Petersburg; *Jewish Autonomous Region*; *Autonomous National Areas*: Nentsy, Khanty-Mansiisk-Iurga, Chukotsk, Iamalo-Nenets.

[4] H Oversloot, 'The Merger of Federal Subjects of the Russian Federation during Putin's Presidency and after' (2009) 34(2) *Review of Central and East European Law* 119.

Nevertheless, 83 is still an unwieldy number, and there have been frequent and ongoing calls for federal restructuring to achieve a smaller number of larger entities. To some extent this has been achieved through the division of Russia in 2000 into seven (since January 2010, eight) 'federal districts', each overseen by a presidential federal representative (*polpred*). Half of the federal districts contain between six and nine federal subjects, and the other half between 11 and 18. The introduction of presidential federal representatives is discussed in chapter four.

Soviet Russia (the RSFSR) was also federal, but there was a significant difference. As with the USSR itself, residual power lay at the centre. Under Article 73 of the current Russian Constitution, residual power resides with the federal subjects. However, this residue is vanishingly small. Article 71 lists matters exclusively in federal jurisdiction, while Article 72 lists those within the joint jurisdiction of the federation and the federal subjects. Very little escapes mention. The 1977 USSR Constitution made a show of declaring the constituent Union Republics to be sovereign with a right of secession, although somehow this was to be exercised without changing the USSR boundaries, as they were exclusively within USSR jurisdiction. By contrast, the 1993 Russian Constitution does not extend a right of secession to any of the federal subjects. There is further discussion of Russia's unique federation in chapter three.

D. Language

The official language in the Russian Federation is Russian, a Slavic language written in the Cyrillic alphabet, although more than 140 other languages and dialects are currently spoken in Russia, and the republics within Russia have the right to assign official status to other languages. In recent years the Russian language has been developing rapidly. A new vocabulary of 'loan words' and resurrected pre-Revolutionary expressions fill the need for terms appropriate to the market economy, introduced from 1990 after years of centralised State economic planning under the Soviet system. A fashion for using terms and expressions coined in the GULAG[5] (the vast system of prison camps developed under Stalin) has broadened the vocabulary in everyday usage.

---

[5] GULAG is the acronym for the Head Administration of Corrective Labour Camps and Colonies (*Glavnoe Upravlenie Ispravitel'no-Trudovykh Lagerei i kolonii*) made famous by A Solzhenitsyn's three-volume *Gulag Archipelago*.

Non Russian-speaking scholars of Russian law need to be wary of the unavoidable interpretation associated with translation of legal materials. There are hazards for a translator rendering a Russian legal text into English. For example, Russian laws are written in the present indicative tense, rather than the future imperative expected by English speakers: 'Thou shalt not kill'. It is therefore impossible to tell from its grammar whether a particular Russian phrase is meant to be descriptive or normative. A translator may choose to make the text of a Russian law sound normative to English ears by the use of 'shall' rather than 'is', but that is a deliberate addition to the original. Thus the first article of the Russian Constitution has been translated as: 'The Russian Federation – Russia is a democratic federated rule-of-law State with a republic form of government'[6]; equally as 'The Russian Federation – Russia shall be a democratic federal rule-of-law State with the republican form of government.'[7] In the first example, it sounds as though the federal rule-of-law situation has been achieved; in the second it may still be an aspiration, but that different nuance is a trick of the translation.

Another characteristic of Russian is that, as with many Continental European languages, there are two words for 'law', *pravo* and *zakon*.[8] English does not have this duality of expression, although it may refer to both 'jurists' and 'lawyers'. The word *pravo* is cognate to the Russian word *pravda*, meaning truth. The name *Pravda* may be familiar as that of the newspaper formerly issued by the CPSU.[9] *Pravo* means law in the general sense, associated with rights, similar in meaning to the Latin *ius*, French *droit*, German *Recht*, etc. The alternative word for law is *zakon*. As with Latin *lex*, French *loi*, German *Gesetz*, this signifies enacted legislation. *Zakon* is not the only Russian word for types of legislation (normative

---

[6] WE Butler, *Russian Public Law*, 2nd edn (London, Wildy, Simmonds & Hill, 2009) 4, and *Russian Law*, 3rd edn (Oxford, Oxford University Press, 2009) 811.
[7] W Burnham and P Maggs, *Law and Legal System in the Russian Federation*, 4th edn (Huntington, NY, Juris Publishing Inc, 2009) 657.
[8] There are two words for Russian as well. *Russkaia* means Russian in an ethnic sense, whereas *rossiskaia* means pertaining to the Russian State, so that an ethnic Tatar woman can be a Russian (*rossiskaia grazhdanina*) citizen but is not Russian (*russkaia*).
[9] In the mid-1970s Professor Feldbrugge, Director of the then Documentation Centre for East European Law at the University of Leiden, commented to the author that Communist Parties in Europe name their newspapers after the principles they most abuse. The Soviet government newspaper was called *Izvestiia*, which means news, leading to the Soviet Russian joke that *Pravda* has no news and *Izvestiia* has no truth.

legal acts – in Russian *normativnye pravovye akty*) but is used for the highest
form of enacted law, passed by the primary legislature either at federal
level or in a subject of the federation. There are many other words
for subsidiary legislation, eg *ukaz, postanovlenie* and *rasporazhenie*, usually
translated as edict, decree and regulation respectively. In his attempt to
translate using a one-for-one equivalence, Butler identified more than
40 different Russian types of legislation and 'long since exhausted the
repertoire of English-language equivalents'.[10]

There are also two Russian words for 'truth' – *pravda* and *istina*. *Pravda*
truth would be that which is capable of proof – 'a conformity with the
known facts or events'[11] – whereas *istina* truth is something felt in the
heart – 'the truth beyond the known facts of the world'.[12] Alexander
Yakovlev, in his *Striving for Law in a Lawless Land: Memoirs of a Russian
Reformer*,[13] contrasts these two concepts to conclude that 'In the Russian
people's consciousness, the law has never been associated with moral
truth.'[14] In his view this dichotomy between law and conscience combined with the absolutism of the autocratic monarchy (*samoderzhavie*)
and the Marxist denial of personal rights – 'any personal rights may be
sacrificed for the good of all'[15] – are historical obstacles to be overcome
in Russia 'to make the change to a better life'.[16] Yakovlev also contrasts
two words for justice, *spravedlivost*, meaning fairness and justice, and
iustitsiia, the Russian version of the Latin word:

> Of course, everyone in Russia understands that the system of justice ought
> to be fair, impartial, and lawful, that it ought to provide justice to people
> with essentially the same meaning that that word conveys in English. But this
> terminological duplicity reflects a specific cultural trait. The idea of justice as
> an objectively existing web of social relations in real-life situations (*spravedliv-
> ost*) exists in public consciousness parallel to (and in a different context

[10]   WE Butler, 'Techniques of Law Reform in the Soviet Union' (1978) 31 *Current
Legal Problems* 209.

[11]   'Appendix 1: *pravda* versus *istina*' in AV Ledeneva, *How Russia Really Works: The
Informal Practices that Shaped Post-Soviet Politics and Business* (Ithaca, NY, Cornell
University Press, 2006) 197.

[12]   *Ibid.*

[13]   A Yakovlev, *Striving for Law in a Lawless Land: Memoirs of a Russian Reformer*
(Armonk, NY, ME Sharpe, 1996).

[14]   *Ibid* at 10, although inexplicably Yakovlev characterises *pravda* as 'moral, sub-
jective and spiritual truth . . . *istina* amounts to factual truth'.

[15]   *Ibid* at 24.

[16]   *Ibid* at 25.

from) the notion of justice as a set of political, state-bound institutions. Historically, the law was not considered to be a real ingredient of normal life but something imposed from above, more often than not a burden, if not actually a yoke.[17]

Sometimes it may be more appropriate to transliterate rather than translate. Thus, for instance, in the following chapters one of the Russian courts will be referred to as *arbitrazh* courts. Using this unusual term flags up their distinctiveness, and avoids the translational trap of calling them Arbitration Courts, which they are not. *Arbitrazh* courts grew out of the Soviet institution of *arbitrazh* tribunals, established to iron out inconsistencies in the nationwide economic plan. At that stage they did not aspire to be courts and focused on practical outcomes, not the balance of legal rights. Now they are fully-fledged courts, applying the same Civil Code as the other domestic courts, but with jurisdiction over entities working in the economic sphere; a relic of their original concern.

Even with straightforward translation, the reader should be careful not to assume the term in English has the same connotation as the original Russian expression. Phrases like 'democratically elected' or 'political party' may signify something rather different in Russia, with a meaning conditional on the historical context of its use.

Equally problematic, although for a different reason, is the expression 'rule-of-law'. The Russian phrase *pravovoe gosudarstvo* is commonly translated as 'rule-of-law State', but this masks the distinction between law as *pravo* (the root of the adjective *pravovoe*) and as *zakon*. The Soviet system from the mid-1960s strove for legality (*zakonnost'*), but that was a long way from 'rule of law'. There has been an analogous debate on meaning amongst Western scholars of the Chinese legal system, comparing concepts of 'thick' and 'thin' law in their approach to a possible rule of law:

> A thin theory law stresses the formal or instrumental aspects of rule of law . . . thick or substantive concepts begin with the basic elements of a thin concept of rule of law but then incorporate elements of political morality.[18]

There is little doubt that Russia fulfils the 'thin' rule-of-law requirements; the extent to which she has developed a 'thick' concept of rule

---

[17] *Ibid* at 10–11.
[18] R Peerenboom, *China's Long March towards Rule of Law* (Cambridge, Cambridge University Press, 2002) 3.

of law is debatable, and that discussion forms the backdrop of this study of the Russian Constitution in context.

E. The impact of social culture

Russia has a diverse population, and it is foolish and patronising to dwell on stereotypes and caricatures. However, there are some general characteristics of Russian society which may inform her legal culture. There is, in general, respect for the aged and a chivalrous, some might say chauvinistic, approach to women. Loyalty tends to be to friends, group or patron, rather than to the State as an amorphous entity. The dividing line between reciprocal assistance and corruption is difficult to draw, as the long-held tradition of mutual exchange of favours still holds sway, and personal trust and other informal relations are given higher priority than formal arrangements. Attitudes to law and legal regulation may appear surprisingly lax to those brought up in North America and northern Europe. In Russia there can be a wide gulf between the 'law in the books' and 'law in action'. This must surely be true in all jurisdictions, but in Russia (pre-revolutionary, Soviet and post-Soviet) there persists an idea that law is made in Moscow, and for many that is a very long way away and local practices may take precedence.

In Russia, prior experience of constitutionalism was comparatively sparse. Compared with her Western European neighbours, Russia had some marked differences in her historical development:

> There had been no feudalism, at least in the form of a balance of interests regulated by law; social classes were defined by service to the state; the Orthodox Church was an extension of government rather than a rival source of authority; and government itself accepted no legitimate limit to the scope of its decisions.[19]

In pre-revolutionary Russia, there were discussions about rights and whether there should be any limitations on the scope of the ruler's power, the interrelation between *pravo* (right) and *zakon* (enacted law), but these tended to be on an abstract, theoretical level, and rarely informed law-making and law application. In post-revolutionary Russia, law was given little respect as a result of the impact of Marxist ideology

---

[19] S White, *Russia's New Politics: The Management of a Postcommunist Society* (Cambridge, Cambridge University Press, 2000) 291.

with its view that law was merely part of the superstructure of society overlaying the essential economic infrastructure at the particular stage of societal development (see chapter two). When the communist ideal was reached, law and State would have withered away. It is therefore not surprising that now, in post-Soviet Russia, there has been unparalleled development of an approach to legality and constitutionality.

F. Russian legal nihilism

Famously, in the mid-1800s, Alexander Herzen described the lack of any kind of legal order in Russia[20]:

> The legal insecurity that has hung over our people from time immemorial has been a kind of school for them. The scandalous injustice of one half of the law has taught them to hate the other half; they submit only to force. Complete inequality before the law has killed any respect they may have had for legality. Whatever his station, the Russian evades or violates the law wherever he can do so with impunity; the government does exactly the same thing.

This legal nihilism was highlighted by President Medvedev in his first annual address to the legislature in November 2008: '[Legal nihilism] did not appear in Russia yesterday. Its roots go deep into our past'.[21] He has set himself to try to eradicate it, but in doing so he is attempting to sweep away a deeply-embedded and longstanding cultural tradition.

In her enlightening description of *How Russia Really Works: The Informal Practices that Shaped Post-Soviet Politics and Business*,[22] Alena Ledeneva also highlights the consequences of the cavalier approach to formal law that has been customary in Russia. She shows how legal rules may be manipulated to subvert their original purpose, and selective enforcement, or non-enforcement, may be used strategically. One example described how electoral campaigns can be affected.[23]

---

[20] '*Du développement des idées révolutionnaires en Russie*' in *Collected Works in Thirty Volumes* (Moscow, 1954–61) vol 7, 121, as cited in Yakovlev, above n 13, at 10.

[21] D Medvedev, 'Russian president Medvedev's first annual address to parliament', *Rossiya TV* verbatim broadcast in Russian, 5 November 2008, translation by (2008) *BBC Monitoring Former Soviet Union*, 5 November, available via Westlaw.

[22] Ledeneva, above n 11.

[23] *Ibid* at 48, 51.

Legal procedures are used to sabotage legality. Control of the media, use of negative campaigning (so-called 'black PR' – *chernyi piar*), collection of and trade in compromising information, and 'mutual support networks' all have a significant impact on the real distribution of power. As Ledeneva convincingly argues, these important informal practices 'are engaged in advancing but also undermining the workings of market and democracy'[24] and must be borne in mind, even though the extent of their impact is not open to measurement.

G. Families of legal systems?

In form, the Russian legal system has many of the hallmarks of a Continental European 'Romanist' system which takes its legal heritage from Roman Law. As with Continental European legal systems and their offspring, in Russia the main branches of law are codified. As a discipline, law is regarded as a science, so that the prestigious Institute of State and Law is part of the Russian Academy of Sciences. Legal academics are more respected than judges, who traditionally have been regarded as functionaries with little social standing, although this is changing.[25] There was academic debate over whether Soviet Russia had a Romanist legal system or led a separate family of Socialist legal systems. Now that debate considers whether post-Soviet Russia is back in the 'Romanist family' or in some separate post-socialist family. Whichever view, if any, prevails, there is at least one characteristic of the Russian legal system which may set it apart from its Continental cousins. There is a stark contrast between the rigorous Russian legal education, and its scientific approach to the study of law, and the traditional low level of regard for law in the general culture. This is a characteristic which Russia's current President Medvedev, a former lawyer, and the Chairmen of its three top courts have set themselves to transform. They see the Constitution as an important instrument in that process.

---

[24] *Ibid* at 27.

[25] The fact that many judges in Soviet Russia were women unfortunately said more about the perceived low status of the post than it did about real equality of the sexes.

II. CONCLUSION

Even for something as fundamental as the Constitution, there may be different views as to the role that it takes, and therefore the extent to which its terms are binding law or merely guidelines. Russian cultural and historical experiences have not created positive expectations for law in general, and the Constitution in particular. The next two chapters expand on the historical background to the current Constitution, before an examination of its substance in relation to the Executive, Legislature and Judiciary in chapters four, five and six. It may then be possible to assess the extent to which post-Soviet Russia is developing a new and effective constitutionalism.

FURTHER READING

HJ Berman, *Justice in the USSR* (Cambridge, Mass, Harvard University Press, 1966).

FJM Feldbrugge, *Russian Law: The End of the Soviet System and the Role of Law* (Dordrecht, Nijhoff, 1993).

O Figes, *Natasha's Dance: A Cultural History of Russia* (London, Allen Lane Penguin Press, 2002).

L Gönenç, *Prospects for Constitutionalism in Post-Communist Countries* (The Hague, Nijhoff, 2002).

E Huskey, 'A framework for the analysis of Soviet law' (1991) 50 *Russian Review* 53.

AV Ledeneva, *How Russia Really Works: The Informal Practices that Shaped Post-Soviet Politics and Business* (Ithaca, NY, Cornell University Press, 2006).

W Partlett, 'Re-classifying Russian Law: Mechanisms, Outcomes, and Solutions for an Overly Politicized Field' (2008) 2 *Columbia Journal East European Law* 1.

J Quigley, 'Socialist law and the Civil Law tradition' (1989) 37 *American Journal of Comparative Law* 781.

A Yakovlev, *Striving for Law in a Lawless Land: Memoirs of a Russian Reformer* (Armonk, NY, ME Sharpe, 1996).

2

History and Nature of the Constitution

Introduction – The Constitution in Pre-revolutionary Times –
The Constitution During the Soviet Era – Conclusion – Further
Reading

I. INTRODUCTION

RUSSIA HAS A rich although frequently turbulent past. This
chapter explores some aspects of it which impact on her present
concept of constitutionality. Written law in Russian dates from
the 11th century, but the first written Constitution was not until 1906,
the Fundamental Law of the Russian Empire. This was nullified after the
Bolshevik revolution in 1917, and a new 1918 Constitution issued for the
period of the proletariat dictatorship. Further Soviet Constitutions
followed, but their role differed from that of Constitutions in bourgeois
States. The reforming *perestroika* era of the late 1980s brought a
reassessment of the value of law. The events leading to the dissolution
of the USSR by the end of 1991 gave pause for thought in Russia as her
leaders worked to avoid an equivalent fragmentation of Russia itself.

  This chapter covers developments up to the end of the USSR. The
following chapter analyses the circumstances leading to the adoption of
the current Constitution, and gives an overview of its structure and
contents. The two chapters together are a backdrop to consideration of
the Executive, Legislature and Judiciary in the subsequent chapters.

II. THE CONSTITUTION IN PRE-REVOLUTIONARY TIMES

A. Early Statehood

In 1988, Russia celebrated her millennium; 1,000 years since the conversion to Christianity of the Russian population under the rule of Prince Vladimir Sviatoslavich ('Saint Vladimir'). This arguably marks the beginning of the Russian State; significant because it links the mythos of Statehood to the acquisition of an official State ideology, here Orthodox Christianity. It has been a persistent theme in Russia to have an explicit ideology to guide the ship of State, although the ideology changed dramatically in 1917, and less dramatically in the early 1990s. The current Constitution forbids an official State ideology, but there is still a quest to conceptualise the political basis of the State, such as the discussions about 'sovereign democracy' in 2006.[1]

The earliest written Russian law is the *Russkaia Pravda*, associated with Vladimir's son, Iaroslavl (ruled 1015–54). The first half of the 'Short Pravda' of Iaroslavl appears to be a compilation of rules based on customary law of the different tribes of his close supporters.[2] The second half, the 'Pravda of Iaroslavl's Sons', is more akin to legislation. Although, as Feldbrugge convincingly argues,[3] it was likely to have been 'new customary law' in response to the particular challenges of the time, it presents itself as legislation based on the Prince's power. The existence of numerous editions of the *Russkaia Pravda* testifies to its widespread use, although in quite what way is beyond recall. During this period of rule of the various Russian principalities by Rurikid princes, the popular assembly of each city, its *veche*, played an important part in the political decision-making process.[4] It was not unknown for a prince to be expelled. *Veche* procedure was chaotic and the requirement of unanimity sometimes led to violence; the stronger side, literally, winning the day.[5] These local assemblies disappeared as the developing Russian State

---

[1] P Moore, 'Kremlin ideologue defends "sovereign democracy"' (2006) 10(216) *Radio Free Europe/Radio Liberty*, 23 November.
[2] See FJM Feldbrugge, 'The *Russkaia Pravda*' in FJM Feldbrugge, *Law in Medieval Russia* (Leiden, Brill, 2009) 32 at 38.
[3] *Ibid* at 58.
[4] FJM Feldbrugge, 'Popular Assemblies in Early Medieval Russia: The *Veche* in Legal History' in Feldbrugge, above n 2, 147 at 152.
[5] *Ibid* at 157.

became more centralised, as a result of, and in reaction to, the imposition of the Mongol Yoke.

B. The Mongol Yoke – autocracy takes root

Public law in medieval Russia was transformed by the conquest by the Mongol-Tatar Golden Horde. This was the nomadic army controlled by the successors of Genghis Khan (died 1227), the so-called Golden Family. Inhabitants of the Russian steppes had frequently suffered depredations from nomadic raiders. However, from 1236, for two and a half centuries, Russia joined much of Asia and (for a shorter time) parts of Eastern Europe under more continual subjugation to the so-called Mongol Yoke. The chroniclers recording this incursion were Orthodox Christian monks, at the interface of a clash of religions, and presented it as wholly negative. In fact, Russia, although cut off from Europe, was put in touch with the wealth of learning in the Muslim east.[6] The Mongol overlords had little interest in interfering with the local civil legal relations. What they wanted was effective payment of tribute, and they organised an efficient administrative system to ensure this, including an impressive empire-wide postal service, the *iam*, the name of which entered the Russian language. The Russian words for money and customs-tariff also have Mongol roots.

The Mongols are blamed for the introduction to Russia of absolute autocracy and a system of universal public service. The Code of Genghis Khan, the *Yasa*, allocated to every subject 'a specific position in the service to the State, from which he could not depart without penalty of death'.[7] Later Russian rulers enthusiastically adopted this principle. Arguably Russia never developed a feudal system equivalent to that of Western Europe, with reciprocal obligations between lord and tenants. Under the Russian system descended from the Mongol approach, obligations were all one way, compulsory service owed to the State.

The ruler credited with throwing off the Yoke was Grand Duke of Muscovy Ivan III (Ivan Vasilevich, known as Ivan the Great, 1440–1505, reigning alone from 1452). As a result of his success he called

---

[6] See CJ Halperin, *Russia and the Golden Horde* (London, Tauris & Co, 1987).

[7] HJ Berman*, Justice in the USSR* (Cambridge, Mass, Harvard University Press, 1963) 195.

himself 'Tsar-Autocrat, chosen by God'. The word 'Tsar' is cognate with the Latin 'Caesar', meaning emperor, and this remained the main title of the ruler of Russia until 1721, when Peter the Great claimed to be Emperor of All the Russias (*Imperator Vserossiysky*), although he also retained the title of Tsar. Just as significant was the other title claimed by Russia rulers of 'Autocrat' (*Samoderzhets*). The Russian word is a compound from *sam* (self) and *derzhat'* (to keep, hold or possess). Legal scholar Alexander Yakovlev expands:

> The word suggests not only that '*l'État c'est moi*,' but 'I hold a state in my own hands, all state power is entirely at my disposal, and my power, by definition, cannot be restricted and need not be justified.'[8]

Nothing before the revolutions of 1917 seriously restricted that imperial autocracy founded on the principle of divine right, and little in the Soviet approach before the mid-1980s changed the culture of unaccountable rulership.

C. Centralisation

In 1453 Constantinople fell to the Ottoman Turks. It had been the centre of the Roman Empire in the East. Ivan III's wife, Sophia Palaiologina, was a descendent of the Emperor of the Eastern Roman Empire, and brought the Byzantine symbol of the double-headed eagle to Russia. In 1510 the monk Filofei wrote to the ruling Grand Duke Vasili III, the son of Ivan III and Sophia, 'Two Romes have fallen. The third stands. And there will be no fourth.' The position of Russia as a 'missionary state'[9] emphasised the unity of Church and State. This idea of the State as repository of the truth and custodian of world destiny was paralleled by the USSR's self-declared position of ideological supremacy.

During Ivan III's long reign the first national Russian law code, the *Sudebnik*, was adopted in 1497, followed by a second version in 1550.[10] Both were mainly concerned with detailed judicial procedure, for exam-

---

[8] AM Yakovlev, *Striving for Law in a Lawless Land: Memoirs of a Russian Reformer* (Armonk, NY, ME Sharpe, 1996) 20.

[9] *Ibid* at 199.

[10] See WE Butler, *Russian Law*, 3rd edn (Oxford, Oxford University Press, 2009) 20.

ple setting appropriate fees. Bribing judges was prohibited. The 1497 *Sudebnik* restricted peasants' freedom of movement from one estate to another. The period during which a peasant could relocate was reduced to a mere two weeks after harvest. The march to complete serfdom had begun.

Ivan III's successor, Ivan IV, became Grand Prince of Muscovy at the age of three in 1533. Crowned Tsar of All the Russias in 1547, he continued to rule until 1584. He was known as *Ivan Groznyi*, Ivan the Terrible, more accurately translated as 'Ivan the Awesome'. Ivan undermined the power of the nobility (the Boyars) by removing their hereditary security of tenure. Wreaking revenge for their disloyalty, perceived or actual, Ivan bound the nobility individually to him by service which they could not exchange with another lord without losing their existing traditional inheritable patrimonial estate (*votchina*). Instead, in return for State service, each noble was granted a non-inheritable estate (*pomestie*) which was completely conditional on the will of the Tsar.

Ivan established the infamous *Oprichniki*, who enforced his command with unrestrained violence. They wore black gowns and rode black horses, the better to intimidate, and had the power to execute anyone they regarded as an enemy of the Tsar. This unaccountable security organisation waging war on the domestic population has resonance with repressions during the Soviet era.

D. Romanovs and the growth of absolutism

Ivan IV killed his heir Ivan in a fit of rage, so was succeeded by his ineffective son Feodor, who ruled 1584–98. Feodor died childless, so a Land Assembly (*Zemskii sobor*) met to elect a successor. These assemblies originated during the time of Ivan IV as a mechanism for consultation and legislation, and were composed of representatives of the nobility, the Church and the mercantile class. The 1598 Land Assembly elected the man who had been advising Tsar Feodor, Boris Gudunov. His short reign (1598–1605) was the beginning of a 15-year period known as the 'Time of Troubles', with weak government, pretenders to the throne (two claimants, 'False Dmitrii' I and II), famine, plague and invasion by Polish and Lithuanian forces. A volunteer army led by a nobleman and a merchant successfully repulsed the latter, and a Land Assembly was convened in 1613 to choose a new Tsar.

The eventual reluctant electee was the 16-year-old Mikhail Romanov, who established the last Russian tsarist dynasty. Mikhail reigned until 1645. His son, Alexei Mikhailovich (ruled 1645–76) presided over a further growth of absolutism.

Tsar Alexei gathered another Land Assembly in 1649 to pass a new law code, the *Sobornoe Ulozhenie*. The draft enactment was discussed for four months at the Assembly, which had two chambers with delegates from over 120 towns in the lower chamber. 'Evidence survives about contested elections in several places.'[11]

Amongst other things, the new code consolidated serfdom, forbidding peasants to leave their lord's estate for any reason, and extending indefinitely the time during which runaways and their descendants could be tracked down and returned to subjugation. Not only serfs were bound. Other subjects were placed in a hierarchy which determined which duties they owed to the State. Absolutism was thus consolidated.

Tsar Alexei's son by his second wife, Peter I (born 1672), became known as Peter the Great in 1721 when he assumed the title of Emperor. He gained a reputation as a great reformer, although he was not universally revered. He set out in March 1697 on his 'Great Embassy', touring Europe for 18 months to gather information. On his return, he enforced on both officials and the military a Western European dress code of trousers rather than robes, and required them to be clean-shaven. In 1712 he had a new capital, St Petersburg, constructed at great cost in both money and lives. Reforms 'from above' were the only method:

> Society on its own lacked any effective levers by which to bring about change. For these reasons, any major reform project could only be implemented by means of administrative intervention of the State.[12]

The tradition of reform from above still persists.

Peter had great zeal to bring order to all levels of his realm. He intensified State control over the people, including an individual poll tax on all male non-nobles, and compulsory military service for most men. He reformed central, provincial and local government. He divided Russia into *Gubernii*, eight of which were established in 1707, increasing to 12

---

[11] Richard Hellie, 'Assembly of the Land' in J Millar (ed), *Russia History Encyclopedia* (USA, Macmillan Reference, 2003), online at <http://www.answers.com/topic/assembly-of-the-land>, accessed 30 August 2010.

[12] A Chubarov, *The Fragile Empire: a History of Imperial Russia* (New York, Continuum, 1999) 19.

by 1718. Each *Guberniia* was presided over by a Governor directly answerable to the Tsar. There was some devolution for local government. Towns were given increased powers to elect local officials, in the hope that this would stimulate trade and reduce the provincial level of bureaucracy.

In 1711 Peter established the Senate, a nine-man committee which evolved to become both an executive organ and also the Supreme Court. It replaced the traditional Boyar *Duma* (advisory council of hereditary nobility). In 2008 Peter's Senate and Synod Building became the seat of the Russian Constitutional Court.

Peter's central government reforms began in 1717 by abolishing the existing chaotic system of governmental departments (*Prikazi*), replacing them with a smaller number of better-organised *Collegia*. Nevertheless, Peter remained in sole overall charge, so the net effect of the reconstruction was more efficient absolutism.

One of Peter's most lasting reforms, initiated in 1711, was the establishment of an organisation to oversee the civil service. In 1722 he formed the Procuracy to act as the 'eye of the Tsar'. It is said that after Peter himself the Procurator-General was the most powerful man in Russia. The modern Russian Procuracy claims its direct descent from Peter's establishment.

Peter also completely reformed the structure of the Orthodox Church, effectively incapacitating the Church's ability to be a separate power base. This contrasted with the Western European position where, in both Catholic and Protestant States, the Church to some extent acted as a counterweight to the temporal power of the Head of State.

In 1714 Peter acceded to the landlords' requests to make their land-holdings hereditary, but still required obligatory State service in return. The 'Table of Ranks' introduced in 1722 consolidated this system. The Table was a list of hierarchical positions in the military and civil service. Those entering State service would begin at the bottom and could work their way up. In theory this rewarded talent and merit, eliminating the monopoly of the old land-owning nobility, but in practice congestion in the higher ranks preserved considerable control by the old order. Nevertheless, the system allowed anyone, even a commoner (although not a serf), to be ennobled, provided that they attained sufficiently high rank. The Table of Ranks survived until the Russian Revolution. Famously, Vladimir Lenin's father progressed sufficiently to be awarded noble status.

Peter's reforms were imposed from above by coercion. They were aimed at modernisation and westernisation, and those goals were in the main achieved. However, their positive impact was on the educated elite, not the mass of the population who remained as serfs. This exacerbated the already existing divide in society. The upper classes were increasingly Europeanised, even to the extent that they would follow the fashion of speaking French or German rather than the vernacular Russian of the lower orders; social stratification and schism was thus further embedded.

E. Failed reform under Anna

Peter the Great was succeeded by his wife (as Catharine I, 1725–27) and his young grandson, Peter II (born 1715, ruled 1727–30), who died of smallpox on the eve of his wedding. The Supreme Privy Council, a body composed of a handful of aristocrats set up as advisers to Catharine I, took charge and offered the imperial throne to Anna Ivanovna, Peter the Great's niece (ruled 1730–40). Before her coronation, Anna signed a set of 'Conditions' restricting the exercise of her imperial power. However, these were not the only proposals under discussion; for a brief period in Moscow there was widespread intensive debate about different forms of government and limitation of autocracy, and 'more than a score of draft reform projects . . . thought over in advance'.[13] Constitutional historian Andrei Medushevski points out that 'a great many of provincial gentry were in Moscow'[14] for Peter II's wedding and they joined in the reform discussions; for perhaps the first time, 'evidence of bottom-up initiative'.[15] When Anna arrived at the Kremlin palace she was presented with a petition for a representative assembly. She apparently acceded, but within hours she tore up both it and the Conditions, secure that her palace guard supported autocracy. Absolute rule was reasserted, although not before the aristocrats at least had had a taste of presenting class demands.

---

[13]   A Medushevsky, *Russian Constitutionalism: Historical and Contemporary Development* (Abingdon, Routledge, 2006) 71.

[14]   *Ibid* at 70.

[15]   *Ibid* at 73.

F. A touch of enlightenment? – Catherine II

Thirty years later, inspiration from western Europe returned through the reign of Empress Catherine II, the Great (1762–96). The daughter of a minor Prussian prince, in 1745 at the age of 15 she married Peter the Great's grandson, Grand Duke Peter. He became Tsar in 1762, but shortly after was assassinated and Catherine was declared Empress. She brought European Enlightenment ideals to Russia, although not their practical implementation. She sent bright young scholars abroad to learn law; Semion Desnitskii and IA Tretiakov both attended Glasgow University, where they came under the influence of Adam Smith and others from the Scottish Enlightenment, before returning to teach at Moscow University.[16] Catherine herself corresponded with Voltaire and sent him, and Frederick II of Prussia (Frederick the Great), copies of a lengthy draft Instruction (*Nakaz*) for her newly-created Codification Commission. She had taken two years to compose the draft in which she incorporated the theories (and indeed verbatim text) of Montesquieu, Beccaria and others. Her draft was in French, which she translated into Russian. The *Nakaz* was subsequently printed in Russian, German, French and Latin, and its circulation gave Catherine a reputation of enlightened autocrat, as it embodied Enlightenment theory. But beyond generating some discussion in high circles, it had little practical impact in Russia.

Catharine's *Nakaz* was sent in 1767 to the All-Russian Legislative Commission which she had established to codify Russia's laws. The Legislative Commission was an innovation, as deputies included elected representatives of all classes except the serfs and the clergy. However, after a year of almost 200 sessions the Commission had not achieved any practical results. The delegates differed too much in their aims and aspirations. Faced with a task completely beyond their experience, they descended into sectarian squabbles. The outbreak of war against the Ottoman Empire in 1768 gave Catherine the excuse to dissolve the

---

[16] See AH Brown, 'The Father of Russian Jurisprudence: the Legal Thought of SE Desnitskii' in WE Butler (ed), *Russian Law: Historical and Political Perspectives* (Leiden, Sijthoff 1977) 117, and W Bowring, 'Russia and Human Rights: Incompatible Opposites?' (2009) 1(2) *Göttingen Journal of International Law* 33 at 37, available online at <http://eprints.bbk.ac.uk/785/2/785.pdf>, accessed 22 March 2010.

Commission, and its failure dissuaded her from future experiments with democratic representation. However, it did expose the opposed aspirations of the different classes. The peasantry wanted relief from taxation. Merchants wanted trade monopolies and the right to own serfs. The nobility's demands were equally self-serving: the end of their compulsory State service, return to full ownership of hereditary estates and complete enserfment of the peasants. In time they achieved these ends. In 1731 landlords holding estates in return for State service gained full proprietory rights. By 1762, already reduced from a lifetime to 25 years, compulsory service for the nobility was completely abolished. These privileges were enshrined in Catherine's 1785 Charter of the Nobility. Unfortunately, the nobility's achievements did not translate into good governance of the peasant majority. There was increased despotism. The Pugachev rebellion's failed attempt during 1773–75 to overthrow the landlords and divide their estates amongst the peasants undermined any sympathy for serf aspirations towards emancipation.

G. Reaction and reform proposals

After Catherine II's death in 1796, her successor Paul I (born 1754) reasserted imperial control over the nobility, restricting their rights to exemption from compulsory service and corporal punishment. He induced such antagonism that he was assassinated in 1801. His son, Alexander I, came to the throne aged 23 and ruled until 1825. His education had been controlled by his grandmother Catherine, and he was tutored by a Swiss, de la Harpe, who nurtured in Alexander her Enlightenment ideals. During the early years of his reign, he surrounded himself with a group of aristocratic reformers. Shortly after his accession he initiated work on a new codification of the law, but this did not come into fruition during his lifetime. Unfortunately neither did the proposals to create a constitutional monarchy drafted for him in 1809 by the extraordinarily able Mikhail Speransky. These were stillborn as a result of the war with Napoleon and aristocratic opposition, but laid a foundation for future changes in the early years of the 20th century. Speransky envisaged a separation of powers, with a hierarchy of courts, elected legislative bodies which he proposed to call *Dumas* and a separate executive branch with different levels of administrative agencies. A State Council would act as an upper legislative chamber and the Tsar would reign over all, as a constitutional monarch. None of this came to pass during Speransky's lifetime. In 1810 the State Council was established but as a legislative consultative body composed of Tsar-appointed officials (Government ministers joined *ex officio*), although the existing Senate (established by Peter the Great) was not abolished. However, reform of the administration was fiercely opposed by those holding rank in the existing system. They gained the ear of Tsar Alexander and persuaded him to dismiss Speransky in March 1812, although he was reinstated and appointed governor-general of Siberia in 1816, which post he carried out very successfully.

As Alexander's reign progressed, he became more involved in the war with Napoleon and its subsequent impact on European politics, and less interested in liberal reforms at home. He left no surviving legitimate children; on his death in 1825 his younger brother, born 1796, became Tsar Nicholas I.

H. Bureaucracy and private law reform

In contrast to Alexander's early liberal education, the formative influence on Nicholas I was his military service during the Napoleonic Wars. He endeavoured to transfer the principles of military discipline to the rule of his empire. He had gained the throne after suppression of the unsuccessful Decembrist uprising, so-called because it took place on 18 December 1825. The leaders of the groups behind the Decembrists were aristocratic reformers hoping for a constitutional monarchy (or, for the more extreme, a democratic republic), and their arrest and punishment inhibited open discussion about constitutional reform, and drove some elements into more extreme secret societies, as any gradual reform seemed increasingly unfeasible. The Decembrists supported Nicholas's elder brother Constantine, who lived in Poland and had previously renounced his claim to the throne. During the uprising, rebel troops and citizen onlookers faced imperial forces across the square outside the Senate Building. After a day-long stand-off, cavalry and canon wreaked slaughter, the uprising was put down and its ringleaders were hanged. It was said that

> the crowd chanted '*Konstantin i Konstitutsiia*'. A British historian has reported wryly that some of the participants knew so little about a Constitution that

they thought the second word in the chant was the name of Constantine's wife.[17]

The year after his accession Nicholas I established totalitarian control. The Third Section of his Chancellery headed a nationwide system of police surveillance and censorship. Government bureaucracy increased, as did the growth of an administrative class dependent on government employment. One positive side-effect of this was increased appropriate higher education to prepare efficient civil servants. This produced suitable candidates for the newly-established advocates' profession a generation later.[18] Work also resumed on a new code of law. A group of lawyers, including Mikhail Speransky, produced

> the greatest systematization … of legislation, in its day, on this planet and far ahead of anything commensurate in continental Europe, England, or the United States.[19]

The work was, in many senses, immense. Published in 1830, the Complete Collected Laws of the Russian Empire (*Polnoe sobranie zakonov Rossiiskoi imperii*) comprised 48 huge volumes containing a chronological collection of the more than 30,000 legislative enactments passed since the 1649 *Sobornoe Ulozhenie*. Merely tracking down the enactments was a daunting task, as few had been printed and there was no systematic record-keeping or central repository. From the Complete Collection the compilers distilled a much smaller Digest, the Code of Laws (*Svod zakonov*), published in 1832.[20] This was a mere 15 volumes, nevertheless impressive. However, it was not until the reign of Nicholas I's son, Alexander II, that the most long-awaited reform, the emancipation of the serfs, took place in 1861.

---

[17] J Hazard, 'Models for a Gorbachev Constitution of the USSR' (1989) 10 *Michigan Journal of International Law* 176 at 179, citing B Pares, *A History of Russia* (New York, AA Knopf, 1947) 318.

[18] See R Wortman, *The Development of a Russian Legal Consciousness* (Chicago, University of Chicago Press, 1976).

[19] WE Butler, 'Review of Whisenhunt, *In Search of Legality: Mikhail M Speranskii and the Codification of Russian Law*' (2006) 7 *Kritika* 658.

[20] See T Borisova, 'Russian National Legal Tradition: *Svod versus Ulozhenie* in Nineteenth-century Russia' (2008) 33 *Review of Central and East European Law* 395.

I. Emancipation of serfs and reform of the legal system

Alexander II (born 1818) came to the throne in 1855, aged 36, when Russia had been waging war for two years against the combined forces of Britain, France, Turkey and Sardinia in what is known in England as the Crimean War. The campaign revealed inadequacies in military and logistic arrangements on both sides, but particularly for Alexander it was clear that the army, mainly composed of conscript serfs, was no match for his more professional adversaries. After a peace settlement in 1856, Alexander set about reforms. He triggered consideration of serf emancipation in an address to the nobility in 1856. On 19 February 1861 he issued the Tsar's Manifesto on 'The Abolition of Serfdom in Russia'.

> This tremendous work could be only compared with the abolition of slavery in the United States which followed four years later. In the Russian case, however, the emancipation was carried out on an infinitely larger scale, and was achieved without civil war and without devastation or armed coercion. It revealed a great paradox: only an autocrat could achieve a 'peaceful' transformation like this; in a democracy, which must compromise on such issues to satisfy pressure groups, such bold actions are much more difficult![21]

Debate about the success or otherwise of the emancipation scheme is beyond this summary; certainly it did not give the peasants the economic freedom that they desired, even less political freedom. It did necessitate reorganisation of local and provincial government. In 1864, an elected assembly (*zemstvo*) was set up in each district and province. Each *zemstvo* nominated an executive board, with representation of five social groups, including peasants, although the board's system of decision-making was by voting weighted to favour the nobility. *Zemstvo* decisions were also completely subordinate to the will of the *Guberniia* Governor. Analogous reforms in 1870 gave each town and city an elected council (*duma*).

After emancipation, peasants had their own system of local government. Each peasant would be a member of a community known as a *mir*.[22] A number of *miry* would compose a larger administrative unit, a *volost'*. The *volost'* would have an elected assembly, and also, importantly, as part of the emancipation scheme, its own court. Thus the peasants

---

[21] Chubarov, above n 12, at 75.
[22] The Russian word *mir* also means world and peace. Tolstoy's famous book *War and Peace* is *Voina i mir* in the original.

had access to courts established specifically for their class, although in reality peasant justice might be effectuated outside the official system and come to light only when imposition of one of their customary penalties was bungled.[23]

The year 1864 was also the year of far-reaching legal reforms which brought to Russia for the first time a professional Bar and a hierarchy of courts, completely separated from the other branches of State, allowing judicial appeals. Jury trials were introduced for serious crimes. In aspiration at least, judges were independent and parties were equal, although this equality of course excluded the peasants who had their own courts. Alexander II's aim was expressed in the words of his decree:

> to establish in Russia fast, just and merciful courts, equal for all Our subjects, to increase judicial power, to give it the necessary independence and, in general, to strengthen in Our people the respect for law without which public prosperity is impossible and which must serve as a permanent guide for the actions of all and everybody, from the highest rank to that of the lowest rank.[24]

J. Reaction and repression

Alexander II had introduced an element of representative democracy in local government. He had been considering a more general political change, with advisory representation in the State Council, when he was assassinated in 1881 by the nihilist group People's Will. His son Alexander III (born 1845) did not share his father's progressive aims. He believed in divine right, and his priorities of nationality, orthodoxy and autocracy[25] left no room for experiments with democratic consultation. He was more interested in centralisation and reduced the powers of the *zemstvo*, placing them under the control of government-appointed land captains. Censorship was strengthened, and the secret police system, the *Okhrana*,

---

[23] See S Frank, 'Popular Justice, Community, and Culture among the Russian Peasantry 1870–1900' in B Eklof and S Frank (eds), *The World of the Russian Peasant: Post-Emancipation Culture and Society* (Boston, Mass, Unwin Hyman, 1990); R Beerman, 'Pre-revolutionary Russian peasant laws' in WE Butler (ed), *Russian Laws, Historical and Political Perspectives* (Leyden, Sijthoff, 1977) 172.

[24] PH Juviler, *Revolutionary Law and Order* (New York, Free Press, 1976) 6.

[25] Trilogy coined in 1833 by Minister of Education Count Sergei Uvarov, and accepted by Nicholas I and his successors.

which had been abolished in the final year of Alexander II's reign, was resurrected. A Russification campaign brought discriminatory legislation against those not of the Orthodox Christian faith and those not ethnically Russian. Any reform to reduce the Tsar's autocracy – propagated under the slogan of the 'people's autocracy'[26] – became anathema.

K. Reluctant reform – 1905–06

Alexander III's sudden death from natural causes in 1894 brought his eldest son Nicholas to the throne. As conservative and anti-Semitic as his father, Nicholas II (born 1868) is said to have lacked the former's strength of character. A series of unfortunate events – famine during 1891–92, repercussions following the slaughter of innocent petitioners on 'Bloody Sunday' in January 1905, failure in war against Japan – compelled Nicolas to concede to constitutional reforms. These came in stages, which unfortunately lagged behind the aspirations of the many different voices exhorting their necessity and were not consistently implemented. Nevertheless, they were ground-breaking.

The first tentative step was the Manifesto of 6 August 1905, which undertook to establish a State Duma as a consultative body, indirectly elected by a restricted franchise. But the Duma in this form was never convoked, and further civil unrest over the summer of 1905 impelled Nicholas to issue his comparatively brief but significant October Manifesto. This obliged the Government to establish for the very first time in the Russian Empire

> the essential foundations of civil freedom, based on the principles of genuine inviolability of the person, freedom of conscience, speech, assembly and association.[27]

However, when incorporated into the second chapter of the 1906 Fundamental Law these rights were not absolute; they were exercised 'as determined by law'.[28]

---

[26] Chubarov, above n 12, at 110.

[27] D Field (tr), Nicholas II, 'Manifesto of October 17, 1905' (Art 1), available at <http://academic.shu.edu/russianhistory/index.php/Manifesto_of_October_17th%2C_1905>, accessed 29 March 2010.

[28] English abridged translation available at 'The Russian Fundamental Laws of 1906', <http://www.dur.ac.uk/a.k.harrington/fundlaws.html>, accessed 1 August 2010.

In the October Manifesto Nicholas also promised that voting rights would be extended to those classes excluded from representation in the previous Duma, and that future electoral laws would be decided by the Legislature, not the Executive (Article 2). He lied. In Article 3 he undertook

> to establish as an unbreakable rule that no law shall take effect without confirmation by the State Duma and that the elected representatives of the people shall be guaranteed the opportunity to participate in the supervision of the legality of the actions of Our appointed officials.[29]

The law extending the franchise as promised was passed on 11 December 1905, and after much committee discussion the appropriately amended Fundamental Law of Russian Empire was adopted on 20 February 1906. However, it was decided that it would be dangerous to publish the new law before the elections for the Legislature, so it appeared on the day the Duma opened, 10 May 1906.

Nicholas had chaired some preparatory discussions, and he reluctantly conceded a small but symbolic alteration in the description of his position. The previous version of the Fundamental Law (Article 4) described the Tsar (Emperor) as 'autocratic monarch with unlimited power'. The word 'unlimited' was deleted in the new version:

> The All-Russian Emperor possesses the supreme autocratic power. Not only fear and conscience, but God himself, commands obedience to his authority.[30]

Thus autocracy was preserved, but the autocrat could agree to share power, and Article 7 acknowledged 'the sovereign emperor exercises power in conjunction with the State Council and the State Duma'. The Emperor had legislative initiative, exclusive in the case of changes to the Fundamental Law, and a right of veto. He retained full executive power. He had the right to appoint and dismiss government ministers, and members, and the Chair, of the Council of Ministers, and controlled foreign policy and the armed forces as commander in chief. Importantly, the Council of Ministers could submit edicts directly to the Tsar for approval and promulgation between Duma sessions.

---

[29] Field, above n 27.
[30] Above n 28.

i. The new Legislature

The new legislative body was bicameral, with the upper chamber formed from a newly-constituted State Council, and the lower chamber consisting of the new State Duma. Under the 1906 Fundamental Law, half the State Council was appointed by the Tsar, and half indirectly elected: by *zemstvo*s, assemblies of nobles, trade unions, universities and the Academy of Sciences. Three members representing the Russian Orthodox Church were appointed by the Church Synod.

The new Duma had 524 members. Elections were also indirect, through a complex system of *'curiae'* – colleges or constituencies – of land-owners, urban dwellers, peasants and workers, for which only male citizens over 25 years old voted. Women, military servicemen, students and criminal defendants or convicts were totally excluded. The *curiae* elected provincial conventions, which elected Duma members for five-year terms. The weighting was deliberately uneven. In the 1906 Duma a group of 2,000 land-owners (mainly gentry), 4,000 urban dwellers, 30,000 peasants or 90,000 industrial workers would each be represented by one member. In the non-Russian regions representation was also weighted to benefit ethnic Russians.

The Duma and the State Council had equal legislative power. After approval by both chambers, bills were sent to the Emperor for consideration. Unless he agreed, no law could enter into force. He could also dissolve the Duma at will, which he did with both the First Duma (27 April to 9 July 1906) and the Second (20 February to 3 June 1907). Little was achieved by either.

Despite the Fundamental Law stipulating that changes to electoral law needed legislative consent, the Government reduced the number of Duma members to 442 and altered the *curiae* composition to enhance land-owner representation. Now one member might represent 230 landowners, '1,000 wealthy business people . . . 15,000 lower-middle-class voters; 60,000 peasants; and 125,000 urban workers'.[31] Dominated by landed nobility, this Third Duma cooperated easily with the Government. It sat for its full five years from 1 November 1907 and adopted more than 2,000 laws, including important land reforms. The Fourth Duma, established 15 November 1912, ceased activity early on 25 February 1917, when the experiment to limit imperial autocracy was

---

[31] Chubarov, above n 12, at 154.

violently brought to an end by revolution. Nicholas abdicated, his brother Grand Duke Michael was unwilling to assume the throne, and administration passed to an ineffective Provisional Government. This fell to the Bolshevik Communists in the 1917 Great October Socialist Revolution.

L. The imperial legacy

Historian Chubarov concludes that:

> Despite the Petrine Europeanization, Catherine's 'enlightened absolutism', Alexander I's liberal aspirations, the liberal reforms under Alexander II and the constitutional experiment under Nicholas II, the basic, essential features of Russia's political system were still practically unchanged in the early twentieth century from what they had been in the seventeenth century.[32]

There was a heritage of mutual mistrust between the population and the Government. There was State control through censorship, restrictive laws against association and the exercise of religious belief (other than Orthodox Christianity), restriction of movement both within and out of the country, and lack of effective channels for expression of political aspirations.

Russia's particular history, with a combination of the Autocrat's sense of divine office and little opportunity for the growth of civic society as understood by Russia's western neighbours, meant that the revolutionaries, and in particular the founders of Soviet Russia, had limited experience of an effective written Constitution, or indeed any sense of constitutionality.

That is not to say that there was no notion of rights in the Russian Empire, but they attached to social groups – the ranks defined by the State – rather than individuals.[33] The idea of natural personal rights was regarded by Russian conservatives as 'harmful to youth'.[34] There was also the preference for gradual 'change from above'

---

[32] *Ibid* at 210.

[33] J Burbank, 'An Imperial rights regime: law and citizenship in the Russian Empire' (2006) 7(3) *Kritika* 397; and Borisova, above n 20, at 305.

[34] Borisova, above n 20, at 318.

by means of refining existing institutions. The establishment of complete 'legality', as the authorities saw it, replaced the need for a constitution – something that was alien to domestic traditions.[35]

The Russian Empire was unusual. Subjugated territories were contiguous with the home State, not overseas. This affected concepts of citizenship and Statehood; issues of diversity were close to home. Some differences were tolerated, for example Alexander I allowed Poland a written Constitution in 1818, but felt his Russian subjects not yet developed enough for one.[36]

In Imperial Russia, approaches to reform tended to divide into two antagonistic views. The Westernisers advocated copying external models, whilst the Slavophiles sought inspiration from existing social traditions. An analogous contrast existed between the 19th-century German romantics, with their idea of progression through the national spirit of a 'people' (*Volk*), and the French rationalists who advocated a natural law approach. Borisova persuasively shows that in the codification debate in early 19th-century Russia, the Russian word *Ulozhenie* (compilation) became associated with theorists sympathetic to the former approach, and *Svod* (Digest) with the latter. Medushevsky sees a similar polarisation in the approach to constitutionalism.[37] On the one hand, liberal aristocrats sought a Constitution imposed from above. On the other hand, revolutionary movements tried to smash the existing system from below. The Decembrists who demonstrated in favour of Constantine after the death of Alexander I epitomised this division. They were split into two groups, the North and South Decembrists, which held opposed views as how best reform should proceed. Neither succeeded.

III. THE CONSTITUTION DURING THE SOVIET ERA

A. End of empire and establishing soviet power

During the turmoil in 1905, workers in St Petersburg established a group to coordinate strike action. It was called the Soviet of Workers' Deputies, the Russian word *soviet* meaning council. The Soviet, roughly based on

---

[35] *Ibid* at 321.
[36] *Ibid* at 330.
[37] Medushevsky, above n 13, at 81 and 87.

the Paris Commune of 1871, became the model for the revolutionaries opposing the Provisional Government after the abdication of the Tsar in March 1917. When Lenin returned to Russia in April 1917, he published his 'April Theses' which called for 'All power to the soviets'. When his Bolsheviks took charge after the October 1917 Revolution, they developed a network of soviets.[38]

Lenin's system of soviets was a way to harness the revolutionary zeal of the masses, forming 'bottom-up' government, although always under the watchful eye of the leading core, the Communist Party. Local soviets (directly elected but with a class-based voting system) indirectly elected Congresses of Soviets up to the top level of the All-Russian Congress of Soviets.

In the form developed from 1936 the soviets were directly elected by universal suffrage. There was a hierarchy, with the USSR Supreme Soviet at the top, the local soviets at the bottom and federal regional soviets in between. Each soviet was a representative agency. It could pass legislation (limited in scope for the lower tiers). It elected from amongst its members an executive committee to act as the administrative agency and exercise full power when the soviet was not sitting. For the Supreme Soviet, this was its Presidium.

The Supreme Soviet also appointed the USSR Council of Ministers (Government), and this headed the hierarchy of executive committees. An executive committee was thus answerable both to its soviet and to the executive committee of the next higher-level soviet. This double tie-in ('dual subordination') worked well to ensure cohesion across the huge Soviet State, particularly as the leading members of these agencies would also be Communist Party members working under Party discipline.[39]

B. Marxist theory on State and law

The revolutionaries' belief in Marxist theory gave them a distinctive perspective on the role of law in society, and consequently a novel view

---

[38] Russia used the Julian calendar, which by 1917 lagged 13 days behind the Gregorian calendar used by almost all of Western Europe, until 1 February 1918, which became 14 February. As a result, Revolution Day, celebrating the Great October Socialist Revolution, was on 11 November.

[39] S Dobrin, 'Soviet Federalism and the Principle of Double Subordination' (1944) 30 *Transactions of the Grotius Society* 260.

of the function of a written Constitution. Karl Marx applied Hegel's theory of dialectics to societal development, although without Hegel's inferred higher Force (God, World Spirit). Marx theorised that the dialectical antagonism between social classes drove society to evolve. He, and particularly Frederick Engels who popularised his theories, postulated five evolutionary stages of society, culminating in communism. At each stage the means of production forms the all-important economic substructure. Law, religion and morals are mere superstructure. Therefore law does not have any intrinsic or enduring quality but is contingent on the society's particular evolutionary stage. In all but communism the ruling class uses law as a tool to subjugate the other classes. The final stage of communism would be achieved once workers in industry realise that they need not be wage slaves and instead take the means of production into their own hands. The ruling class would be eliminated, and workers would own both the means of production and the fruits of their labour. Elimination of parasitic groups (such as capitalists and religious organisations) would allow the communist principle 'from each according to his ability, unto each according to his needs'.

Engels financially supported Marx and popularised Marx's theory. Engels' 1884 book, *The Origin of the Family, Private Property and the State*, highlighted the 'withering away of the state' as communism is achieved:

> Society, which will reorganise production on the basis of a free and equal society of producers, will put the whole machinery of state where it will then belong: into the museum of antiquities, by the side of the spinning-wheel and the bronze axe.[40]

Importantly, Marx claimed that his theory of societal development was scientifically proven, so progress to communism is inevitable. This has two important repercussions. First, the end justifies the means if one were attempting, as Lenin was, to accelerate progress. Secondly, society develops in stages, therefore any written Constitution need only be appropriate for that stage, rather than an immutable expression of the will of some founding fathers.

---

[40] F Engels, *The Origin of the Family, Private Property and the State* (Moscow, Progress Publishers, 1968) 170. Engels based his 'scientific' conclusions on the work of an American evolutionist anthropologist, Lewis H Morgan, whose research was later discredited as being overly speculative and disproved by ethnological and archaeological findings.

Soviet theoreticians extended Marx and Engels' simple five stages of societal evolution, particularly as the Soviet State endured in a mainly hostile world without yet achieving communism. It became a tradition for the Party leader to enhance the ideology with a new stage, and this was often marked by a new Constitution.[41] Lenin introduced the 'dictatorship of the proletariat', where the proletariat, lead by the Party vanguard, would take over the existing State structure and accelerate progress towards socialism. Under the dictatorship of the proletariat the maxim is 'he who does not work, neither shall he eat' (Article 18, RSFSR Constitution of 1918).

Unlike Marx, Soviet theory treated socialism as a separate stage to be traversed before communism. Stalin, who was Party General Secretary from March 1922 to March 1953, declared when he introduced the draft 1936 USSR Constitution that 'the complete victory of the socialist system in all spheres of the national economy is now a fact'.[42] Antagonistic classes had been eliminated, leaving the two fraternal classes, workers and peasants, symbolised by the hammer and sickle in Soviet iconography.

The 1936 Constitution was adopted at a time when the official line called for stability of law to achieve 'socialism in one country' under conditions of 'capitalist encirclement'. It was therefore 'more akin in both style and content to the "bourgeois" constitutions so much despised in the early years'.[43] The timing of its adoption was significant. Stalin was prepared to overlook the class war to have more influence on the world stage. The USSR had joined the League of Nations in 1934 on Germany's exit, and was keeping a wary eye on Nazi developments. As well as its external 'propaganda' role,[44] the Constitution also signalled stability for the domestic population decimated by forced collectivisa-

---

[41] A Evans, 'Developed socialism in Soviet ideology' (1977) 38 *Soviet Studies* 409; K Ruutu, 'Past, present and future in Russian constitutional politics: Russian Constitutions in conceptual historical perspective' (2010) 35 *Review of Central and East European Law* 77.

[42] JV Stalin, 'On the Draft Constitution of the USSR' from Collected Works, vol 14 (London, Red Star Press, 1964), available at <http://www.marxists.org/reference/archive/stalin/works/1936/11/25.htm> accessed 7 January 2011.

[43] AL Unger, *Constitutional Development in the USSR: a Guide to the Soviet Constitutions* (London, Methuen, 1981) at 79.

[44] The word *propaganda* exists in Russian but does not have the same negative overtones it has in English. The Constitution propagates information, hence it is a *propaganda* document.

tion and industrialisation. It was a welcome distraction; as Areyah Unger notes,

> the coincidence in time between the adoption of the constitution and the terror of the so-called Great Purge is too striking to go unmentioned.[45]

In 1961 the Communist Party led by Khrushchev adopted a new Party Programme, asserting that the USSR had reached a further stage of 'full-scale construction of communism' with the unification of workers and peasants into a 'State of the whole people', and a reduced role for the State in the expectation of a rapid progression to communism. Opposed and ousted by Party colleagues in October 1964, Khrushchev's utopian predictions were quietly ignored.

His successor, Brezhnev, in the 1970s moved the utopian goal even further away through the further refinement of 'developed socialism', which the USSR marked by the adoption of the 1977 USSR Constitution. Neither of the next two Party leaders, Andropov, who took up office on the death of Brezhnev in November 1982, and Chernenko (Party First Secretary from February 1984 to March 1985), held office long enough to have an impact on theory, but the next and last Party General Secretary, Mikhail Gorbachev, who was in charge of the Party until he resigned that post in August 1991, instigated a new Party Programme and reassessment of the application of Leninist principles in his *perestroika* movement, discussed in section III.E. below.

C. Function of a Soviet Constitution

It is difficult to reconcile a notion of constitutionalism with Marxist theory. Both Marx and Lenin, particularly in the latter's pre-revolutionary writings, described the State as a tool of oppression by the ruling class. Lenin wrote in 1917, in *The State and Revolution*, that the bourgeois State should be forcibly smashed, to be replaced by a proletarian State which would be subject to the withering depicted by Engels. Faced with having a State to run, Lenin modified his view to allow the possibility of the proletariat taking over the existing State structure to create a workers' State.

---

[45] Unger, above n 43, at 83.

As the workers' State embodies the will of the working people, it can never be in conflict with the people, so there is no need for any mechanisms to protect the people from State actions. This reasoning also undermines any requirement for separation of powers. There is but one power – that of the people – and it is administered on their behalf by appropriate State agencies. The doctrine of separation of powers was thus decried by Soviet theoreticians as a 'bourgeois fiction' (although from 1936 the convenience of separation in the administration of power was acknowledged).

Of infinitely more significance to the functioning of the Soviet State than any Constitution was the fact that, prior to 1990, the USSR was a single-party State. The Communist Party ruled, and it did so through total control – of personnel in key positions, and of citizens' economic life as well as their social and political activities. Nevertheless, the Party had decided that Constitutions were important symbolic acts, so the Soviet State was graced with not one but many. In 1988 Butler could write, '[a]t the moment, 36 constitutions are in force on Soviet territory'.[46] Not only the USSR but each of its (then) 15 Union Republics, and the autonomous republics within some of those, had a Constitution. Unsurprisingly, their substantive wording was remarkably similar.[47]

What, then, was the purpose of a Soviet Constitution? It did not work well as a legal document. It was not directly applicable. It could not be pleaded in court and, although described as 'Basic Law', subordinate legislation was occasionally inconsistent. However, any Constitution is a political as well as a legal document, and this aspect was particularly strong for Lenin, who famously asserted: 'Law is a political measure, is politics.'[48] A Soviet Constitution acted as an educative 'propaganda' document for both internal and external audiences. It depicted a functioning workers' State, enhancing its legitimacy. A new Constitution would mark achievement of a new stage, but paradoxically at the same time it would be aspirational, a blueprint for the future.[49]

---

[46]   WE Butler, *Soviet Law*, 2nd edn (London, Butterworths, 1988) 143.

[47]   See WB Simons, 'Introduction' in WB Simons (ed), *Constitutions of the Communist World* (Leiden, Brill, 1980).

[48]   '*Zakon est' mera politicheskaia, est' politika.*' V Lenin, '*O Karikature na Marxism i ob "imperialisticheskom kapitalisme"*', in V Lenin, *Polnoe Sobranie Sochinenip*, 5th edn (Moscow, Politicheskaia Literatura, 1973) vol 30, at 99. English translation, 'A Caricature of Marxism and Imperialist Economism' from V Lenin, *Collected Works*, vol 23 (Moscow, Progress Publishers, 1964), available at <http://www.marxists.org/archive/lenin/works/1916/carimarx/4.htm#v23pp64h-048>, accessed 7 April 2010.

[49]   Simons, above n 47, xi–xvi.

One clear function of a Soviet Constitution was to set out the structure of State agencies, although not always with complete candour. Given that separation of powers did not fit with the official ideology, it is unsurprising that State agencies were not neatly divided between the standard trilogy of legislative, executive and judicial. Particularly in the idealistic 1918 RSFSR Constitution, there was no attempt to delineate between the two central agencies, the All-Russian Congress of Soviets and its Central Executive Committee (CEC). They were jointly specified to have 'jurisdiction over all matters of general State importance' listed in Article 49, as well as 'any other matter which they deem within their jurisdiction' (Article 50). There were also gaps: no mention of the CEC's Presidium, nor of other important bodies such as the Bolshevik party (as it was known at the time) or the *Cheka*, the Extraordinary Commission for Combating Counter-Revolution, the first in a long line of Soviet State security organisations.

From 1936, Soviet terminology made a distinction between agencies of State power and agencies of State administration. The agencies of State power were the soviets. Over time their full name had changed. In 1918 the soviets were of 'workers', soldiers' and peasants' deputies'; by 1936 they were of soviets of 'working people's deputies'; and in 1977 they were just 'people's deputies' as the 'State of the whole people' had been achieved.

The highest agencies of State power in the USSR and in each of its Union Republics were their Supreme Soviets. The USSR Supreme Soviet was bicameral, consisting of the Soviet of the Union and the Soviet of Nationalities (the RSFSR Supreme Soviet was unicameral). The Presidium of the USSR Supreme Soviet had an ill-defined role, apart from the fact that it was the

> permanently functioning agency of the Supreme Soviet of the USSR accountable to it for all its activity, and exercising the functions of the highest organ of state power of the USSR in the interim between its sessions, within limits prescribed by the Constitution. (1977 Constitution, Article 119)

The Chairman of the USSR Presidium was the formal Head of State. Union Republic Supreme Soviets had their equivalent Presidia.

Agencies of State power legislated: 'Legislative power of the USSR shall be exercised exclusively by the USSR Supreme Soviet' (1936 Constitution, Article 32), 'Laws of the USSR shall be adopted by the USSR Supreme Soviet or by a nationwide referendum held by decision of the USSR Supreme Soviet' (1977 Constitution, Article 108). But many other agencies could also pass legislative acts, for example the Presidium of the USSR Supreme Soviet could issue edicts and adopt decrees (1977 Constitution, Article 123), and the USSR Council of Ministers issued decrees and regulations 'on the basis and in execution of laws of the USSR and other decisions of the USSR Supreme Soviet and its Presidium' (1977 Constitution, Article 133).

At the local level, soviets' executive committees were the 'executive and administrative agencies'. The highest executive and administrative agencies were the Councils of Ministers (of the USSR and of its Union Republics), known as 'Councils of People's Commissars' until February 1947. These formed the Government.

The first Soviet Constitution, the Russian Socialist Federated Soviet Republic (RSFSR[50]) Constitution of 1918, was the most overtly political, with its clear expression of Marxist aspirations. It did not mention courts or justice. It was symbolic: 'of grandiose, colossal, world historical significance . . . formulated . . . as the Constitution of every nation where there is a proletariat and poorest peasantry'.[51] The General Provisions made clear in its first article (Article 9):

> The fundamental aim of the Constitution . . . designed for the present transitional period, is to establish a dictatorship of the urban and rural proletariat and the poorest peasantry in the form of a powerful All-Russian Soviet government with a view to crushing completely the bourgeoisie, abolishing the exploitation of man by man, and establishing socialism, under which there will be no division of classes and no state power.[52]

Lenin, a disaffected lawyer who regarded law as a transitory phenomenon associated with class oppression, nevertheless thought there was a value in asserting the new State's ideals in a Constitution. However, it was not important enough to pack the drafting committee; of its 15 members, only three were leading Bolsheviks:

---

[50]   The position of Socialist and Soviet in the acronym RSFSR switched in 1936 to indicate the victory of socialism; GP van den Berg, 'Power-Sharing Compacts under Russian Constitutional Law' in R Sharlet and F Feldbrugge (eds), *Public Policy and Law in Russia: In Search of a Unified Legal and Political Space* (Leiden, Nijhoff, 2005) 43, fn 9.

[51]   Speech by drafting committee member Yu Sledkov presenting the draft to the Fifth Congress of Soviets, cited in Unger, above n 43, at 11.

[52]   *Ibid* at 28.

It was to be the last time that members of non-Bolshevik parties and of an overt opposition group within the Bolshevik party would participate in the work of a Soviet constitutional commission, and it deserves to be recorded for that fact alone.[53]

The creation of the Union of Soviet Socialist Republics in 1922 lead to the first USSR Constitution in 1924. As the soviet system had spread to other regions of the former Empire, Constitutions similar in principle to the RSFSR Constitution were adopted: in the Ukraine and Belorussian Soviet Socialist Republics in 1919, in the Azerbaidzhan SSR in 1921, and in the Armenian and Georgian SSRs in 1922. In 1922, Bukhara and Khorezm adopted Constitutions which declared they were Soviet People's Republics, although with no mention of socialism.[54] From August 1922 the Communist parties of all the republics set up committees to work out a federal union. The Party Central Committee established a special commission headed by Stalin, in charge of nationalities policy, to formulate proposals. These led to the Union Treaty of the USSR of 30 December 1922. The extent to which this was the 'voluntary union' it claimed to be is doubtful.

> In 1922 seven Republics signed a Treaty. But it was only after the Communist Party in each of these Republics had become dominant, with the support of the Red Army. So on the surface there were agreements with these Republics, but in essence there was nothing but Party directives.[55]

The 1924 Constitution gave each Union Republic in the new Union the right of free secession (Article 4), although it was said that this provision had 'merely declaratory and not legislative character'.[56] Union Republics amended their Constitutions to take the USSR Constitution into account. In Russia this was done in 1925.

The 1936 'Stalin' Constitution marked a substantial shift in approach to State and law. The economic basis of the State had changed to full central planning, and the Stalinist theory of 'socialism in one country' required a strong State backed by strong law. The focus on the withering away of law previously associated with EB Pashukanis and NV Krylenko

---

[53] *Ibid* at 9–10.
[54] J Hazard, 'The Soviet Constitution: an Introduction' (1943) 3 *Lawyers Guild Review* 27 at 34.
[55] Yakovlev, above n 8, at 138.
[56] Unger, above n 43, at 54, citing S Dranitsyn, *Konstitutsiya SSSR i RSFSR*, 2nd edn (Leningrad, 1924) 85.

was replaced with the more positivist approach of AIa Vyshinskii. Émigré lawyer Dr Samuel Dobrin[57] noted in a contemporaneous article that

> The word 'revolution' or 'revolutionary' is not even once mentioned in the new Constitution; evidently revolution is left to Mussolini and Hitler.[58]

The resultant Constitution was a masterpiece. It was drafted principally by Bukharin,

> who less than two years later, in the last of the notorious show trials of the 1930s, was condemned to death for a variety of highly treasonable acts, including espionage, terrorism and conspiracy to dismember the USSR. It is a telling reflection of the surrealist character of Stalinist constitution making that the work of a man convicted of such grave crimes against the state became the supreme law of the land.[59]

Written in beautiful Russian, the 1936 Constitution presents an idyllic picture of a well-ordered State with citizens' rights and duties set out for the first time at USSR level (see section III.D.i. below). However, what was omitted was almost as significant as what was included. For example, articles on the formation of the renamed USSR Legislature fail to mention that only one candidate would be put up for each seat. Stalin 'apparently envisaged several candidates for a position, even though there would be only one political party'[60] but decided against this, supposedly out of a 'developing fear of European war'.[61] From then on until the *perestroika* reforms discussed in section III.E. below, Soviet elections were characterised by a system of pre-election selection, with the potential candidates subject to vetting by the Party, ensuring that agencies at all levels of State were filled with right-minded people.

One ironic side-effect of this careful pre-election selection of the single electoral candidate was that the USSR Supreme Soviet (at least during the Brezhnev era) was much more representative of the general

---

[57] Dobrin, 'a member of the Russian Bar in practice in Russia until the revolution of 1917 and legal adviser to Soviet organizations in the United Kingdom from 1925 until 1930': *In Re Banque des Marchands de Moscou (Koupetschesky)* [1958] Ch 182 at 186.

[58] S Dobrin, 'The New Soviet Constitution' (1936) 22 *Transactions of the Grotius Society* 99.

[59] Unger, above n 43, at 80.

[60] Hazard, above n 54, at 40.

[61] *Ibid.* See also GP van den Berg, 'A new electoral law in the Soviet Union' (1978) 4 *Review of Socialist Law* 353 at 354.

population by gender, age and ethnicity than legislatures in western democracies. It also existed only for show. It met twice a year for two or three days, as a grand jamboree with deputies in national costume, while the more serious legislative work was carried out by the Supreme Soviet's Presidium, which had full power whenever the Supreme Soviet was not in session.

Even with single-candidate elections, it was not impossible for an individual to fail to be elected. If enough brave people went into the polling booth and crossed off the candidate's name before putting their ballot in the box, the candidate would not gain the required majority vote. Van den Berg, writing in 1978,[62] knew of only one instance when a candidate for a USSR or Union Republic Supreme Soviet was rejected, although Unger notes that, although rare, it was not unknown in local elections; in 1939, '125 out of a total of 1.3 million failed to get elected; in 1977 the equivalent figures were 61 out of 2.2 million'.[63]

In 1962 Khrushchev initiated drafting a post-Stalin Constitution to take into account the USSR's 'enhanced international status at the centre of a world system of socialist states',[64] but the process foundered, amongst other reasons, because there was insufficient unanimity about federal reforms to fit Khrushchev's reorganisation of the planned economy on a more regional basis (his *Sovnarkhoz* reforms). After his ouster in 1964, Brezhnev took over as Constitutional Drafting Commission Chairman, but little was done for almost 10 years. It is not clear why there was this hiatus, nor why in the spring of 1977 the Constitutional Commission was revived, leading to a draft being published on 4 June for public discussion. According to official figures, 140 million participants proposed 400,000 changes. The result was one new article (Article 102, that electors mandate their deputies) and some other alterations, but the main aim of the public campaign was to legitimise the new Constitution by mass involvement. Even though orchestrated, this was generally successful.

The text of the 1977 USSR Constitution contains grammatical errors.[65] However, it is more true to life than the previous Constitution,

---

[62] Van den Berg, above n 61, at 356. It was in the October 1939 elections for the National Assembly of Western Belorussia.

[63] Unger, above n 43, at 113.

[64] *Ibid* at 175.

[65] S Pomorski, 'The Language of the Soviet Constitution of 1977: A Note' (1981) 7 *Review of Socialist Law* 331.

in that the real precedence of the Communist Party is indicated by its inclusion in Article 6 as the 'guiding and directing force of Soviet society'. There were minor changes in the State framework, for example Supreme Soviet terms were increased from four to five years, but as they merely acted as stage-managed 'rubber stamps', this had no tangible impact apart from the sham of the elections being less frequent. (Local soviets' terms were increased from two to two-and-a-half years.) In 1977 Brezhnev began a tradition that the Party General Secretary would also be Chairman of the USSR Supreme Soviet Presidium, therefore Head of State. Although this role carried no executive power, western media occasionally referred to the post-holder by the honorific title of President, although the USSR did not adopt a presidential system until 1990 (see section III.H. below).

A parallel Constitution was passed in the RSFSR in 1978 (replacing a 1937 Constitution). The 1978 Constitution (much amended) remained in force in Russia until the adoption of the current Constitution on 12 December 1993.

D. The Soviet law in individual rights

The Soviet approach to Marxist theory not only impacted the role of a Constitution, it also affected the treatment of individual rights.

i. Early Soviet rights

Treatment of rights in the 1918 Constitution combined a reaction against pre-revolutionary religious discrimination with overt political discrimination. The Constitution was in two parts. Part One was the Declaration of the Rights of the Working and Exploited People, drafted by Lenin and presented to the Constituent Assembly, which rejected it. The door to the Constituent Assembly was barred three days later by sailors loyal to Lenin, while its members were out at lunch. 'Thus ended the only genuinely elected legislative body during the whole period of Soviet rule.'[66]

---

[66] D Barry and C Barner-Barry, *Contemporary Soviet Politics: An Introduction* (1977) at 21, cited in R R Ludwikowski, *Constitution-making in the Region of Former Soviet Dominance: with full texts of all new constitutions ratified through July 1995* (Durham, NC, Duke University Press, 1996) 17.

Despite its name, the Declaration did not deal with rights but flagged up political objectives, such as nationalisation of land and other natural resources, moving towards State ownership of enterprises, railways and banks; repudiation of debts 'contracted by the governments of the Tsar, the landlords and the bourgeoisie'; bringing about peace, granting independence to Finland[67] and proclaiming the right of self-determination for Armenia. By the early 1920s the Declaration was outdated: 'Indeed Lenin himself, shortly after its publication, had baptised it "a child of the revolution in a very bad hat." '[68]

Some rights were included in the General Provisions. The freedom of conscience article allowed both religious and anti-religious propaganda (Article 13), as the new State distanced itself from the religious intolerance of the Tsarist regime. However, as the Constitution was geared to 'establish a dictatorship of the urban and rural proletariat and the poorest peasantry . . . with a view to crushing completely the bourgeoisie' (Article 9), there could be no equality. Discrimination was evident, for example at all levels representation was heavily weighted against rural inhabitants. Both active and passive franchises were severely restricted on class grounds. Any individual or group could be deprived of their rights if 'used to the detriment of the interest of the socialist revolution' (Article 23).

The 1924 USSR Constitution dealt exclusively with the formation of the union and State structure, with no section on individual rights. It did specify that there would be a Supreme Court (Chapter 7) with powers to review the activity of Union Republic Supreme Courts and protest to the Central Executive Committee (CEC) when USSR legislation or the interests of other Union Republics were violated. It could also, at the request of the CEC, give an opinion on the constitutionality of any orders issued by the Union Republics, and resolve legal disputes between Union Republics (Article 43).[69]

The Russia Constitution amended in 1925 to take into account the USSR Constitutions did not contain the Declaration of the Rights of the Working and Exploited People; it did keep the franchise restrictions.

---

[67] On Finnish constitutional history, see J Husa, *The Constitution of Finland: A Contextual Analysis* (Oxford, Hart, 2010).

[68] B Mirkine-Guetzévitch, 'The Public Law System of the Sovietic Dictatorship'(1930) 12 *Journal of Comparative Legislation and International Law* 248 at 256.

[69] PH Solomon, 'The USSR Supreme Court: History, Role, and Future Prospects' (1990) 38 *American Journal of Comparative Law* 127.

The 1936 USSR Constitution introduced universal suffrage. Since the victory of socialism there was no longer any need to discriminate on the basis of 'race or nationality, religious persuasion, educational qualification, domicile, social origin, property status and past activities' (Article 135), so all citizens aged 18 or over could vote, 'with the exception of the insane and persons convicted by a court of law to deprivation of electoral rights'. Chapter X dealt with Fundamental Rights and Duties of Citizens; for the first time rights were awarded on the basis of citizenship, not class. This chapter contained the one mention of the Communist Party, in Article 126, as the 'vanguard of the workers and the leading core of all organisations'. The approach to rights was similar to that in the 1977 Constitution, discussed below.

ii. *Rights under the 1977 USSR Constitution*

The developed USSR was proud of its law on individual rights. Rights in the 1977 Brezhnev Constitution had moved up in priority as compared with the 1936 Stalin Constitution, where the chapter on citizens' rights and duties was tenth out of 13. By 1977, rights were more prominent, symbolised by the fact that, of the nine sections of the 1977 Constitution, 'The State and the Individual' was the second, preceded only by the 'Fundamentals of the Social Order and Policy of the USSR'. Not only had rights become more prominent, but they also bore a closer relationship to practical reality than earlier. By 1977

> preoccupation with human rights had become a major international concern – not least owing to the activities of the dissident movement in the USSR itself.... [T]he Soviet Union had become a party to formal international commitments, most notably the two 1966 UN Covenants on Economic, Social and Cultural Rights and on Civil and Political Rights (ratified by the USSR in 1973) and the 1975 Helsinki Final Act. More important, the post-Stalin leadership of the USSR greatly expanded both the material welfare and the legal security of Soviet citizens. In regard to both socio-economic rights and civil liberties, therefore, the new constitution was able to incorporate changes already accomplished and in large part embodied in ordinary legislation.[70]

In keeping with Marxist priorities, economic rights were listed before social and political rights, and the focus was on practical implementation. Particularly for economic rights, each substantive article had a

---

[70] Unger, above n 42, at 194.

second paragraph detailing the measures to guarantee its exercise. Supporters of the Soviet concrete approach to rights regarded it as superior. They criticised bourgeois States' theoretical rights; what good is a right to work, when the capitalist economic system assumes inevitable unemployment? By contrast, the Soviet centrally-planned economy was designed to ensure that everyone capable of working did indeed exercise that right (1977 Constitution, Article 40), which was simultaneously a duty (Article 60). There were other duties. Article 66 exhorted parents to 'be obliged to be concerned about the upbringing of children, to prepare them for socially useful labour, and to raise worthy members of socialist society'. In return, 'Children shall be obliged to be concerned about parents and to assist them.'

Equality was a much-vaunted principle. Article 34 called for equality of citizens, irrespective of

> origin, social and property position, racial and national affiliation, sex, education, language, attitude to religion, type and nature of occupation, place of residence, and other circumstances.

Equality of nationality was important within the federal multi-ethnic Soviet State, and equality of sex allowed women to take their place in the national workforce. In fact, 'Equality of Citizens' was so important that it had a separate chapter, comprising the first half-dozen articles of the section on rights.

But the rights in the 1977 Constitution were not 'human rights'. They were neither inherent nor inalienable, but were based on the theory of 'dependent rights'. As the title of the chapter suggested in its reference to 'Rights, Freedoms and Duties', and as Article 59 made absolutely explicit, 'The exercise of rights and freedoms shall be inseparable from the performance by a citizen of his duties'. The phrase 'human rights' did appear in the 1977 Constitution, but only in the chapter on Foreign Policy, where 'respect for human rights and freedoms' was embedded in Article 29 as one of the principles guiding relations between the USSR and other States, particularly those which were not following the Socialist path. It followed the principle of 'non-interference in internal affairs'.

The rights articles in the 1977 Constitution did not have direct application in court. Additional legislation was needed to create a legally-actionable right. The right to appeal to a court actions of officials, based on Article 58(2), was brought into operation only 10 years later (see chapter six for further developments on citizens' appeals).

Another feature of the 1977 Constitution, and its 1936 predecessor, was that the socio-political rights contained very clear words of limitation. For example, Article 47 'guaranteed freedom of scientific, technical and artistic creativity' only 'in conformity with the aims of communist construction'; similarly for the right to unite in social organisations in Article 51. Freedoms of speech, press, assembly and meetings, street processions and demonstrations (Article 50) were guaranteed if exercised 'in conformity with the interests of the people and in order to strengthen and develop the socialist system'. Activities which did not appear (to the State) to serve these lofty purposes were criminalised. Article 52 on freedom of conscience was asymmetrical, giving freedom to 'profess any religion or none, to perform religious worship, or to conduct atheist propaganda' but not freedom to conduct religious propaganda. Those whose belief systems encouraged active proselytising, such as Jehovah's Witnesses, could be prosecuted.

Perestroika brought a complete change in approach to rights; no longer dependent, they transformed to human rights. This development is discussed in chapter six.

E. *Perestroika*

In March 1985 the young Mikhail Gorbachev became Party General Secretary. He was the first lawyer in the Party Politburo since Lenin. Already a rising star when Brezhnev's successor Andropov died – Gorbachev organised Andropov's funeral, symbolising that he was the heir apparent – he bided his time and placed his supporters strategically in the Party during the brief tenure of Brezhnev's old friend Chernenko as Party leader. Gorbachev was brought in as a reformer. He had succeeded in improving agriculture in his home territory of the south Russian Stavropol Territory (he had studied agronomics as well as law).

There was a 20-year generation gap between the previous three Party General Secretaries and Gorbachev. The missing generation had been decimated during the Great Patriotic War: '[O]f the male babies born from 1920 to 1925, the peak fighting generation, only 3 per cent survived.'[71] A mere 54 years old when he took charge of the Party,

---

[71] M Walker, *The Waking Giant: the Soviet Union under Gorbachev* (London, Penguin, 1987) xix.

Gorbachev had the youth and energy to push through dramatic changes in the governance of the USSR. Although the Party's primary motivation in choosing Gorbachev was economic reform, his vision also included social and political reform. He advocated '*perestroika*', that is restructuring or reconstruction, in all areas of Soviet life, whilst attempting to remain true to the Leninist vision of progress. *Perestroika* watchwords included *glasnost'* (openness to speak out), *demokratizatsiia* (democratisation) and *gumanism* (humanism).

Gorbachev brought with him knowledge of, and respect for, law. Significant for the growth of constitutionalism, he encouraged the aspiration towards the rule of law. A year after Gorbachev had taken up office, the CPSU held its 27th Party Congress, at which a framework for economic reforms and new Party Programme were agreed. Once the Party had endorsed the principles, plans for significant economic reforms quickly followed. At that stage the economic reforms aimed to encourage 'socialist competition', initiative and democracy in the workplace, but still within the overall structure of a planned economy; the central authorities were not yet ready to relinquish price control.

In June 1988 the CPSU held the 19th Party Conference to discuss the requirements for the next stage of *perestroika*. The Conference was the first for 47 years (as contrasted to the five-yearly Party Congresses). Six 'Theses' proposed by the Party Central Committee were discussed by Party members elected to attend, resulting in Resolutions highlighting the requirements to advance *perestroika* in each sector.[72] The Resolution on Legal Reform was groundbreaking. It opened with an acknowledgement that there should be a socialist rule-of-law State (*sotsialisticheskoe pravovoe gosudarstvo*), with reforms 'to ensure the supremacy of the law in all spheres of the life of society'.[73] The Russian adjective usually translated as rule-of-law or law-governed (*pravovoe*) comes from the word for law in its most expansive sense (*pravo*), implying an inherent value (see chapter one). Linking that to the concept of a socialist State was radical, indeed almost oxymoronic. Amongst other things, the Resolution recognised the presumption of innocence, previously problematic as a concept given the investigative nature of Soviet criminal procedure,

---

[72] On Progress in the Implementation of the Decisions of the Party Congress, Democratisation of Soviet Society and the Reform of the Political System, the Struggle against Bureaucratism, Relations between Nationalities, *Glasnost'* and, lastly, Legal Reform.

[73] Resolution 1 passed 1 July 1988, reported in *Pravda* and *Izvestiia*, 5 July 1988.

called for adversariality in trials, strengthened the independence of judges and said that 'it would be useful to institute a constitutional supervision committee'. Although it had no legislative authority, as a policy document from the ruling CPSU the Resolution on Legal Reform was taken seriously, and over the following years all its recommendations were enacted with only minor digressions. The tradition of reform from above held strong.

The Resolution on Democratisation also led to far-reaching reforms. A new form of democracy was advocated, with multi-candidate elections of representatives[74] to a completely revised Legislature. After discussions on a draft published on 22 October, amendments were introduced to the 1977 Constitution on 1 December 1988 which transformed the back half of the Constitution (chapter 12 onwards, dealing with the 'Soviets of People's Deputies and the Procedure for Electing Them', details of which are to be found in section III.F. below). This was the nearest there was to a new Constitution for *perestroika*. Apart from a change in the constitutional position of the CPSU, also discussed in section III.F. below, which required amendment to Articles 6 and 49, the first 11 chapters remained untouched by the dramatic legal reforms. The Brezhnev approach to individual rights was not excised from the USSR Constitution despite a transformation in rights laws during the idealistic *perestroika* period, discussed in chapter six.

F.   The December 1988 Amendments to the 1977 USSR Constitution

i.   *The USSR Congress of People's Deputies*

The December 1988 amendments introduced the USSR Congress of People's Deputies (CPD) as a completely new 'highest agency of State power', replacing the bicameral USSR Supreme Soviet. The Supreme Soviet had directly-elected deputies, but they had stood as sole candidates and had kept their prior jobs as their representative duties were minimal; Supreme Soviet sessions lasted only two to three days, twice a year. The much smaller, indirectly-elected Supreme Soviet Presidium, which exercised power in between those sessions, was also superseded.

---

[74] Butler, above n 46, at 154 recalls that '[i]n the 1987 elections, as an experiment, multiple candidates were nominated in selected districts'.

The new CPD was large. It consisted of 2,250 delegates (the old Supreme Soviet had 1,500). It had a term of five years, meeting at least once a year. Although unicameral, delegates gained their seats in one of three ways. One-third of delegates were elected from electoral districts based on population, one-third from the different federal subjects of the USSR[75] and, as a complete innovation, one-third were put in post by particular 'social organisations' listed in the new Law on Elections of People's Deputies of the USSR passed at the same time.[76] (Under the previous system, social organisations had had merely the right to propose candidates.) Candidates for election to the first two types of constituencies should be at least 21 years old[77] and 'ballots may include any number of candidates' (Article 100). In the other third, social organisations were left to decide how they each would fill their allotted seats. As the leading 'social organisation', the CPSU was allocated 100 seats. For the first time, it had a formal role in the structure of the State, ironic given that one of Gorbachev's *perestroika* goals was to reduce the Party's hands-on day-to-day governance and return it to being the 'guiding and directing force' (Article 6, 1977 Constitution). The Party put up 100 candidates for its 100 seats, with Party leader Gorbachev heading the list. This champion of democratisation was thus never subject to election by the population. He gained his CPD seat through Party selection, and from there in March 1990 was appointed USSR President by the CPD, without resort to a General Election (see section III.H. below).

The tripartite method for forming the USSR CPD undermined the principle of equality. As with the previous bicameral Supreme Soviet, any citizen aged 18 and over had the right to vote for a constituency deputy as well as representatives of each of the different levels of federal subject where they lived (Union Republic, territory, etc). The serious inequality came from 'social organisation' representation. Depending on how many

[75] On the basis of 32 deputies from each Union Republic, 11 from each autonomous republic, 5 from each autonomous region and one from each autonomous national area.

[76] The social organisations eligible were listed in the draft Constitutional amendments, but in the final form they were put instead in the USSR Law on Elections of People's Deputies. As well as the CPSU, there were trade unions, *Komsomol* (the Young Communists' League), veterans and women's groups, and other social organisations such as stamp collectors, cinema fans, book lovers and musicians.

[77] The 1988 constitutional amendment said that the deputies to Union Republic CPDs need only be 18 years old. In 1989 this was deleted, leaving Union Republics free to set their own age restrictions.

of these a citizen belonged to, he or she might have a hand in selecting differing numbers of representatives – or none at all – for that third of the Congress deputies. The Soviet response to criticism of this uneven input was 'We'll do it our way'; they saw no problem with their innovative method of increased representation of the most socially active citizens.

There were two other important characteristics of the new CPD deputies. First, although the elections were multi-candidate, they were not yet multi-party. The CPSU still had the monopoly of political power, although the new 'informal organisations' which *perestroika* encouraged could nominate candidates. Secondly, the CPD deputies would be paid. There was initial controversy as to whether the rate of pay should be uniform or should be linked to each deputy's individual loss of earnings. Uniformity won. For the first time in the USSR there were professional democratic representatives; the start of a political elite.

ii. *The USSR Supreme Soviet*

The constitutional amendments reformed the Supreme Soviet to be 'the permanently functioning legislative, administrative, and control agency of State power of the USSR' (Article 111). Despite an old name, this was a new body, although bicameral like its namesake. The two chambers were of equal size, with equal rights, and the Supreme Soviet's 542 members were CPD deputies elected in a secret ballot from amongst themselves. The new Soviet of the Union was formed of deputies from electoral districts based on population and social organisations, and the Soviet of Nationalities of deputies from the federal subjects[78] and also social organisations. The Supreme Soviet sat twice a year for 'as a rule, three to four months' duration' (Article 112). In theory, one-fifth of its membership should have been replaced annually (Article 111), but during its two years' existence this was never done.

The Presidium of the Supreme Soviet was revamped, with a much-reduced role, as the 'agency accountable to the USSR Supreme Soviet which ensures the organisation of the work' of the CPD and Supreme Soviet (Article 118). Its composition was mainly *ex officio* and its duties mainly honorific, but it could issue edicts, adopt decrees and declare war. Importantly, it was given the power to

---

[78] 11 from each Union Republic, 4 from each autonomous republic, 2 from each autonomous region and one from each autonomous national area.

effectuate control over the observance of the USSR Constitution and ensure the conformity of Union Republic constitutions and laws to the USSR Constitution and laws. (Article 119(5))

The draft Constitutional amendments had eliminated this role, because one of the other reforms was to establish a completely new body to supervise constitutionality, the Constitutional Supervision Committee (CSC) (see chapter six). However, in the autumn of 1988 the Union Republic of Estonia passed legislation claiming ownership of natural resources in Estonia, and supremacy of local law. The Presidium declared the Estonian legislation void, as contrary to the USSR Constitution. This was a more powerful sanction than the CSC would have had, and this useful tool for maintaining central control was reinstated.[79]

The power of Constitutional amendment was reserved exclusively to the CPD, but the Supreme Soviet otherwise had a very broad remit, including deciding 'other questions relegated to the jurisdiction of the USSR except those which are relegated to the exclusive jurisdiction of the USSR CPD' (Article 113(20)). It could adopt laws and decrees, the only restriction being that they should not contradict CPD legislation.

The Chairman of the USSR Supreme Soviet was designated as the 'highest official' (Article 120) and was awarded for the first time some specific powers, including to issue regulations. The Council of Ministers (Government) was formed by the ministers being appointed by the Supreme Soviet at a joint session of both chambers, although it was accountable to both the CPD and the Supreme Soviet.

Elections to form the new CPD were held in March 1989. The results were dramatic. A politicised public in a nearly 90 per cent turnout took the opportunity to reject a number of high-profile Party members, for example the Leningrad Party Secretary Iurii Solov'ev. Boris Yel'tsin stood in Moscow Number One constituency and gained over 89 per cent of the vote, in spite of, or more likely because of, a Party campaign to discredit him[80] (although he did not resign from the Party for another

---

[79] See J Henderson, 'The Soviet Constitutional Reforms of December 1 1988: An Analysis of the Changes from Draft to Law' in R Plender (ed), *Legal History and Comparative Law: Essays in Honour of Albert Kiralfy* (London, Frank Cass, 1990) 73 at 90.

[80] See B Yeltsin (trans M Glenny), *Against the Grain* (New York, Simon & Shuster, 1990).

year). He then managed to secure a seat in the Supreme Soviet because a liberal deputy from Siberia relinquished his seat in Yel'tsin's favour.[81]

A number of run-off elections were needed, as the existing requirement, devised for single-candidate Soviet elections, that the winner should gain at least 50 per cent of the votes, had not yet been removed. Even those who won a clear plurality rarely had an absolute majority. But on 25 May the first convocation of the new CPD opened (it ran until 9 June). The sessions were televised, but this exercise in *glasnost'* (openness) had to be curtailed as people were shirking work to watch the novel spectacle of public political debate; a 20 per cent fall in industrial production was recorded during the CPD's first few days.[82]

G. The 1989 amendments

In December 1989 there was a small but important change to the previous year's reforms. Originally each Union Republic was to set up its own CPD, structured analogously to the USSR CPD. But the Union Republics were beginning to rebel. They successfully lobbied for the removal of the requirement that they should allocate seats to social organisations in their CPDs. In fact Russia was the only Union Republic to set up a CPD, but the 1989 amendments allowed it to be formed on the basis of only two types of constituency, not three: electoral districts based on population, and electoral districts based on federal subjects. The Communist Party (and other social organisations) had no specifically allocated seats in Russia. Further Russian developments are explored in the next chapter.

H. The 1990 amendments – from a parliamentary to a presidential system

The pace of change accelerated. The initial *perestroika* motivation had been economic – to bring innovation into the centrally State-planned economy. By the end of 1989 the Party decided that the economic reforms were not far-reaching enough, and the time had come to turn

---

[81] DD Barry, *Russian Politics. The Post-Soviet Phase* (New York, Peter Lang, 2002) 29.
[82] *Ibid.*

their back on State planning and move to a market economy. This was a momentous decision. No other State in the world had had such a complete State monopoly of ownership of industry, land, natural resources, railways, roads and other forms of communication. There was no blueprint on how best to change the economic basis of the largest State in the world. The Party decided it would be expedient to have an executive President to take the necessary decisive steps for the transformation. Gorbachev may also have felt that 'the proposal for a President would assist in shifting power from the Party to the state'.[83]

So on 14 March 1990 the USSR Constitution was amended again, with three significant reforms.[84] The constitutional position of the CPSU was changed (discussed below). The categories of ownership were revised in preparation for the capitalist economy. The USSR Presidency was introduced in a new chapter inserted into the Constitution, just after the chapter on the CPD and the Supreme Soviet, and just before that on the Council of Ministers.

The Constitution defined the USSR President as Head of State. No one could be President for more than two terms (absolutely). The postholder must be a USSR citizen aged 35–65, elected for a term of five years by universal, equal and direct suffrage by secret ballot. In fact no General Election was held. During discussion in the CPD the fear was raised of civil war in the event of a contested election. It was decided that the President would be appointed instead by the Congress itself. Initially more than one candidate was put forward, but by the time the vote was taken Mikhail Gorbachev, Party General Secretary and Supreme Soviet Chairman, was the sole candidate. Once President, Gorbachev stood down as Supreme Soviet Chairman, but retained his Party position. The presidential powers in Article 127-3 were quite extensive, including submitting to the Supreme Soviet candidates for important posts, ie Chairman of the Government (Council of Ministers); of the People's Control Committee; of the Supreme Court; the Procurator General, and the Chief State Arbitrator (at this stage State *Arbitrazh* had not yet been transformed into a court; see chapter six). The CPD subsequently confirmed the appointments. The President could also recommend to the Supreme

---

[83] AM Yakovlev with D Gibson, *The Bear that Wouldn't Dance: failed attempts to reform the constitution of the former Soviet Union* (Manitoba, Legal Research Institute, 1992) at 56.

[84] WE Butler, *Basic Documents on the Soviet Legal System*, 2nd edn (New York, Oceana, 1991) at 3.

Soviet and CPD dismissal of the same officials, with the exception of the Supreme Court Chairman. The President had unqualified power to 'suspend the effect of decrees and regulations of the Council of Ministers'. He was Commander-in-Chief, could appoint and replace the USSR Armed Forces High Command, and appoint judges of military tribunals. He could declare war in the event of an armed attack on the USSR, although he should 'immediately submit that question for the consideration of the USSR Supreme Soviet'. He could declare martial law or the more limited regime of an 'extraordinary situation', although not without qualification.

The President would head a new body, the Federation Council, to consider federal issues (Article 127-4). The Federation Council would consist of the highest State official of each Union Republic. The heads of the smaller federal subjects could also attend its meetings, as could the Chairmen of the Supreme Soviet and its two chambers.

There would also be a Presidential Council to assist in working out internal and external policy. The Government Chairman was a member *ex officio*; other members were appointed by the President. The President was given power to issue edicts 'on the basis of and in execution of the USSR Constitution and laws'. He had inviolability, but this could be withdrawn if he violated the USSR Constitution and laws by a two-thirds vote in the CPD, at the initiative of the CPD or Supreme Soviet, taking into account an opinion of the Constitutional Supervision Committee. The Constitution did not mention a Vice-President at this stage.

On 26 December 1990 further reforms refined the new arrangements. The post of Vice-President was added, the candidate to be proposed by the President and elected at the Presidential elections (Article 127-4). As there were no such elections, the chosen candidate Gennadii Ianaev (Yanaev) was put into post by the CPD. This was a fateful appointment. Less than eight months later Ianaev was one of the group of eight who attempted to oust Gorbachev in the unsuccessful August Putsch of 1991 (see section I below) which precipitated the dissolution of the USSR. (In the autumn of 1993 Yel'tsin as Russian President also had a rebellious vice-president: see chapter three. Under the current Russian Constitution there is no such post.)

The December 1990 reforms changed some terminology; the Government was now called the Cabinet of Ministers and its head the Prime Minister. Presidential power was also slightly increased. Individual ministers were no longer subject to scrutiny on appointment by the

Supreme Soviet, only the Government as a whole had to be approved. The reform-minded Presidential Council was eliminated. The background to these changes was Gorbachev increasingly using his presidential powers and downplaying his position as Party General Secretary, whilst the Union Republics had become less tolerant of central USSR authority and demanded more autonomy, if not complete independence.

i. Change in constitutional position of the Communist Party (CPSU)

One dramatic impact of *perestroika* was the successful call for the CPSU to relinquish its seven-decades' monopoly on political power. When it was passed in 1977, Article 6 of the Constitution gave the CPSU an unrivalled constitutional position as the 'guiding and directing force of Soviet society and the nucleus of its political system and State and social organisations'. Article 7 allowed 'Trade unions, the All-Union Leninist Communist Youth League, cooperative and other social organisations' also to 'take part in the administration of State and social affairs and in deciding political, economic and socio-cultural questions'. Despite some bitter opposition, a meeting of the Party Central Committee in February 1990 approved the elimination of the Party monopoly.[85] On 14 March, Articles 6, 7 and 51 (on the right to associate) were changed to allow citizens to unite in political parties. As a face-saving compromise the new Article 6 retained mention of the Party:

> The Communist Party of the Soviet Union, other political parties . . . and other organisations . . . shall participate in working out the policy of the Soviet State and in the administration of state and social affairs.

Article 7 now provided that these bodies should operate within the framework of the Constitution and Soviet laws, and forbade those

> which have the purpose to forcibly change the Soviet constitutional system and integrity of the socialist State, undermine its security, and inflame social, national, and religious dissension . . .

There were no other amendments to the first 11 chapters of the Constitution. As explained in chapter six, the approach to rights was overhauled during the *perestroika* era, but there was no new Constitution for *perestroika* and the existing USSR Constitution was not appropriately updated.

---

[85] Barry, above n 81, at 41.

I. March 1991 – end of December 1991 – the USSR Disintegrates

President Gorbachev presided over unprecedented economic, social and political reforms in *perestroika* USSR. His Achilles' heel was federal relations; he could not understand why any part of the USSR would want independence from the world's biggest superpower, and he underestimated the strength of individual national aspirations. In 'an attempt to relegitimise the authority'[86] of the USSR, he initiated a referendum in March 1991 on whether it was 'necessary to preserve the USSR as a renewed federation of sovereign republics'. Six Union Republics boycotted it: the three Baltic republics, plus Armenia, Georgia and Moldova. Russia took the opportunity to ask its population whether they wanted a President (see chapter three). Support for a renewed USSR by those who voted was high, at 76.2 per cent of the 75.4 per cent turnout.[87] The nine Union Republics which had held the referendum, plus the USSR, worked towards a new USSR Union Treaty.

The new Treaty was due to be signed by Gorbachev on 20 August 1991. It acknowledged greater powers for the Union Republics. Concern about this led a group of leading government and Party members to resist by forming the eight-man Committee on the State of Emergency (CSE). The CSE was composed of Vice-President Ianayev, KGB head Vladimir Kriuchkov, Minister of Internal Affairs Boris Pugo, Defence Minister Dmitrii Iazov, Government Chairman Valentin Pavlov, Deputy Head of the Security Council Oleg Baklanov, Head of the Peasants' Union Vasilii Starodubtsev and Aleksandr Tiziakov, a leading representative of State industry. The CSE attempted to seize control on 19 August while Gorbachev was away at his summer retreat at Foros. Rather than returning to Moscow as planned, Gorbachev found himself under house arrest with all the phone lines cut. His wife Raisa suffered a minor stroke. The CSE declared Gorbachev to be indisposed, and tried to transfer power to Vice-President Ianaev. However, their strategy was not well planned. They did not have the military wholeheartedly on their side and they failed to appreciate the importance of blocking all radio transmissions. At least one CSE member was clearly drunk during television broadcasts. Boris Yel'tsin, President of Russia, rallied opposition

---

[86]   R Sakwa, *Russian Politics and Society*, 4th edn (Abingdon, Routledge, 2008) 22.
[87]   *Ibid.*

to the CSE and within a few days the abortive putsch had failed. However, it proved a turning point for the USSR.

Gorbachev returned to a changed political landscape. The Party had been heavily involved in the putsch, and a betrayed Gorbachev resigned as Party General Secretary on 24 August. The agencies of State power also changed. The USSR CPD disbanded itself (on full pay until 1994), as did the Supreme Soviet Presidium. The Supreme Soviet was replaced by a State Council consisting of the Council of Republics and Council of the Union. One of the first actions of the State Council was to declare the three Baltic republics of Estonia, Latvia and Lithuania to be independent. The Cabinet of Ministers was replaced by the Inter-Republican Economic Committee (with a Chairman). The Presidency was retained, but the Vice-Presidency was abolished. But these changes at the centre were beginning to be irrelevant. The Union Republics, and particularly Russia, had lost faith in the USSR and began to reorganise themselves without it (see chapter three).

On 25 December 1991, Gorbachev resigned the USSR Presidency, acknowledging that the country of which he was Head of State was ceasing to exist. By the end of 1991 the USSR had dissolved.[88] The Union Republics became independent States, even if they did not yet have their own currency and some were still home to large sections of Russian armed forces. After 74 years, the Soviet experiment had fizzled out.

IV. CONCLUSION

Those preparing the current Constitution 'drew expressly' on the Basic Law of 1906.[89] However, Russia's constitutional heritage was not an auspicious background for her current Constitution, which advocates democracy, rule of law, and the highest value for individuals and their rights and freedoms. All previous Constitutions, in various ways, negated those principles.

For most of Russia's history, she was isolated from Western Europe, but not ignorant of developments there. Peter and Catherine looked

[88] See DD Barry, 'The USSR: a Legitimate Dissolution?' (1992) 18 *Review of Central and East European Law* 527.
[89] WE Butler, *Constitutional Foundations of the CIS Countries* (London, Simmonds & Hill, 1999) xxiii.

west for inspiration, although the application of their discoveries did little to diminish absolutism. During the Soviet era, legal education included history of political doctrines, which encompassed western enlightenment philosophy and 'State law of bourgeois countries'. Students were taught about these to criticise them, but it also gave them a grounding in alternatives to their own regime's approach to State and law.

Reform from above was a recurrent theme, but during earlier centuries in Russia the gulf between rulers and ruled was almost unbridgeable. Citizens had little scope to influence governance positively, and learned to ignore, or subvert, the official system. That practice, of working around rather than with established rules, still casts a long shadow over the current Russian legal system.

FURTHER READING

R Beerman, 'Pre-revolutionary Russian peasant laws' in WE Butler (ed), *Russian Laws, Historical and Political Perspectives* (Leiden, Sijthoff, 1977) 172.

J Burbank, 'Legal culture, citizenship, and peasant jurisprudence: perspectives from the early twentieth century' in PH Solomon (ed), *Reforming Justice in Russia, 1864–1996* (Armonk, NY, ME Sharpe, 2005).

——, 'An Imperial rights regime: law and citizenship in the Russian Empire' (2006) 7(3) *Kritika* 397.

WE Butler, 'The pre-revolutionary heritage' in WE Butler (ed), *Russian Law*, 3rd edn (Oxford, Oxford University Press, 2009).

FJM Feldbrugge, *Russian Law: the End of the Soviet System* (Dordrecht, Nijhoff, 1993).

J Hazard, 'The Evolution of the Soviet Constitution' in DD Barry (ed), *Toward the "Rule of Law" in Russia? Political & Legal Reform in the Transitional Period* (Armonk, NY, ME Sharp, 1992).

A Medushevsky, *Russian Constitutionalism: Historical and Contemporary Development* (Abingdon, Routledge, 2006).

A Nove, 'Some Aspects of Soviet Constitutional Theory' (1949) 12 *MLR* 12.

AL Unger, *Constitutional Development in the USSR: a Guide to the Soviet Constitutions* (London, Methuen, 1981).

AM Yakovlev with D Gibson, *The Bear that Wouldn't Dance: failed attempts to reform the constitution of the former Soviet Union* (Manitoba, Legal Research Institute, 1992).

3

Overview of the 1993 Constitution of the Russian Federation

Introduction – Background to Adoption of the 1993 Constitution
– Overview of the Constitution's Contents – Conclusion – Further
Reading

I. INTRODUCTION

THIS CHAPTER GIVES overviews of both the political context
of the adoption of the 1993 Constitution and the Constitution
itself. By the end of 1992 the 1978 Russian Soviet Federated
Socialist Republic (RSFSR) Constitution had been amended over 400
times and accurate editions were non-existent. It was marred by internal
inconsistencies, and was no longer appropriate as the Constitution of an
independent Russia aspiring to separation of powers and rule of law. It
was clear that a new Constitution was indispensible; the problem was
how best to produce one. By the autumn of 1993 a political stalemate in
Russia induced President Yel'tsin to take drastic steps which resulted in
the present Constitution, as well as a new Legislature and revised
Constitutional Court. Despite his actions raising doubts about the
legitimacy of the new Constitution, the text adopted was sufficiently
close to rival drafts to be acceptable to the warring political factions, or
at least it was preferable to the alternatives of either an extensively
hacked Soviet Constitution or no Constitution at all.

II. BACKGROUND TO ADOPTION OF THE 1993 CONSTITUTION

A. Yel'tsin takes charge in Soviet Russia

Chapter two ended with the dissolution of the Soviet Union by 31 December 1991, leaving Russia as an independent State. Before that landmark date, the 1978 RSFSR Constitution had been altered to take account of *perestroika* reforms. On 27 October 1989 it was amended to institute a new Russian Legislature, the RSFSR Congress of People's Deputies (CPD). The CPD was to have 1,068 deputies elected by multi-candidate elections, 900 from constituencies based on population and 168 from Russia's different federal subjects.[1] The CPD would indirectly elect a reformed RSFSR Supreme Soviet to be the 'permanently functioning legislative, administrative and control agency of state power of the Russian Federation' (Article 107, as amended).

Elections for the first Russian CPD (denoted by Roman numeral I) were held on 14 March 1990. The previous March, Boris Yel'tsin had been elected to the USSR CPD, and by 1990 he had also become a member of the USSR Supreme Soviet. However, he decided that his future lay in Russian not Soviet politics, so he stood as a candidate to the new Russian CPD representing his home region of Sverdlovsk. He won easily, getting more than 72 per cent of the vote despite competition from 11 other candidates.

Yel'tsin planned to use the platform of the I CPD to strengthen Russia's position within the USSR. His first move, promised during his electoral campaign, was to become the CPD Chairman. Although the position had little formal executive power, it gave scope for political leverage, an art in which Yel'tsin excelled. His ambition was nearly thwarted by the agenda for the I CPD's 16 May inaugural session specifying immediate election of the Chairman. This would have given the advantage to the incumbent Russian Government Chairman of three years' standing, Alexander Vlasov, a career Party and government official, who also aspired to the Chairman's post. However, by a vote of 495 to 494 the deputies decided to delay the election, giving Yel'tsin and others over

---

[1] 84 were from the autonomous units (4 from each autonomous republic, 2 from each autonomous region, 1 from the autonomous area) and the other 84 from the territories, regions, and the cities of Moscow and Leningrad which have special federal status.

a week for frenzied campaigning. The Chairman would be elected by secret ballot, with the winner needing over half the votes of the existing 1,060 deputies. The first two ballots were inconclusive, but in the third round Yel'tsin gained 535 votes, four more than the majority he needed. Vlasov came second with 467 votes. Yel'tsin was formally instated as the Russian CPD Chairman on 5 June 1990.

On 8 June, the CPD had voted by 809 to 48 to send an appeal to the legislatures of the other 14 Union Republics which made up the USSR, proposing that they all begin work on a new Union Treaty. This effort to build a new Treaty 'from the bottom up' was as fruitless as Gorbachev's 1991 efforts to gain approval of a centrally-drafted Treaty.

B. Russia's Declaration of State Sovereignty, 12 June 1990

Within a week of Yel'tsin becoming its Chairman, on 12 June the CPD passed the 'Declaration on the State Sovereignty of the RSFSR'.[2] The result of the overwhelming roll-call vote of 907 to 13 was met with a rousing ovation. Three months earlier the Lithuanian Socialist Republic had adopted a 'Declaration of Independence', but the Russian deputies stressed that, in contrast, the Russian Declaration of Sovereignty did not claim independence from the USSR but merely asserted Russia's supremacy in case of conflict with the USSR, including primacy of Russian over Soviet law.

Ironically, on the same day the CPD deputies had voted by 704 to 206 to keep the words 'Soviet' and 'Socialist' in Russia's formal name (RSFSR). Conservative forces were also at work when the I CPD elected the 252 deputies to make up the Supreme Soviet. Yel'tsin's closest allies failed to get seats, a situation which may have sown the seeds of future conflict between this smaller, more permanently active State agency and Yel'tsin after he became President in June 1991.

The Declaration of Sovereignty stopped short of proclaiming immediate total control of laws on its territory. However, it said that Russia was a 'sovereign State' (Article 1) having 'full power . . . except for those [matters] which it voluntarily transfers to the jurisdiction of the USSR.' It claimed 'the supremacy of the RSFSR Constitution and laws of the

---

[2] Translation in WE Butler, *Russian Public Law*, 2nd edn (London, Wildy, Simmonds & Hill, 2009) 1.

RSFSR throughout the territory of the RSFSR', with the suspension of contrary USSR legislation (Article 5). In its Declaration's assertions Russia was stoking up the dispute as to where residual power lay in the federal USSR, and inflaming the so-called 'war of laws' between increasingly rebellious Union Republics and the USSR, where laws would be inconsistently applied in both, for example tax legislation in the first half of 1991.[3] The Declaration was to be the basis of a new Russian Constitution and Union Treaty (Article 15), and Article 13 articulated that 'the separation of legislative, executive, and judicial power shall be a major principle of the functioning of the RSFSR as a rule-of-law State' and

> rights and freedoms provided for by the RSFSR Constitution, USSR Constitution, and generally-recognised norms of international law shall be guaranteed to citizens and stateless persons residing on the territory of the RSFSR. (Article 10)

These principles are in the 1993 Constitution.

C. Constitutional amendments on the way to a new Constitution

On 15 June 1990, the I CPD amended Article 6 of the 1978 RSFSR Constitution to allow different political parties to exist. The CPSU had already lost its constitutional monopoly under the 1977 USSR Constitution on 14 March 1990 (see chapter two). Despite the fact that the majority of the deputies to the I CPD were Party members, the revised Russian article made no mention of the Communist Party, as the USSR reform did in its face-saving compromise wording. In late June 1990 a separate Russian Communist Party was established for the first time since the USSR came into existence. In the interim the CPSU had been expected to represent simultaneously USSR and Russian interests. Perhaps not coincidentally, the I CPD passed a law on 20 June forbidding any leader of an agency of State power in Russia from holding simultaneously office in a political organisation.

On 16 June 1990 the I CPD set up a Constitutional Commission to draft a new Constitution. It was composed of 102 deputies. Yel'tsin was nominally the chairman, but rarely attended. Oleg Rumiantsev, a deputy

---

[3] WE Butler, *Russian Law*, 3rd edn (Oxford, Oxford University Press, 2009) 571.

and well-known constitutional lawyer, was appointed Executive Secretary and chair of the smaller, more active working group of around 15 deputies. As a result, the Commission became known informally as the Rumiantsev Commission.

On 15 December 1990 the RSFSR Constitution was amended to incorporate changes consistent with the Declaration of Sovereignty, so that the Preamble now included Russia's claim to sovereignty and that it was a 'democratic rule-of-law State within the renewed USSR'.

Legislation to create a Presidency in Russia was passed on 24 April 1991. The Russian population had been asked on 17 March whether they would like a presidency via an opportunist question added to the USSR referendum seeking support for a 'renewed Union'.[4] The response had been positive and the Russian Constitution was appropriately amended on 3 June 1991, inserting a completely new chapter (Chapter 13-1). The first presidential election was held on 12 June 1991 and Boris Yel'tsin won decisively with 57.30 per cent of the votes cast, beating five other candidates.

There were further constitutional amendments on 1 November 1991. Amongst other things, the State flag and provisions about the State anthem were changed. The previous RSFSR flag was the Soviet Union's red flag with a gold hammer and sickle and gold star in the top left-hand corner, with the addition of 'a light blue stripe, one eighth of the overall width, down the flagpole side' (Article 181, 1978 Constitution). This was replaced by the historic Russian tricolour, with horizontal stripes in white, blue and red, which had reappeared on the barricades protesting against the attempted putsch by the Committee for the State of Emergency in August 1991 (see chapter two). In keeping with the changes to the Legislature, power to decide the State anthem was given to the revised Supreme Soviet; in the previous version of the Constitution it had belonged to the Presidium of the old Supreme Soviet. In fact, Yel'tsin himself chose a new anthem in December 1993; a wordless tune by the 19th-century composer Mikhail Glinka (which later caused embarrassment for triumphant Russian athletes at the 1998 Olympic Games). It has since been replaced by the melody of the Soviet national anthem with new words.[5]

---

[4] See R Sakwa, *Russian Politics and Society*, 4th edn (Abingdon, Routledge, 2008) 22.
[5] J Henderson, 'Signs and Portents' (2002) 8 *European Public Law* 321.

In the meantime, Yel'tsin continued to undermine the USSR. On 8 December 1991 he met with his counterparts from Belarus' and the Ukraine in a hunting lodge in Belovezhskaia Pushcha in Belarus', where they jointly signed the 'Minsk Agreement'. This established the Commonwealth of Independent States (CIS) comprised of their three republics, and also declared that 'the USSR as a subject of international law and geopolitical reality terminates its existence'.[6] It also stated that the signatories are 'endeavouring to build democratic rule-of-law States'[7] and that

> from the moment of signature of the present Agreement, the application of the norms of third states . . . including the former USSR, shall not be permitted. (Article 11)

The Russian Supreme Soviet ratified the Agreement on 12 December 1991, although allowing that 'norms of the former USSR shall apply on the territory of the RSFSR until the adoption of respective legislative acts of the RSFSR', except where contrary to the existing Russian Constitution and legislation, and to the Agreement itself. On the same day, 'being guided by the Declaration on State Sovereignty of the RSFSR' and exercising its power 'to ratify and denounce international treaties of the Russian Federation' (Article 109(15) of the Russian Constitution), the Supreme Soviet adopted a decree 'On the Denunciation of the Treaty of the Formation of the USSR of 30 December 1922'.[8]

Just over a week later, on 21 December 1991, all the remaining Union Republics of the USSR with the exception of Georgia and the three Baltic Republics – Estonia, Latvia and Lithuania – signed the Alma Ata Declaration which brought them into the CIS.[9] (At the time Georgia was on the brink of civil war, and the Baltic Republics had no interest in the CIS. The signatories were Azerbaidzhan, Armenia, Belarus', Kazakhstan, Kyrgyzstan, Moldova, the Russian Federation, Tadzhikistan, Ukraine and Uzbekistan.)

On 25 December 1991 – the same date that Mikhail Gorbachev resigned his USSR Presidency, recognising that the USSR was unravel-

---

[6] Preamble, Agreement on the Creation of the Commonwealth of Independent States, in WE Butler (ed and trans), *Basic Legal Documents of the Russian Federation* (New York, Oceana, 1992) 3.

[7] *Ibid.*

[8] Butler, above n 2, at 3.

[9] Butler, above n 6, at 7.

ling, which it did by the end of the month – the Legislature gave Russia a new name. No longer the RSFSR, she was now the Russian Federation, or alternatively Russia, although the Constitution was not brought up to date until the following April.

D. Independent Russia

Moving into 1992, the pace of change did not diminish for newly-independent Russia. Two significant events in the spring of that year affected the existing Constitution.

First, on 31 March 1992 three treaties were agreed between Russia and almost all of the subjects of the Russian Federation (the exceptions being Tatarstan and the then Chechno-Ingushetiia).[10] Collectively these treaties became the new Treaty of the Federation for Russia, and as such were approved by the Russian CPD on 10 April. According to the CPD decree, the content of the Treaty was incorporated as an integral part of the existing Constitution. Article 1 of the Concluding and Transitional Provisions of the current 1993 Constitution preserves the Treaty to the extent that it does not contradict the Constitution.

Secondly, on 21 April 1992 the chapter in the Constitution on individual rights was completely replaced. Almost in its entirety, the Russian Declaration of the Rights of Man and Citizen of November 1991 was incorporated into the Constitution as the revised Chapter 5. This imported into the 1978 Russian Constitution a contemporary human rights law, consistent with international legal provisions and explicitly based on the notion of inalienable, inherent rights (see chapter six for the change in approach to rights).

At the same time, Russia's name in the Constitution was changed, replacing RSFSR with Russian Federation. Chapter seven became 'The Russian Federation, a sovereign state' instead of 'RSFSR – Union Republic within the composition of the USSR'. Ironically, despite the fact that the USSR no longer existed – and as noted above, Russia had formally denounced the 1922 Treaty of the Formation of the USSR – the Preamble to the Constitution at this stage still kept the wording inserted consequent to Russia's Declaration of Sovereignty, that Russia 'declares its resolve to create a democratic rule of law State within a

---

[10] Butler, above n 2, at 682.

renewed USSR', although this was deleted the following 9 December. Reference in Article 4 to compliance with the Constitution of the USSR, and the State arms with the motto 'proletariat of the world, unite', remained until the new Constitution in December 1993.

E. Draftsmen get to work

As noted in section I. above, tinkering with the 1978 RSFSR Russian Constitution had created an inconsistent and almost unworkable document. That Constitution had been written in a different era with different priorities. There had been multiple amendments as those priorities changed, and the switch in 1991 from a parliamentary to a presidential system set up internal conflicts. What was needed was a new Constitution for Russia's new circumstances. It was noted in section II.C. above that one of the early acts of the I CPD was to establish a Constitutional Commission, which came to be known as the Rumiantsev Commission. It agreed a draft outline by August 1990, which it published that November (the first 'Rumiantsev draft').

The Rumiantsev Commission was not the only body interested in framing the new Constitution.[11] The legislative faction 'Communists of Russia' postponed the CPD debate on the 'Rumiantsev draft' and issued its own more traditional proposal by the end of 1990. Saratov University's Faculty of Law also published its own draft. A compromise draft was prepared by the Rumiantsev Commission in time for the III CPD (28 March to 3 April 1991), but by then a Russian Presidency had been agreed in principle, which necessitated a rethink.

There were further attempts to get agreement on a constitutional draft in the changed context following the failed putsch in August 1991 (see chapter two). On 10 October 1991 the Rumiantsev Commission presented a second draft to the Supreme Soviet, but it failed to gain enough votes to be put on the V CPD's agenda for approval. The depu-

---

[11] See S Believ, 'The Evolution in Constitutional Debates in Russia in 1992–1993: a Comparative Review' (1994) 20 *Review of Central and East European Law* 305; R Moore, 'The path to the new Russian Constitution: a comparison of executive–legislative relations in the major drafts' (1995) 3 *Demokratizatsiya* 44; GP Smith, *Reforming the Russian Legal System* (Cambridge, Cambridge University Press, 1996) 86; J Kahn, *Federalism, Democratization, and the Rule of Law in Russia* (Oxford, Oxford University Press, 2002) 133; Sakwa, above n 4, at 55.

ties thought there were unresolved separation of powers issues relating to both the relationships between the Executive and Legislature, and between Russia and its federal subjects. The Rumiantsev Commission managed to get a slightly revised draft presented to the V CPD 'for discussion' on 2 November 1991. This resulted in the V CPD instructing the Commission to prepare yet another draft to present to the VI CPD the next spring.

The third draft from the Rumiantsev Commission was published on 24 March 1992, and although approved on 18 April by the VI CPD, it was not universally appreciated:

> Whereas the Communists call Rumiantsev's draft 'bourgeois,' Professors Sobchak and Popov call it 'socialist,' the hardline Democrats call it 'eclectic,' and the national-patriots call it 'Russophobic.'[12]

By this time Russia's new Treaty of the Federation of 31 March 1992 had been agreed by almost all Russia's federal subjects, which reduced some of the conflicting tensions over the federal formulation in the drafts.

Ten days before the VI CPD meeting in April, an alternative draft was published by the mayor of St Petersburg, Anatolii Sobchak, and fellow leading jurist Sergei Alekseev. They severely criticised Rumiantsev's draft, feeling that it

> insufficiently protected the civil rights and liberties of Russian citizens, inadequately provided for separation of powers . . . and was unclear on a 'national state structure'.[13]

Both Sobchak and Alekseev had worked from 1989 on a proposed new USSR Constitution, and this draft Russian Constitution 'relied heavily on the model Constitution developed by Andrei Sakharov prior to his death in early 1990'.[14] Sobchak and Alekseev advocated that the Constitution should be ratified by a Constitutional Assembly, claiming that the CPD had no legitimacy, having been elected in 1990 at a time when the CPSU was the only legal political party.

A rival draft was published on 30 April 1992 by the Presidential Administration, under the guidance of Yel'tsin's legal adviser Sergei

---

[12] Smith, above n 11, at 88, citing A Kostyukov, (1992) *Megapolis-Express*, 22 April, at 3.

[13] *Ibid.*

[14] *Ibid* at 89.

Shakhrai. In Shakhrai's draft, the President would head a strong Executive and be elected for a six-year term.[15] Despite formally being Chair of the 'Rumiantsev Commission', Yel'tsin supported this 'Presidential draft', to the annoyance of the Commission and the VI CPD, which refused to debate it although it approved its 'general outline' and rejected the other drafts.[16]

The Rumiantsev Commission came forward with another draft on 11 November 1992, but this was not adopted by the VII CPD in December. Events in the spring of 1993 (outlined in section II.F. below) evidenced the sharpened conflict between President and Legislature, and a further 'Presidential draft' was released by Alekseev, Shakhrai and Sobchek on the eve of the 25 April 1993 referendum gauging support for President and Legislature. This Presidential draft was presented to the Rumiantsev Commission on 6 May 1993, which promptly rejected it on 7 May, when it also published its own revised version downgrading the President from leading the executive branch to merely ceremonial Head of State. This draft was to be finalised by 15 October and discussed in a special CPD convocation on 17 November 1993. But warring over the increasingly personalised rival drafts was transforming into direct confrontation, and 'the constitution, no longer above the political conflict, became simply another instrument in it'.[17]

F. President versus Legislature

While the competing versions of the Constitution were being drafted, a dispute between President Yel'tsin and the Legislature was crystallising. On one level the root of the problem was the inconsistent wording of the much-amended 1978 RSFSR Constitution. The President was the 'highest official . . . and head of executive power' (Article 121-1, 1978 Constitution as amended), whilst the Russian Congress of People's Deputies was 'the highest agency of State power' (Article 104). Thus

---

[15] *Ibid.*

[16] L Gönenç, *Prospects for Constitutionalism in Post-Communist Countries* (The Hague, Nijhoff, 2002) 160.

[17] RB Ahdieh, *Russia's Constitutional Revolution: Legal Consciousness and the Transition to Democracy 1985–1966* (University Park, PA, Pennsylvania State University Press, 1997) 53.

two different branches of State were deemed 'highest' (*vysshim*), with no mechanism for resolving conflicts.

When Yel'tsin was inaugurated as President on 10 July 1991, he gained wide-ranging power to issue edicts and regulations 'with regard to questions relegated to his jurisdiction' (Article 121-8, amended Constitution), provided they conformed to the Russian Constitution and laws (*zakony*). However, the CPD had unqualified power to repeal presidential as well as Supreme Soviet legislation (Article 104(14)), and the Supreme Soviet could repeal any presidential edict that the Constitutional Court, newly established in 1991, ruled against (Article 109(19)).

> Thus the extensive powers of an executive presidency were enshrined in law, but so too were a number of slow-acting time-bombs.[18]

On 2 November 1991, after considerable debate, the V CPD awarded Yel'tsin additional powers for one year to appoint ministers without legislative approval, and to instigate urgent economic reforms with minimal legislative oversight. Local elections were also suspended until 1993, and the President was given power to appoint regional executive heads.[19] Using his expanded powers, Yel'tsin appointed himself Government Chairman on 6 November, as a prelude to 'shock tactic' economic reforms. On the same day he issued presidential edict No 169 to ban completely in Russia both the CPSU and the Russian Communist Party (on 23 August he had suspended the RCP, and on 25 August had authorised seizure of property of both, in response to Party involvement in the failed putsch against Gorbachev). Challenge to the legality of Yel'tsin's edicts led to a seven-month-long hearing at the Constitutional Court from May to November 1992, with the result a 'score draw' that Yel'tsin was in part justified, but not as regards the Russian Party or seizure of all the assets.

The stringent economic reforms introduced in January 1992 undermined Yel'tsin's popularity. Pushed forward by free market economist Egor Gaidar leading a group of academic economists with little practical experience – scathingly labelled by Vice-President Rutskoi as 'the boys in pink shorts'[20] – the harsh measures alienated the sizable body of uncommitted CPD deputies who had supported Yel'tsin's advocacy of

---

[18] R Sakwa, *Russian Politics and Society*, 2nd edn (London, Routledge, 1996) 141.
[19] PJS Duncan, 'The Democratic Transition in Russia: From Coup to Referendum' (1993) 46 *Parliamentary Affairs* 491 at 502.
[20] E Huskey, *Presidential Power in Russia* (Armonk, NY, ME Sharpe, 1999) 30.

Russian Statehood but neither his radical economic reforms nor his assumption of strong executive power.[21] By April 1992, despite endorsement by almost all of the federal subjects of the new Federation Treaty, Yel'tsin had lost the backing of a stable ruling majority in the central Legislature, and indeed the confidence of his own Vice-President Rutskoi who sided with the 'industrial lobby'.[22] Backtracking on reforms in the second half of 1992 did not win back Yel'tsin's popularity.

The two-week December 1992 meeting of the VII CPD was dramatic, both politically and legally. On the positive side, on 9 December 1992 the VII CPD passed significant amendments to the 1978 Constitution in relation to the legal system: unlimited terms of office for federal judges, new local Justices of the Peace courts, and the possibility of jurors 'considering a civil or criminal case' once enabling legislation was passed. The article which specified that there should be equality before the law now also required the 'principle of adversariality'. The principle of separation of powers was made explicit. For the first time private ownership gained constitutional approval. Some aspects of the federal structure were also tidied up, for example including Moscow and Saint Petersburg as 'cities of federal significance'. Unfortunately these important steps on the way to a reformed legal, economic and social structure were almost overshadowed by Russia's 'first constitutional crisis of the post-Soviet era'.[23] A power struggle between Yel'tsin and the Legislature was prevented from eruption only through skilful mediation by the Constitutional Court Chairman Zor'kin.

Within the first few days of the CPD meeting, opponents to Yel'tsin had unsuccessfully tried twice to amend the Constitution to take away the presidential power to appoint ministers. Although a majority supported the resolution both times, it was less than the two-thirds required. The first stage of an impeachment attempt was similarly thwarted, but it left Yel'tsin in no doubt that he would have difficulty getting the required vote of confirmation of economic reformer Egor Gaidar as Government Chairman (he had been Acting Chairman since June). On 8 December, Yel'tsin therefore proposed a deal. In return for the CPD confirming Gaidar in post, Yel'tsin would agree that four other key ministers, in

[21] *Ibid* at 29.
[22] A Rahr, 'The Roots of the Power Struggle' (1993) 2 *Radio Free Europe/Radio Liberty Research Report* 9 at 10.
[23] Huskey, above n 20, at 30.

charge of the so-called power ministries of foreign affairs, defence, security and internal affairs, would also be subject to appointment by the Supreme Soviet, on nomination by the President.

On 9 December, Article 121-5(5) of the Constitution was amended to that effect. But there were other constitutional changes: the Government (Council of Ministers) was also made accountable to the CPD and the Supreme Soviet as well as the President (Article 122 as amended); Article 109(19) was amended to allow the Supreme Soviet to suspend a presidential edict pending a ruling by the Constitution Court; and Article 121-6 was also inserted, specifying that if the President used his powers to 'change the national-State structure of the Russian Federation or to dissolve or suspend the activity of any legally elected agencies of State power', his authority as President would immediately cease. Having thus built in an insurance against intemperate Presidential actions, the CPD promptly reneged on the prior tacit understanding and did not endorse Gaidar as Government Chairman. The secret ballot vote was 467:486, leaving Gaidar 54 short of a majority of votes of the 1,041 CDP delegates needed for confirmation. Yel'tsin was understandably furious. On 10 December he warned of a 'creeping coup' by the reactionary Legislature (the Supreme Soviet) headed by 'legislative dictator' Khasbulatov (its Chairman), and said he would turn to the people with a referendum on 24 January, asking:

> Whom do you entrust to lead the country out of the economic and political crisis, to revitalize the Russian Federation – the present composition of the Congress or the President of Russia?[24]

The loser(s) would face new elections the following spring. The next day the Legislature amended the law on the referendum to ban any referendum that would result in the dissolution of a high State body, including the CPD, the Constitutional Court or the office of President.

At this point Constitutional Court Chairman Zor'kin stepped in and, with difficulty, persuaded the two antagonists, Yel'tsin and Khasbulatov, to discuss a possible compromise.[25] They each brought six supporters to form a 14-man commission which Zor'kin chaired. The resulting nine-point agreement was accepted by the CPD; Yel'tsin and Khasbulatov

---

[24] 'Excerpts of Yeltsin Speech to Congress' (Associated Press translation), *AP Online*, 10 December 1992, available via Westlaw.
[25] See, eg, account by F Kaplan, 'Yeltsin, Congress leaders reach compromise' *Boston Globe*, 13 December 1992, available via Westlaw.

were given a standing ovation when they shook hands. Under the agreement, a referendum on a new Constitution would be held on 11 April, although the questions were not yet determined. Yel'tsin agreed that his candidate for Government Chairman would be one of three selected by the CPD from a Yel'tsin shortlist of five; in return, his extra presidential powers would be extended for another three months. The constitutional amendments allowing immediate termination of presidential power if he tried to change the 'national-State structure' or suspend the Legislature, and additional Supreme Soviet oversight of presidential legislation, were made conditional on the referendum about the basic provisions of a draft new Constitution, and would not enter into force until then.

A few days later, on 14 December, Yel'tsin surprised many by replacing acting Government Chairman Gaidar with the more cautious Viktor Chernomyrdin, despite Gaidar being one of the three that the Legislature approved from his shortlist. However, Yel'tsin's retreat and sacrifice of Gaidar did not appease the CPD for long.

In March 1993 Yel'tsin asked for his extra powers to be renewed, but the VIII CPD refused and instead adopted proposals from the VII CPD meeting in January–February to reduce them. It also reneged on the agreement to hold a referendum on 11 April. A furious Yel'tsin stalked out of the Legislature and declared he would hold his own referendum anyway on 25 April. Within three hours he submitted two questions to the Central Elections Commission to be put to the popular vote: whether Russia should be a presidential republic, and whether citizens should have the right to own land.

Yel'tsin's patience had worn thin. On Saturday 20 March 1993 he announced on television that he had signed a decree 'On special procedure for governing the country' which threatened dissolution of the Legislature. Unwisely, Russian Constitutional Court Chairman Zor'kin called a meeting of the Court, and on Tuesday, 23 March, by 9 judges to 3, condemned Yel'tsin's speech before seeing the transcript. When it appeared five days after the broadcast it was much less threatening, and Zor'kin was criticised for failing to follow proper procedure.

On 26 March the IX CPD opened a special session to consider taking action against Yel'tsin, but a vote on 28 March to impeach him for exceeding his presidential powers in initiating a referendum failed. The 617 votes in favour were 72 short of the necessary two-thirds majority.

The impending stalemate was resolved by a joint agreement that a referendum would be held on 25 April, but with four questions:

1 Do you have confidence in the President of Russia, BN Yel'tsin?
2 Do you approve of the socioeconomic policy being carried out by the President and the Government since 1992?
3 Do you consider it necessary to hold early elections for the President?
4 Do you consider it necessary to hold early elections for the people's deputies of the Russian Federation?

The CPD asserted that all four questions raised constitutional issues, and under the Law 'On the Referendum of the RSFSR' of 16 October 1990 therefore required approval of more than half of the total electorate, not merely the majority of those who voted. Yel'tsin disagreed. On 8 April 1993, a group of people's deputies who supported Yel'tsin's view asked the Constitutional Court to adjudicate. On 21 April 1993 the Court ruled that questions 1 and 2 primarily concerned a moral and political assessment, and were not clearly associated with amending the Constitution or other law, and therefore needed only a simple majority of those who had voted, not the total electorate. In contrast, questions 3 and 4 involved early termination of the powers of the President and deputies, whose terms were set in the Constitution. A positive response therefore required the agreement of the majority of eligible voters. The decision was not unanimous. Judge Morshchakova thought that none of the questions raised any constitutional issues, and therefore a simple majority of those who voted should apply to all four. Judge Ametistov agreed with the majority decision of the Court in relation to the first two questions, but nevertheless entered a special opinion on the legal force of any referendum outcome. He pointed out that the CPD itself had not passed the decree establishing the referendum by a qualified majority, and therefore it would be unconstitutional for any outcome to affect the Constitution. The majority Court ruling was a disappointment to Yel'tsin's supporters, although they had confidence that they could nevertheless gain a strong showing.

Yel'tsin and the Russia's Choice faction supporting him organised a campaign using the slogan '*Da. Da. Net. Da!*' (Yes. Yes. No. Yes!) to remind his supporters how they should vote. Overall Yel'tsin succeeded. He gained a positive vote of 58.67 per cent of the votes cast for question 1 (confidence in the President) and 53.0 per cent for question 2 (approval of his policies). For question 3, 49.5 per cent said they did not want early presidential elections, whereas for question 4, 67.2 per cent of those who voted (constituting about 43 per cent of the total electorate) agreed that there should be early elections for people's deputies.[26] According to the official results, 64.5 per cent of eligible voters took part.

The referendum results had little immediate practical impact. No new elections were called for the Legislature, which Yel'tsin later said was his biggest mistake. But the popular vote of support for him had profound political importance. Yel'tsin justified his controversial actions in October 1993 (see section II.G. below) by a claim of legitimacy based on the referendum endorsement of him and his policies in April. In his view, that popular support was more significant than the fact that he acted in breach of his legal powers as President when he closed the Legislature, called elections for its replacement and instituted the new Constitution.

At the time, the April referendum results gave Yel'tsin confidence to push ahead for a draft new Constitution. In May he decreed that there would be a Constitutional Assembly (*Konstitutsionnoe Soveshchanie*) convening on 5 June 1993 to formulate a new Constitution based on the 1990 Declaration of State Sovereignty and the 1992 Federal Treaty, starting with discussion around the presidential draft Constitution. Before the Assembly met, suggestions for additions or amendments were solicited from the federal subjects.

Formation of the Assembly was by invitation, not election. It was composed of

> 700 regional and republican officials, top political party figures and interest group leaders to debate and revise a draft constitution. . . . Twenty-one of Russia's 22 republics and all 67 regions (krais and oblasts) were represented.[27]

Representatives were selected by regional administrators, 'most of whom were loyal to the president'.[28] Several of the Constitutional Court judges were also Constitutional Assembly members, and they were instrumental in making sure that the draft approved included a relatively strong federal Constitutional Court, despite some reduction in the Court's proposed powers.[29] All in all, the Constitutional Assembly was 'a veritable "who's who" of Russia'.[30]

[26]   *Izvestiia*, 25 May 1993.

[27]   D Semler, 'Special report: Summer in Russia beings no real political progress' (1993) 2 *East European Constitutional Review* 20. Only Chechnya refused to take part.

[28]   Smith, above n 11, at 94.

[29]   A Trochev, *Judging Russia: Constitutional Court in Russian Politics, 1990–2006* (Cambridge, Cambridge University Press, 2008) 73–74.

[30]   Ahdieh, above n 17, at 57 in fn 42, quoting an interview on 21 July 1993 with E Kovaldin, adviser to the President, Gorbachev Foundation and expert witness to

Establishment of the Assembly was not unanimously welcomed. Opponents said that it was merely a rubber stamp, and the 10 days allotted were insufficient to revise the draft Yel'tsin had put forward. Also, Yel'tsin had no specific power to create such a body. The Supreme Soviet Chairman, Ruslan Khasbulatov, 'remained adamantly opposed to the conference, characterising it as "one way of unconstitutionally adopting a Constitution"'.[31] The Deputy Chairman Ryabov and the Chairman of the Council of Nationalities Ramazan Abdulatipov were more conciliatory. They acknowledged that Yel'tsin had acted unconstitutionally in taking the authority to summon a Constitutional Assembly, but nevertheless urged members of the Legislature to participate. The Supreme Soviet compromised by agreeing to the Assembly but maintaining that it should consider the parliamentary draft.

According to Yel'tsin's Chief of Staff Sergei Filatov, the Constitutional Assembly had three goals: to produce a single draft Constitution; to establish the method for its adoption; and to take a preliminary decision on how the new Legislature should be elected. The 762 diverse representatives were subdivided into five working groups (on Federal Organs of Power; Subjects of the Federation; Political Parties; Entrepreneurs and State Enterprises; and Municipalities). Legal Academician Vladimir Kudriavtsev led a 60-member 'Constitutional Arbitration Commission' which analysed each group's reports to produce the final revised draft.[32] Assembly meetings were

> often contentious. Delegates proposed more than 5,000 amendments. . . . Communist MP Yuri Slobodkin attempted to offer a draft but was removed from the assembly for disorderly conduct. The Supreme Soviet's official draft was given a late and limited hearing. The Speaker of the parliament, Ruslan Khasbulatov, attended the convention, but after being booed during his opening speech he declared the assembly a sham and stormed out of the meeting, taking with him about 70 participants from local parliaments.[33]

By Yel'tsin's deadline of 16 June an agreed draft had not been achieved, so the main Assembly took a 10-day break while Kudriavtsev's group continued work. Their reconciled draft was approved by the reconvened

the 1993 Constitutional Conference.

[31] Moore, above n 11, at 50.

[32] *Ibid.* Kudriavtsev had successfully urged the USSR CPD to adopt the USSR Declaration of the Rights of Man on 5 September 1991 (see ch 6).

[33] Semler, above n 27.

Constitutional Assembly on 26 June. Although based originally on the presidential draft, it incorporated a number of elements from the parliamentary draft, for example a chapter on the 'Foundations of the Constitutional System'. The term of presidential office was set at four years (matching that of the Legislature), not five as in both presidential and parliamentary drafts. The Duma's role as primary legislator was spelled out much more clearly than in either of those drafts. The approved Constitutional Assembly draft was issued on 14 July. It was then sent to the legislature of each federal subject for comment.

On 16 July the Supreme Soviet received a report on the Assembly draft from Oleg Rumiantsev, chair of the parliamentary Constitutional Commission. Despite the fact that the draft incorporated many elements of the earlier parliamentary draft, the Supreme Soviet refused to ratify it and insisted on issuing its own amended version. Moore suggests that this decision was Khasbulatov's, based on his principled stand that only the Legislature could adopt a Constitution. 'Accepting the documents that resulted from a presidential initiative was, therefore, tantamount to a surrender.'[34]

In an attempt to forestall Yel'tsin bypassing the legislature with a new Constitution, the Supreme Soviet resolved that a Constitution could only be adopted by a two-thirds majority in the CPD or a referendum. The rules set by the Law on the Referendum for constitutional amendment are strict. They require at least 50 per cent participation and ratification by a majority of the electorate, not just of those voting; a near impossibility, practically, leaving CPD approval as the only legal option. The Supreme Soviet also set about undermining Yel'tsin's economic reforms.

Proposals for a Federation Council as an upper house of the new Legislature constituted *ex officio* by regional leaders were being discussed in late August, and Yel'tsin's Government announced that it would be established in September, with or without CPD approval.[35]

By September it became clear that the options for amicable resolution of the political and legal impasses between President and Legislature were extremely limited. There was also dissent within the presidential administration; on 1 September Yel'tsin peremptorily (and unconstitu-

---

[34] Moore, above n 11, at 54.
[35] Semler, above n 27, at 23. See also Kahn, above n 11, at 135.

tionally) dismissed his Vice-President Rutskoi with whom he had been feuding for some months.[36]

The desire to achieve an agreed draft Constitution was not completely dead. On 8 September a new Constitutional Working Group was formed with Ryabov at its head, 16 deputies including Rumiantsev and six experts to reconcile the Conference draft with the new parliamentary draft by 15 September. On 16 September, Ryabov gave the results.

But it had become apparent to Yel'tsin that under the existing constitutional and legal arrangements the chances of getting any draft either past a hostile Legislature or through the strict referendum procedure were vanishingly small. As opposition to him grew in the Legislature, so did the likelihood of impeachment. He decided that it was time for political resolution of the stalemate.

G. Dénouement

On 21 September Yel'tsin issued presidential edict number 1400, 'On step-by-step [*poetapnoi*; 'stage-by-stage' is an alternative translation] constitutional reform in the Russian Federation'. This mildly-titled provision suspended both the existing RSFSR Constitution and the Legislature, specifying that there would be elections on 12 December for a new federal Parliament for Russia and a simultaneous national plebiscite to approve the new Constitution. The Preamble to the edict cited the April referendum results as justification, contrasting the activities of the CDP and Supreme Soviet which

> are destroying the very foundations of the constitutional system of the Russian Federation: democracy, the separation of powers, and federalism . . . The security of Russia – and its people – is more precious than formal compliance with contradictory regulations created by the legislative branch of power.

Neither the Legislature nor the Constitutional Court accepted Yel'tsin's edict. On 21 September the Presidium of the Supreme Soviet declared

---

[36] Huskey, above n 20, at 31 describes the aftermath of Rutskoi refusing to agree to Yel'tsin's decree of 20 March: 'When Sergei Filatov, the head of the Executive Office of the President, greeted Rutskoi, the Vice-President responded: "I won't shake your hand, you scum". According to Rutskoi, the following day Filatov reduced the Vice-Presidential staff to six persons.' (N Mishin, AV Rutskoi, *Aleksandr Rutskoi: Lefortovskie protokoly*.(Moscow, Paleia, 1994) at 33)

that Yel'tsin had acted in breach of Article 121(6) and therefore forfeited his powers to Vice-President Rutskoi. The following day the Supreme Soviet held an emergency session in the Russian parliamentary building, the White House, and confirmed Yel'tsin's loss of presidential authority from 20:00 hours the previous day. The Constitutional Court also held an emergency session at which a majority declared Yel'tsin's edict *ultra vires*. An inquorate X CPD was hastily assembled and declared Yel'tsin's action to be a *coup d'état*. But the practicalities were on Yel'tsin's side. He controlled the main media, the armed forces and security services, and he had informal assurances that Western powers were sympathetic to his cause. The deputies were urged to leave the White House, and when they refused, they were blockaded in. Power and water were cut off. Attempts at mediation failed, and by 4 October the siege was brought to a dramatic and bloody end by Special Force units storming the White House. Rutskoi, Khasbulatov and others were arrested.[37]

Yel'tsin issued a flurry of edicts to give more details of the new arrangements. On 1 October, elections were set for 12 December to the 450 seats of the new State Duma. On 7 October, 'pending the adoption of a new Constitution', the Constitutional Court was suspended by an edict prepared after consultation with deputy Court Chair Vitruk.[38] Elections to the Federation Council as part of the new Legislature, the Federal Assembly, were set by an edict of 11 October to be held at the same time as the elections to the other legislative chamber, the State Duma.

On 15 October Yel'tsin decreed that a national plebiscite would be held on 12 December to adopt the new Constitution. It was a shrewd political move to harness popular opinion through a plebiscite; if successful it would give the incoming Constitution legitimacy, and gain Yel'tsin a demonstration of support for his policies and, by extension, himself.[39] Furthermore, by specifying in the edict the terms of the plebiscite, requiring a plurality of votes with a turnout of at least 50 per cent of registered voters, Yel'tsin avoided the existing 1990 Law on the

---

[37] And subsequently released before trial under a Duma amnesty on 23 February 1994, along with those convicted as a result of the August 1991 putsch attempt.

[38] Trochev, above n 29, at 75. Vitruk did not always see eye to eye with Court Chairman Zor'kin.

[39] S Avak'ian, *Konstitutsiia Rossii* (Moscow, RIuID, 2000), available online at <http://constitution.garant.ru/science-work/modern/1776651/chapter/3/#300>, accessed 2 August 2010, no pages given, text near note 220.

Referendum, which in any event did not give the President power to initiate a referendum and for constitutional issues demanded approval by 50 per cent of registered voters.

A 'State Chamber' of the Constitutional Assembly was set up on 15 October to finalise the draft Constitution. This 250-strong body included representatives of the federal subjects, as well as legal and constitutional experts. A 'Social Chamber' was set up the same day to get views from various political and social organisations, although its input was

> not evident. Actually modifying the draft Constitution was done by a small circle of people from the President's associates and individual scholar-experts. On controversial issues a decision was taken by the President himself, some final provisions went into the text in his formulations.[40]

The draft Constitution was published on 10 November. The rules for campaigning for the election had been issued in an edict on 29 October. All registered parties were given equal time on State-owned media, including one hour free on national television. However, discussion of the draft Constitution was strenuously discouraged by the President and his First Deputy Government Chairman and Press and Information Minister Shumeiko.[41]

Having elections on the same ballot as the plebiscite raised the conundrum of would happen if the draft Constitution failed to be endorsed by sufficient votes. However, it seems that steps were also taken to make sure that this was extremely unlikely. There are substantial grounds for belief that ballot boxes were stuffed to ensure a sufficiently respectable mandate.[42] These suspicions could not be substantiated as the Central Electoral Commission (CEC) had the ballot papers destroyed within an usually short time after the election, but the CEC head Nikolai Riabov was reported to have admitted later in private conversation a turnout of

---

[40] *Ibid*, text between notes 223 and 224, author's translation. See also Trochev, above n 29, at 75.

[41] W Slater, 'Russia's plebiscite on a new constitution' (1994) 3(3) *Radio Free Europe/Radio Liberty Research Report*, 21 January, 1 at 4.

[42] See, eg, V Tolz and J Wishnevsky, 'Election queries make Russians doubt democratic process' (1994) 3(13) *Radio Free Europe/Radio Liberty Research Report*, 1 April; T Barber, 'Yeltsin referendum "rigged"', *Independent*, 9 April 1994, available online at <http://www.independent.co.uk/news/yeltsin-referendum-rigged-1368955.html>, accessed 17 May 2010.

only 46.7 per cent.[43] The official result issued by the CEC on 20 December was that 54.8 per cent of the electorate had voted; and of those, 58.4 per cent had approved the Constitution. The plebiscite thresholds were passed, therefore the Constitution entered into force on the date of its official publication, 24 December 1993.

In the political circumstances of the time, few wished to query the legitimacy of the new Constitution. It was widely accepted that it was better to have a Constitution than none, and the draft presented was an improvement over the much-amended and practically unworkable rump of the 1978 Constitution. Also, as Moore has shown, the draft submitted for approval contained many elements on which there was general political consensus. In the event, either because of that consensus or because of a conspiracy of silence from both ends of the political spectrum by those who had been elected to the new Federal Assembly, no formal query was raised concerning the correctness of the published results.

Aside from deliberate falsification, another factor may have favoured adoption of the Constitution.

> An alternative explanation may be that many voters inadvertently voted for the Constitution. The format of the ballot was negative rather than positive, meaning that one had to indicate approval by crossing out 'no,' leaving 'yes' untouched. This was unlike the rest of the large ballot in which one indicated one's choice of party or individual candidate by placing a cross in the box next to the name. It is possible that some of the voters failed to read the instructions carefully and unintentionally voted in favour of the draft. This is a classic electoral technique to inflate the support of an unpopular measure. In the absence of exit polls or other methods of determining the intentions of voters, however, we cannot draw any definitive conclusions beyond the numbers themselves.[44]

Thus, there is doubt about the formal legality of the 1993 Constitution. However, it fits with a long Russian tradition of radical change imposed from above by a reforming figure with power. In this particular case there was an intention to make a break with the past, and whether this was achieved legitimately or not is of no lasting importance if there is a political consensus for the outcome, as apparently there was here. The

---

[43] R Sharlet, 'Transitional Constitutionalism: Politics and Law in the Second Russian Republic'(1996) 14 *Wisconsin International Law Journal* 495, fn 2.

[44] Moore, above n 11, at 57.

general population was content to accept a peaceful resolution of their 'Time of Troubles'[45]; practical politics trumped concerns over formal legality.

III. OVERVIEW OF THE CONSTITUTION'S CONTENTS

A. Introduction

Unsurprisingly, given the changed circumstances, the 1993 Constitution differs significantly from its predecessors. For one thing, it is unique in Russia for its method of adoption. Earlier Constitutions had been voted into force by the Legislature or its smaller executive body. As described in section II.G. above, this one was adopted by national plebiscite held on the same date as the elections to the new Legislature. Ironically, compared with Soviet Constitutions, there was comparatively little discussion in the public media of the final draft. In the fraught conditions of the autumn of 1993, it was a stipulation of eligibility for broadcast rights on State media that there would be no discussion of its terms.[46]

This Constitution for an independent, post-socialist Russia emphasises in a simple way its discontinuity from previous Constitutions by a different name. All earlier Constitutions included in their official title the expression Fundamental Law (*Osnovnoi Zakon*).[47] They acted as the basis for further legislation, but in practice could be overridden. Now the Constitution is paramount over domestic legislation.

There is also a changed relationship with international law, discussed in section III.C.v. below, and the Constitution newly introduces 'federal constitutional laws', which resemble 'organic laws' in Continental legal systems. It was sensible to specify certain important topics which needed particularly detailed and careful legislative consideration, not possible at the time of the Constitution's adoption. They are discussed further in chapter five.

---

[45] Reference to the name given in Russia to a 15-year period at the beginning of the 17th century characterised by extreme social and political unrest.

[46] Slater, above n 41.

[47] Alternative translation, 'Basic Law'. The 1906 pre-revolutionary Constitution used an equivalent expression: *Osnovnyie Gosudarstvennye Zakony Rossiiskoi Imprerii* – Fundamentals of State Law of the Russian Empire.

B. Size and structure

Turning to an overview of the Constitution, compared with the previous 1978 Constitution it has about the same word-count – around 9,400 words in the Russian text – but has fewer articles and is less elaborate in structure. The old Constitution had 185 articles in 11 overall sections, subdivided into 22 different Chapters. The current Constitution has only two sections: the substantive text is in Section I, with nine Chapters containing 137 articles; Section II has nine Concluding and Transitional Provisions.

i. Preamble

The 1993 Constitution follows tradition by having a Preamble. All the previous USSR Constitutions except that of 1936 (and RSFSR Constitutions except that of 1937) had one, or an equivalent. The 1993 Preamble sets out, briefly but in very grand style, the 'official view' of the social and historic context for the adoption of the Constitution, emphasising rights and freedoms, State unity and sovereignty, and the democratic basis of Statehood. The Preamble differs in form from the rest of the provisions; it is not broken up into numbered articles or paragraphs, and it is not included in the list of contents. However, it is more than a mere poetic introduction to the Constitution. The Constitutional Court cited it to support a number of rulings, for example in 1998 over the appointment of the Government Chairman (see chapter four).

ii. Section I: Chapters 1 to 9 – Order of Exposition

Following the tradition for codified legal systems, the order of topics gives an indication of their relative importance. In Section I, the first chapter, 'Foundations of the Constitutional System' (Articles 1–16), sets out the principles regarded as so fundamental to an independent Russia that they should be almost impossible to amend (see section III.G. below on 'Amendment Procedures'). Next comes 'Rights and Freedoms of Man and Citizen' (Chapter 2, Articles 17–64), entrenching human rights. The order is similar to that of the 1977 USSR and 1978 RSFSR Constitutions, although, as discussed in chapter six, the approach to rights has been transformed since then. The 1993 Constitution also parallels the previous Constitutions by dealing next with federation: 'The Federated Structure' (Chapter 3, Articles 65–79).

Then there is a change as compared to earlier Constitutions. There was no President when the 1977 USSR and 1978 RSFSR Constitutions were adopted. When each was amended to introduce a presidential system, the relevant chapter was inserted after the chapter on the Legislature. The current Constitution instead puts 'The President of the Russian Federation' first (Chapter 4, Articles 80–93); then the Legislature, 'The Federal Assembly' (Chapter 5, Articles 94–109); followed by 'The Government of the Russian Federation' (Chapter 6, Articles 110–117). This symbolic placement of the President, before the Legislature and separate from the Government, reflects the distinctive position of the Russian Head of State (see chapter four).

Of the central State agencies, the Judiciary come last: 'Judicial Power' (Chapter 7, Articles 118–29). Even though relegated by this late positioning to the 'Cinderella' role, the Judiciary are nevertheless honoured by use of the emphatic word *vlast'* (power) for the first time in a Russian Constitution in the title of their chapter. Members of the Judiciary are not mere functionaries, as they tended to be in pre-revolutionary and Soviet times, but form an autonomous branch of State power.

Local Self-Government is found in the penultimate chapter (Chapter 8, Articles 130–133); and finally Chapter 9 covers Constitutional Amendments and Revision of the Constitution (Articles 134–137).

iii. Section II: Concluding and Transitional Provisions

Section II has nine Concluding and Transitional Provisions. It specifies entry into force on the date of official publication. This was on 25 December 1993, and simultaneously the previous Constitution lost force. The Federation Treaties of 1992, and other treaties between federal agencies of State power and the federal subjects, and between the latter, are preserved, although if any provisions contravene the Constitution, the Constitution applies.[48] This rather strange form of wording preserved the effects of some careful political bargaining in the early 1990s, while not compromising, in theory at least, the supremacy of the Constitution. It meant that the phrase 'Sovereign Republics'

---

[48] Kahn, above n 11, at 139, has a table showing the 'Major Contradictions between the Federal Treaty and the Constitution'.

which appears in part of the Federation Treaty was preserved, despite the Constitution implicitly not assigning sovereignty to any of the Federation's constituent units.[49]

Existing legislation not contrary to the Constitution was preserved, as was the existing President's term of office. The powers of courts were to be based on the new Constitution, but judges retained existing tenure. Existing procedure would apply to juries in criminal trials until passage of a new federal law, and similarly the requirement of judicial oversight of pre-trial detention would not operate until there was new criminal procedure legislation. On the basis of this, the Constitutional Court ruled in March 2002 that it was unconstitutional to delay implementation of the transfer of pre-trial oversight from the Procuracy to the courts, which the 2001 Code of Criminal Procedure had originally set for January 2004, rather than July 2002 when the rest of the new Code would come into force.

The Transitional Provisions with most immediate impact set the term for members elected to the Legislature in 1993 as only two years, and that exceptionally during that period members of the Duma could simultaneously serve in the Government (provision 9), although they would forfeit their deputy immunity if they did. Such 'compatibility' would not be allowed after the 1995 Duma elections, when 19 elected deputies relinquished their seats to take up a government post.[50] The temporary relaxation of separation of powers was justified by the 'excruciatingly small' pool of people with sufficient skills to fill both functions separately, and because compatibility encourages the Executive to cooperate with the Legislature.[51]

C. Chapter 1: Foundations of the Constitutional System

Highlights from the 16 articles of this chapter evidence a strong desire to break with the past.

---

[49] Unattributed editorial, 'A Protracted Farewell to Sovereignty' (2009) *Nezavisimaya Gazeta Online* in Russian, 29 June, available in translation via Westlaw under title 'Russia: Moscow Removing Last Vestiges of Sovereignty From Ethnic Republics'.

[50] Sakwa, above n 4, at 114. See also B Whitmore, 'Running on a Unified Platform of Power' (2003) 46 *RFE/RL Political Weekly*, 19 November 2003.

[51] S Holmes and C Lucky, 'Storm over compatibility' (1993/4) 2(4)/3(1) *East European Constitutional Review* 120.

i. Articles 1–7: the basics of the State and society

Russia declares herself to be a 'democratic federated rule-of-law State with a republican form of government' (Article 1) and asserts that 'man, his rights and freedoms have the highest value' (Article 2). Both these provisions step away from Russia's past. Democratic credentials are reinforced in Article 3, which puts 'its multinational people' as the sole source of power. Article 4 affirms that the 'Constitution and federal laws shall have supremacy throughout the entire territory of the RF.' In practice implementation of this principle has not been comprehensive; particularly during the 1990s, some federal subjects openly flouted central control, encouraged for political reasons by President Yel'tsin. When Putin took over as President in spring 2000, he set himself to redress this (see chapter four). Article 5 specifies the types of federal subjects which make up Russia. Republics have their own constitution and legislation. Each of the others – territories, regions, cities of federal significance, the autonomous region and autonomous national areas – has its own charter and legislation. Despite this clear differentiation (and the fact that some autonomous national areas are subordinate to other units), Article 5(4) declares that 'all subjects shall be equal between themselves in mutual relations with federal agencies of State power'. This became patently untrue during the Yel'tsin era, when many federal subjects made inter-governmental treaties with the federal authorities, exacerbating the already existing asymmetric federalism (discussed further at section III.E.ii. below). Article 6 confirms a single, uniform, federal citizenship. Despite this, the constitutions of some republics within the federation claimed local citizenship; for example, the Republic of Tyva amended its constitution to eliminate Tyva citizenship only following a local referendum in April 2010.[52]

Article 7 specifies that Russia is a 'social State whose policy is directed towards the creation of conditions ensuring a life of dignity and the free development of man'. Its second paragraph says that labour and health shall be protected, and a minimum wage established. It also commits the State to support the family, the disabled and elderly, with a system of social services and other State benefits. This article suggests an element of continuity; although 'social' not socialist, there is a commitment to social justice ahead of the individual rights guaranteed in Chapter 2 of

---

[52] 'Tuva starts poll to bring its Constitution in line with All-Russian', *Itar-Tass World Service*, 11 April 2010, available via Westlaw.

the Constitution. The mechanics of the various social security guarantees is not specified, either here or in Article 39 which guarantees social security provisions. In 2004–05 there was unrest when the State transferred from benefits-in-kind to cash payments[53]; interestingly, in-kind benefits were retained for State officials and judges.

ii. Articles 8–9: economic fundamentals

Before its dissolution, reforms in the USSR created a basic framework for the development of a market economy. The USSR constitutional provisions on ownership were amended in March 1990 (see chapter two) so that shareholding became possible, and legislation was passed creating new types of legal entity. No longer would the State have a monopoly on ownership of the means of production. New USSR Fundamental Principles of Civil Law, drafted to suit the needs of the market economy, were adopted in May 1991. Unfortunately they were set to come into force one year later, by which time the USSR no longer existed. However, pending adoption of a new Russian Civil Code to replace the increasingly inappropriate RSFSR Code of 1964, in July 1992 Russian legislation gave these USSR Fundamental Principles legal force throughout Russia, except where they conflicted with Russian legislation passed after 12 June 1990 (the date of Russia's Declaration of Sovereignty). The 1964 Code would still be applied where there was no new legislation and the Fundamental Principles were silent. This stopgap measure served until the staged introduction from 1 January 1995 of Russia's new Civil Code and ancillary legislation. While still part of the USSR, in March 1991 Russia adopted a Law on Competition and Limitation of Monopolistic Activity, and in December 1991 a Law on Enterprises and Entrepreneurial Activity, both going further towards sensible regulation of a market economy than had USSR legislation.

In December 1992 the then Russian Constitution was amended to introduce 'private ownership' (*chastnaia sobstvennost'*), exercised by individuals and newly-formed companies. This term, previously associated

---

[53] See J Bransten, 'Refashioning the Social Safety Net' (2004) 4(31) *Radio Free Europe/Radio Liberty Russian Political Weekly*, 16 August; L Belin, '[Duma] Alters Course on Social Benefits for Official Heroes' (2005) 9(127) *Radio Free Europe/Radio Liberty Newsline*, 11 July, available at <http://www.hri.org/news/balkans/rferl/2005/05-07-11.rferl.html>, accessed 17 July 2010.

with capitalist exploitation, had been avoided in Soviet reforms, although citizen's personal ownership (*lichnaia sobstvennost'*) had been expanded.

In 1993, Yel'tsin was determined to embed this transition to a market economy and the expanded ownership rights into the Constitution. Article 8 guarantees unity of economic space, free movement of goods, services and financial assets, competition and freedom of economic activity, and gives equal recognition to private, State, municipal and other forms of ownership. Article 9 includes the provision that 'land and other natural resources may be in private, State, municipal and other forms of ownership'. There was no historical Russian tradition of private owner-ship of land, and it remained controversial, delaying the passage of a new Land Code until Autumn 2001, and inspiring separate treatment of agricultural land, with a Law on Agricultural Land Transactions coming into force in January 2003.[54] Some constitutions of federal subjects, for example the Marii El republic, resisted private land ownership until forced to come into line with federal law during President Putin's reas-sertion of central control (see chapter four).

iii. Articles 10–12: separation of power

The 1993 Constitution declares in Article 10 that:

> State power in the Russian Federation shall be effectuated on the basis of separation into legislative, executive, and judicial. Agencies of legislative, executive, and judicial power shall be autonomous.[55]

Butler has carefully translated *samostoiatel'nyi* as 'autonomous' as the usual Russian word for 'independent' is *nezavisimyi*. Most translations into English ignore the distinction. The three branches of State should exercise their powers autonomously from each other although they are not independent. For example, appointment to high office is commonly through nomination by one entity, for example the President, and con-firmation by another, typically one of the chambers of the Legislature. This is the Russian version of 'checks-and-balances'.

---

[54] See L Skyner, 'Political Conflict and Legal Uncertainty: the Privatisation of Land Ownership in Russia' (2001) 53(7) *Europe-Asia* Studies 981; Z Lerman and N Shagaida, 'Land Policies and Agricultural Land Markets in Russia' (2007) 24 *Land Use Policy* 14; and SK Wegren, 'Russia's Incomplete Land Reform' (2009) 64 *Russian Analytical Digest*, 15 September, at 2, available at <http://www.res.ethz.ch/analysis/rad/details.cfm?lng=en&id=106025>, accessed 21 July 2010.

[55] Butler, above n 3, at 707.

Neither autocratic imperial Russia nor Soviet Russia aspired to an ideal of separation of powers. In imperial times,

> the combination of powers was the main, essential feature of the state; the separation of powers was subordinate, less significant and decisive.[56]

Soviet theory presented separation of powers as a bourgeois fiction. The guiding principle under socialism was the unity of State power, and there was no clear demarcation in the powers of the central State agencies (see chapter two).

The aspiration to separation of powers preceded the 1993 Constitution. It was first made explicit in the 1990 Declaration on the State Sovereignty of the RSFSR (see section II.B above). In December 1992, Article 3 of the 1978 Constitution was amended to declare that

> the system of State power in the Russian Federation is based on the principles of the separation of legislative, executive, and judicial power[57]

but Article 2, which gave undivided State power to the Soviets of People's Deputies, remained unaltered. Such inconsistency was typical of the 1978 Constitution in its later years. Nevertheless, the separation under the amended 1978 Constitution was taken seriously enough to act as the basis for Constitutional Court decisions in March and April 1993.[58]

Article 11 lists the federal agencies of State power but leaves delineation of power between federal and subject agencies of State power to 'the Constitution, the Federation Treaties and other treaties on the delineation of power'. This left open the possibility of 'power-sharing treaties' between the centre and individual federal subjects, which indeed occurred, particularly in 1994–98 (see section III.E.ii. below). Article 12 recognises local government as autonomous within the limits of its powers, but says it is not regarded as being within the system of agencies of State power. This flags up a contrast with the Soviet system, where there was 'unity of State power' down the whole hierarchy of soviets. As with

---

[56] AM Yakovlev, *Striving for Law in a Lawless Land: Memoirs of a Russian Reformer* (Armonk, NY, ME Sharpe, 1996), citing pre-revolutionary author NM Kokunov, *The Russian State Law* (1914).

[57] Translation from WE Butler, *Constitution (Basic Law) of the Russian Federation – Russia* (London, The Primrose Academy, 1993) 7.

[58] GP van den Berg, 'Russia's Constitutional Court: a Decade of Legal Reforms. Part Two: the Constitution of the Russian Federation Annotated' (2002–3) 28 *Review of Central and East European Law* 301–02.

other separation of powers, this reform pre-dated the Constitution. A USSR law of 5 April 1990, and a Russian law of 6 July 1991, both incorporated the principle of local government as a self-standing political and administrative level, not formally part of the organisation of State agencies. A law of 28 August 1995, enacted after a 'protracted legislative process and much controversy',[59] gave a framework for local self-government which left considerable legislative scope to regional administrations. This has now been superseded by the federal law of 6 October 2003, 'On the general principles of organisation of local self-government in the Russian Federation', which reorganised the units of local self-government but has had serious implementation problems, causing inconsistency and delay in the imposition of deadlines. It has not resolved inevitable tensions between centralisation and local autonomy, but further discussion of this is beyond the scope of this book.[60]

iv. Articles 13–14: ideological diversity and the secular State

Article 13 trumpets ideological diversity: '[N]o ideology may be established as State or obligatory.' (Article 13(2)) Political diversity and a multi-party system are recognised, and social associations are equal before the law. However, associations advocating social, racial, national and religious enmity are prohibited. Article 14 declares the Russian Federation to be secular, with no State religion, and that religious associations are separate from the State and equal before the law.

The prior Soviet Constitution allowed freedom of conscience and freedom to worship although not proselytise, but it was inherent in the 'guiding and directing' role of the Communist Party 'armed with Marxism-Leninism' (Article 6, 1977 USSR Constitution) that there was an official State ideology. In pre-revolutionary times Orthodox Christianity had a special position (see chapter two).

---

[59] H Wollmann and E Gritsenko, 'Local self-government in Russia' in C Ross and A Campbell (eds), *Federalism and Local Politics in Russia* (London, BASEES/ Routledge, 2009) 227 at 228.

[60] Insightful discussion in chapters of *ibid*. Apart from Wollmann and Gritsenko, see JF Young, 'Russia's elusive pursuit of balance in local government reform', *ibid* at 248, and A Campbell, 'Vertical or triangle? Local, regional and federal government in the Russian Federation after law 131', *ibid* at 263. See also B Bowring, 'Enhanced Local Self-government as a Means of Enhancing Minority Governance' in M Weller and K Nobbs (eds), *Political Participation of Minorities. A Commentary on International Standards and Practice* (Oxford, Oxford University Press, 2010).

The current situation not as clear-cut as the constitutional article suggests. The Russian federal law on Freedom of Conscience and Religious Associations of 26 September 1997, 'acknowledging the special role of Orthodoxy'[61] and 'respecting Christianity, Islam, Judaism and Buddhism and other religions which comprise an integral part of the historical heritage of the peoples of Russia', ensured those groups an advantage in organising registration. The law also made a careful distinction between a religious association and a religious group, and whilst it was true that the associations are equal, they have more rights than the groups, for example legal personality and a consequent right to own property.[62]

There is formal separation of Church and State, but the Orthodox Church has an important role in Russian public life and has succeeded, for example, in encouraging teaching in State schools of a core curriculum on the 'Fundamentals of the Orthodox Culture'.[63] The date 28 July is now a public holiday, commemorating the adoption of Christianity in 10th-century Russia.[64] Not everyone sees religious incursion as negative:

> Such an insistence [in the Constitution] on the distance between the state institutions and religious associations obviously deprives the state institutions of necessary support for spiritual interaction between the state and its components. This Article of the new Constitution provides grounds for arguing in some publications that atheism is a kind of ideology promoted by the secular state.[65]

Russia has a long tradition of having an official faith, and many see the neutrality of the Constitution as a creating a dangerous vacuum into which undesirable belief systems could flow.

---

[61]   Butler, above n 2, at 122.

[62]   J Henderson, 'Freedom of Conscience in Russia' (1998) 4(2) *European Public Law* 174.

[63]   PL Glanzer and K Petrenko, 'Religion and Education in Post-Communist Russia: Russia's Evolving Church-State Relations' (2007) 49(1) *Journal of Church and State* 53 at 61. See also RC Blitt, 'How to Entrench a De Facto State Church in Russia: A Guide in Progress' (2008) *Brigham Young University Law Review* 709.

[64]   K O'Flynn, 'For Russia's Future Priests, an Education in Church-State Ties' (2010) *Radio Free Europe/Radio Liberty*, 28 July, available at <http://www.rferl.org/content/For_Russias_Future_Priests_An_Education_In_ChurchState_Ties/2112024.html>, accessed 5 August 2010.

[65]   Believ, above n 11, at 309.

v. Article 15: direct effect, publication, and the status of international law

Article 15(1) asserts that the 1993 Constitution 'shall have the highest legal force, direct effect, and be applied throughout the entire territory of the Russian Federation.'[66] This provision is hugely significant, although not unproblematic. (See 'Turf Wars' in chapter six, section V.) Earlier Constitutions needed further legislation before constitutional principles could be applied in court. Article 15(1) continues, 'laws and other legal acts applicable in the Russian Federation must not be contrary to the Constitution of the Russian Federation.'[67] Ensuring observation of this has also caused headaches for the federal authorities, and the extent to which the Procuracy can complain to court about constitutionality of local legislation has been disputed.[68]

Article 15(3) requires that:

Laws shall be subject to official publication. Unpublished laws shall not be applied. Any normative legal acts affecting the rights, freedoms, and duties of man and citizen may not be applied if they have not been published officially for general information.

This provision is slightly disingenuous. The requirement of official publication before application applies to laws (*zakony*), not other forms of legislation, except for those affecting the rights of 'man and citizen'. So, for example, publication for general information is not required for applicability of tax regulations relating to legal entities.

Articles 15(4), combined with Article 17, which opens the chapter on the 'Rights and Freedoms of Man and Citizen', creates the interesting scenario that the Constitution is not completely autonomous. According to Article 15(4):

Generally-recognised principles and norms of international law and international treaties of the Russian Federation shall be an integral part of its legal system. If other rules have been established by an international treaty of the Russian Federation than provided for by a law, the rules of the international treaty shall apply.

[66] Butler, above n 2, at 7.
[67] *Ibid.*
[68] See JA Corwin, 'Tatarstan Asks Constitutional Court to Resolve Battle with Prosecutors' (2002) 6(188) *Radio Free Europe/Radio Liberty Newsline*, 4 October.

Article 17 adds:

> The rights and freedoms of man and citizen shall be recognised and guaranteed in the Russian Federation according to generally recognised principles and norms of international law and in accordance with the present Constitution.

As Butler points out in his book *Russian Law*:

> The formal recognition of generally-recognised principles and norms of international law, that is, customary norms of international law, to be an integral part of the Russian legal system is one of the most momentous changes of the 20th century in the development of Russian law.[69]

Further, Article 15(4) 'places international law ahead of the Constitution and, in so doing, confers upon international law a special status in the Russian legal system'.[70]

The contrast to the Soviet dualist approach, where international law applied only if specifically enacted into domestic law, is conspicuous:

> The 1977 Constitution did not allow the direct operation of international law in the domestic setting . . . the Soviet legal order remained closed to international legal norms . . . By relying on the doctrine of transformation, the Soviet Union was able to sign numerous international treaties, including treaties on human rights, and still avoid implementing some or all of their provisions in the domestic legal order.[71]

Article 1 of the November 1991 Russian Declaration of the Rights of Man and Citizen, incorporated in April 1992 as Article 32 of the amended 1978 Constitution, gave priority to generally recognised international norms on human rights over domestic Russian law.

> For the first time in its history, Russia adopted a general constitutional principle incorporating certain international norms into its domestic law.[72]

Despite being limited to human rights provisions, this was revolutionary.

The constitutional provisions including international law as an integral part of the Russian legal system go even further, but have created controversy over whether Article 17 puts generally-recognised principles

---

[69] Butler, above n 3, at 693.
[70] *Ibid* at 695.
[71] GM Danilenko, 'The New Russian Constitution and International Law' (1994) 88 *American Journal of International Law* 451 at 458.
[72] *Ibid* at 461.

and norms of international law above contrary domestic law, but the same level as constitutional law, or whether it confers on them a special status above the Constitution. The first of these propositions has been demonstrated in court practice, but not yet the second. This controversy over special status has persisted, despite some tidying up by a Supreme Court Plenum decree in October 2003 distinguishing between treaties adopted by federal law and by subordinate legislative acts.

Adding to the complication, apparently both the Russian Constitutional Court and the Supreme Court have worked out their own method of defining what are 'generally-recognised principles and norms of international law', by citing international treaties 'or even non-binding international instruments, particularly UN General Assembly resolutions'.[73] This bypasses the usual requirement for general international law to be demonstrated by the actual practice of States, and allows rather more certainly than is warranted.

D. Chapter 2: Individual Rights in the Constitution

Reforms during the *perestroika* era transformed the approach to individual rights (see chapter six). Before 1991, as described in chapter two, the Soviet approach was based on the theory of dependent rights. The current Constitution takes the inherent rights approach, first enshrined in the USSR in its Declaration of the Rights of Man of September 1991. The Russian Declaration of the Rights of Man and Citizen of November 1991 took the same approach and was incorporated into the then Constitution in April 1992. Thus the rights revolution had already occurred before the 1993 Constitution was adopted. Nevertheless, its significance cannot be overstated. A more detailed discussion of the enumerated rights is to be found in chapter six.

---

[73] GM Danilenko, 'Implementation of International Law in CIS States: Theory and Practice' (1999) *European Journal of International Law* 51 at 62.

E.   Chapters 3 and 8: Russia as a Federal State; Local Competence

i.   Russia's federal heritage

A thorough review of the developments of the Russian Federation is beyond the scope of this book.[74] However, it is appropriate to highlight the main features.

The USSR had the formal trappings of a treaty federation, including a declaration that it was a voluntary association of sovereign States and that its constituent Union Republics had the right to secede.[75] The political and practical reality was extremely different. The USSR functioned as a unitary State, with its monolithic Communist Party and centralised State-planned economy. The important characteristics of a sovereign State in the standard Western sense (defined territory, distinct population and independent government) applied only to the USSR as a whole and not to any of the Union Republics.[76] Even their theoretical right of secession was nullified by the fact that any change in the State boundary was under the exclusive jurisdiction of the USSR.

However, that theoretical right led logically to Stalin's criteria for a Union Republic: that it must be located on a border (as well as having a compact and sufficiently large population). This excluded the Tatars and Bashkirs,

> who in terms of size and compactness of population deserved to become republics. This remains a source of bitterness for Tatarstan to this day.[77]

Stalin gained one advantage from the assertion of Union Republics' sovereign Statehood. When the United Nations Organisation was being established in 1945, he claimed the right to 17 seats: one for the USSR and one for each of the then 16 constituent Union Republics.[78] The story goes that the United Kingdom countered this with an assertion that His Majesty's Government would establish diplomatic representa-

---

[74] See M Nicholson, *Towards a Russia of the Regions*, Adelphi Paper 330 (Oxford, Oxford University Press, 1999) and Kahn, above n 11.

[75] See H-J Uibopuu, 'International legal personality of Union Republics of the USSR' (1975) 24 *International and Comparative Law Quarterly* 811.

[76] *Ibid* at 813; and H-J Uibopuu, 'Soviet Federalism under the New Soviet Constitution' (1979) 5 *Review of Socialist Law* 171 at 175.

[77] Sakwa, above n 4, at 238.

[78] The well-known 15, plus the Karelo-Finnish Union Republic which existed from 1940 to 1956. See AL Unger, *Constitutional Development in the USSR: a Guide to the Soviet Constitutions* (London, Methuen, 1981) at 159.

tion in one of the central Asian Union Republics. This would not have been welcomed, and a compromise was reached that the USSR, Ukraine and Belorussia would have UN membership (including a permanent Security Council seat for the USSR), but the other Soviet Union Republics would not.[79] Stalin thus gained control of two extra votes in the UN General Assembly.

During the *perestroika* era, Union Republics attempted to put meaning into the empty words of the USSR Constitution awarding them sovereignty. Gorbachev even instigated passage of a USSR Law on Secession of 3 April 1990, although the cumbersome procedure specified was never used.[80] In September 1991, following the abortive August putsch, the three Baltic republics of Estonia, Latvia and Lithuania were acknowledged as independent by the USSR's State Council, without further ado (see chapter two).

The USSR bequeathed on the RSFSR a complex federal structure, with one group of federal subjects supposedly based on an ethnicity principle and another group based on territory. Added to that, a sizable number of the ethnic federal subjects were contained within territorial units; so-called *matreshka* federalism, named after the Russian nesting dolls. For example, in May 1990, Russia had 88 federal subjects of which 15 were nested inside the other 73. The territorial-based units were the 49 regions, the two cities of federal significance, Moscow and St Petersburg, and the six provinces (similar to regions, except they were once border areas).[81] The ethnically-based units were the 16 autonomous republics (autonomous soviet socialist republics, ASSRs), five autonomous regions within provinces and 10 autonomous national areas (within provinces or regions).

The 'parade of sovereignties' of Union Republics in the USSR from November 1988, when many issued Declarations of Sovereignty, encouraged the 16 autonomous republics within federal Russia also to strive for greater status. In 1990, 14 of them declared themselves sovereign,[82]

---

[79] Uibopuu, above n 75, at fn 165, confirms that in 1947 an approach was made to the Ukrainian SSR; 'no reply was received'.

[80] Except by the breakaway Trans-Dniestr region of Moldova (Pridnestrovie); see 'The USSR Law on Secession', available at <http://pridnestrovie.net/ussr_law.html>, accessed 28 July 2010.

[81] Sakwa, above n 4, at 240.

[82] Kahn, above n 11, at 103. There is a table of dates of the 'parade of sovereignties' *ibid* at 104.

although what they meant by this was not consistent. By 3 July 1991 the amended 1978 Constitution referred to them as republics (in the 24 May version they were still ASSRs). At the same time, four out of the five autonomous regions became republics, leaving the sole survivor the already anomalous far-eastern Jewish autonomous region – where Jews make up only 4.2 per cent of the population and represent only 1.7 per cent of Russia's Jews.[83]

This mismatch of name and ethnicity of the population is common; in only seven of Russia's 21 republics is the titular nationality (to use the Soviet term) the majority, and in only two of the 10 autonomous national areas (Russians are the majority in the others).[84] Russians are the majority in eight republics; in the remaining six, no group has an overall majority. Neither do the ethnically-based units correspond to the number of different ethnic groups which live in the Russian Federation, put at 182 in the 2002 census (with Russians making up about 83 per cent of the total population of around 140 million). Officially, more than 75 minority languages are taught in more than 10,000 schools in Russia.[85] Four autochthonous groups have more than 1 million members (Tatars, 5 million; Chuvashians, 1.6 million; Bashkirs, 1.6 million; and Chechens, 1.1 million); 22 ethnic groups number between 100,000 and half a million, 28 groups between 10,000 and 100,000, and 24 groups with fewer than 10,000.[86] People of ethnicities belonging to another State, such as Ukraine, Armenia, Azerbaidzhan, and Belarus, comprise 20.2 per cent of the total population.[87] There is also great variation in the dispersal of different groups; nearly 9.7 million live outside their nominal ethnic republic.[88] Another major disparity is relative prosperity. The 10 most prosperous federal subjects have an average per capita income four times that of the 10 least prosperous.[89]

---

[83]   Sakwa, above n 4, at 242.

[84]   Table, *ibid* at 243, based on figures from 1991.

[85]   'Council Of Europe Concerned About Russia's Minorities' (2007) 7(9) *Radio Free Europe/Radio Liberty Russia Report* 8 May.

[86]   On the protection on 'small peoples', see also B Bowring, 'Legal and policy developments in the Russian Federation in 2007 with regard to the protection of minorities' (2006/2007) 6 *European Yearbook of Minority Issues* 529.

[87]   Figures from A Heinemann-Grüder, 'Federal discources, minority rights, and conflict transformation' in C Ross and A Campbell (eds), *Federalism and Local Politics in Russia* (London, BASEES/Routledge, 2009) 54 at 61.

[88]   Sakwa, above n 4, at 242.

[89]   Nicholson, above n 74, at 26, with data from 1996.

ii. Federative relations in independent Russia

In the lead-up to the 1993 Constitution, there were two tensions affecting Russia's federal relations: fear and greed. The USSR had recently
disintegrated, and there was fear that the Russian Federation might suf-
fer a similar fate. The USSR's breakup had been triggered by reaction to
the more confederative USSR Federal Treaty which Gorbachev was
about to sign; not welcomed by the Communist 'old guard', ironically
their actions in forming the Committee for the State of Emergency
impelled USSR to the very fate they had sought to avoid (see chapter
two).

Nevertheless, Yel'tsin was happy to encourage regional autonomy, to
spite the USSR. In 1990 he had told the federal subjects to 'take as much
autonomy as you can swallow'.[90] The republics obliged and passed constitutions claiming greater powers than the federal Constitution allowed.
Yel'tsin was content to turn a blind eye in return for political support.

Despite this centrifugal tendency, in March 1992 Yel'tsin gained agreement from almost all of the Russian federal subjects to three new treaties,
which defined the jurisdictions of the central agencies of State power and
those of the federal subjects.[91] The dissenters were the traditionally independent Tatarstan and the then Chechno-Ingushetiia, although there
were also specific reservations by Kaluga and Leningrad regions. One
treaty was with 'the sovereign republics within the Russian Federation',
one with the territories, regions, and cities of Moscow and St Petersburg,
and the third with the one autonomous region and the autonomous
national areas. Collectively, the three became the new Russian Federation
Treaty, which was incorporated into the then Constitution on 10 April
1992.

The differences between the three separate treaties are subtle. The
first used the phrase 'sovereign republics' in its title and Preamble.
Article III(1) stated that the republics 'shall possess the entirety of State
power on their territories, except for those powers which have been
transferred to the jurisdiction of federal agencies', clearly staking a claim
to a confederal arrangement. The second part of the same article
declared that the republics are 'autonomous participants of international and foreign economic relations'. The treaties for the other federal

---

[90]   Cited in Kahn, above n 11, at 148. Kahn quotes Yel'tsin reasserting this on 11
May 1994, *ibid* at 142 and 156.
[91]   Butler, above n 2, at 682.

subjects also had this, but there was no equivalent claim to be the original source of State power.

The lists of issues in federal and in joint jurisdiction in the three treaties are almost identical, although the order of joint jurisdiction issues is different for the republics' treaty compared to the other two. Only in the republics' treaty is 'citizenship of the Russian Federation' mentioned as being within federal jurisdiction. The implication is that there could be citizenship of a republic, and indeed many of the republics' constitutions asserted this.

The 1993 Constitution defines issues in federal jurisdiction in Article 71 and joint jurisdiction in Article 72, and Article 73 assigns any residual issues to the jurisdiction of the federal subjects. Federal executive agencies are also allowed to transfer to federal subjects 'part of their powers if this is not contrary to the Constitution and federal laws' (1993 Constitution, Article 78(2)). The Constitution no longer describes republics as 'sovereign', although the lists of issues in Articles 72 and 73 are almost identical to those in their 1992 treaty. Apart from loss of the mention of federal citizenship, the only other difference is that intellectual property regulation has moved from joint jurisdiction to federal jurisdiction, and court organisation, which was confusingly mentioned in both lists in the republics' treaty, is now firmly under federal control. As mentioned earlier, the Federation Treaty has a residuary life thanks to the Concluding and Transitional Provisions, but only in so far as it conforms to the Constitution.

By asserting equality of all federal subjects, and making no distinction in the allocation of relative powers, the 1993 Constitution enhanced the federal subjects other than republics. Republics kept the right to have a constitution (see chapter one) but lost some jurisdiction.

But their loss became more apparent than real. Constitutional Article 11(3) allows inter-governmental treaties (*dogovory*) between federal subjects and the Federation. This led to a spate of backdoor reclamation of jurisdiction through individually negotiated treaties.[92] There were also individual agreements (*soglashenii*) between governments on more spe-

---

[92] S Kjeldsen, 'The Treaty process evolves – Russian bilateral power-sharing treaties' (1998) 24 *Review of Central and East Europe Law* 363 at 366 (looking at the first 35): 'Since mid-1966 . . . all the sixteen most recent treaties, except one, have a clause stating that they rank higher than federal legislation.' See also Kahn, above n 11, at 174, Table 6.5, examples of supremacy clauses.

cific areas such as banking and currency policy; for example, during 1993 Tatarstan concluded agreements on oil and petrochemical trans-port, foreign economic relations and ownership.[93] Many agreements were negotiated in the run-up to the Federation Treaty.[94]

Treaties were initially only between the centre and republics, but from January 1996 regions and territories also took advantage; between February 1994 and June 1998, 42 treaties were signed between the cen-tre and 46 federal subjects.[95] There were also 'hundreds of bilateral agreements at lower levels, most of which were kept secret in order to stop the competition for favours from getting out of hand'.[96] After mid-1995, treaties tended to contain 'regional wish lists' rather than extraordinary claims to jurisdiction.[97] However, the overall effect was an uneven 'contract federalism' which created asymmetry in the Russian federal structure. About half of the federal subjects negotiated deals, some gaining more privileges than others. The richer units in particular negotiated themselves the best deals.

Tatarstan led the way on 15 February 1994, followed by most but not all of the other republics.[98] The last substantive treaty was with Moscow on 16 June 1998, although there are later treaties which terminate exist-ing treaties, the latest being in May 2003.[99]

No new treaties had been signed for a year when on 30 July 1999 (less than three weeks before Putin became President Yel'tsin's last Government Chairman) a new federal law came into force that Putin helped to draft.[100] The law set out a standard procedure for concluding treaties and agree-ments, and by its Concluding Provisions federal subjects were given three years to bring existing treaties into conformity with the Constitution and federal law.

---

[93] WE Butler and JE Henderson, *Russian Legal Texts* (London, Simmonds & Hill, 1992) 73. See Kahn, above n 11, for background and issues.

[94] Table of agreements in Kahn, above n 11, at 167.

[95] Table with dates in PJ Söderlund, 'The significance of structural power resources in the Russian Bilateral treaty process 1994–1998' (2003) 36 *Communist and Post-Communist Studies* 311 at 317.

[96] Nicholson, above n 74, at 21.

[97] Kjeldsen, above n 92, at 383.

[98] For comparison of provisions, see *ibid* and Kahn, above n 11, at 164.

[99] Butler, above n 3, at 101, fn 22.

[100] R Sakwa, *Putin: Russia's Choice* (New York, Routledge, 2004) 133.

Of course, after years spent disregarding similar passages in the Federation Treaty, Constitution and countless federal pronouncements, these old mantras had a hollow ring. There was no rush to reform.[101]

That was before the change of President in Russia. One of Putin's first goals once in office in 2000 was to rein in the errant federal subjects and restore central control. He brought discipline to Russia's federal structure through changes to federal fiscal arrangements[102] and other ways discussed in chapter four. Treaties began to be revoked. By April 2002 Putin could report that of 42 federal subjects with treaties, 28 had already revoked them.[103] Major amendments in July 2003 to the October 1999 federal law 'On the general principles of organisation of legislative (representative) and executive agencies of state power of subjects of the Russian Federation' included a provision that existing treaties would lapse by July 2005 unless specifically reconfirmed by the federal legislature. Bilateral treaties have not entirely disappeared. After quite protracted negotiations, Russia and Tatarstan agreed a new treaty in July 2007 (recall that Tatarstan was not a party to the Federation Treaty and had its own previous treaty with Russia). However, the disparities in federal relations of the 1990s are much reduced.

Nevertheless, it has taken the best part of a decade to tidy up. As late as mid-2009, 13 federal ethnic units still claimed sovereignty in their constitutions, despite a condemnatory Constitutional Court ruling eight years earlier.[104] After the Court sent a reminder on 9 June 2009, the republic of Sakha (formerly Yakutia) passed an amendment on 17 June removing the claim to sovereignty from its constitution, and it was hoped, although not expected, that the others would follow suit.[105] Over the next few years they all did.

---

[101]   Kahn, above n 11, at 236.

[102]   N Melvin, 'Putin's Reform of the Russian Federation' in A Pravda (ed), *Leading Russia: Putin in Perspective. Essays in Honour of Archie Brown* (Oxford, Oxford University Press, 2005) 208.

[103]   Sakwa, above n 100, at 145.

[104]   'A Protracted Farewell to Sovereignty' (2009) *Nezavisimaia Gazeta Online* in Russian, 29 June, available in translation via Westlaw under the title 'Russia: Moscow Removing Last Vestiges of Sovereignty From Ethnic Republics'.

[105]   P Goble, 'National Republics Resist Moscow's Demand To Amend Constitutions' (2009) *Radio Free Europe/Radio Liberty Feature*, 23 June, available online at <http://www.rferl.org/content/National_Republics_Resist_Moscows_Demand_To_Amend_Constitutions/1760801.html>, accessed 29 July 2010.

One other development in Russian federal relations should be noted here. Since 2005 the number of federal subjects has reduced to 83 though voluntary mergers, based on the provisions of a federal constitutional law passed on 17 December 2001, 'On the procedure of acceptance into the Russian Federation and formation within its composition of a new subject of the Russian Federation'.[106] The result is that there are now only four autonomous areas, not 10, and the *matreshka* nesting of units within others has consequently also reduced, leaving only three 'nested' areas. Merger procedure can be initiated only by neighbouring federal subjects, and requires agreement of the affected populations through a referendum, followed by legislation sponsored by the President.[107] The most recent merger was in March 2008, and although there have been discussions about others, no further steps have been taken so far.

F. Chapters 4 to 7: the Federal Agencies of State Power

The contents and effects of these central constitutional chapters are dealt with in the following three chapters of this book. The chapters follow the order in the Constitution, except that details of Government are included with those of the President in the chapter on 'Executive Power'.

G. Chapter 9: Amendment Procedures

Three of the nine chapters in Section I are entrenched, that is, need an extraordinary procedure, outlined below, for their amendment. The three special chapters are: Chapter 1, Foundations of the Constitutional System; Chapter 2, Rights and Freedoms of Man and Citizen; and Chapter 9, Constitutional Amendments and Revision of the Constitution. Entrenchment was an innovation. Planning for a potentially more argumentative multi-party era, it was clearly felt important that the fundamentals of the constitutional order and the rights and freedoms of man

---

[106] Butler, above n 2, at 698.
[107] For a case study, see O Oracheva, 'Unification as a political project' in C Ross and A Campbell (eds), *Federalism and Local Politics in Russia* (London, BASEES/ Routledge, 2009) 82.

and citizen should be especially protected, and the simple 'workaround' of changing the amendment procedure precluded. Article 135(1) specifies that Chapters 1, 2 and 9 may not be revised by the Federal Legislature. An amendment proposal requires a three-fifths vote of all the members of the Legislature,[108] 'then in accordance with a federal constitutional law a Constitutional Assembly shall be convoked' (Article 135(3)). So far no federal constitutional law has been passed on the formation of a Constitutional Assembly. It may be that an appropriate 'bespoke' law would be passed if and when amendment of an entrenched chapter is sought. The Constitutional Assembly would either confirm the status quo, or work out a draft new Constitution which 'shall be adopted by the Constitutional Assembly by two-thirds of the votes of the total number of members or shall be submitted to an all-people's referendum'. The article defines a positive referendum result as approval by more than half of those who voted, with a turnout of at least 50 per cent, the same requirements as secured the current Constitution.

The other six constitutional chapters can be amended by qualified majorities in the Federal Legislature (two-thirds in the Duma and three-quarters in the Federation Council), plus ratification by the legislatures of at least two-thirds of the federal subjects. For the first 15 years of the Constitution's existence, no such amendment was made, and many commentators had expressed the view that the Constitution was virtually immutable. Then in December 2008, with impressive speed, the national and regional legislatures gave their required approval to a bill instigated by President Medvedev[109] increasing the presidential term of office from four years to six, and that of the Duma from four years to five, and adding slightly to the Duma's prerogatives. The reform could smoothly pass the hurdle of legislative approval because of overwhelming support for Medvedev by deputies in the Unified Russia party with a majority in the Duma of over two-thirds and control of 79 of the 83 regional legislatures. Under the terms of earlier Constitutions, constitutional amendment was by qualified majority of two-thirds of the votes of each of the chambers of the Supreme Soviet (for the 1936 and 1977 Constitutions;

---

[108] A Constitutional Court decision of 12 April 1995 addressed the issue of how such votes should be counted. The majority Court decision was that each chamber votes separately and the qualified majority is of the number that the Constitution specifies for the chamber, not actual attendance.

[109] Policy stated in Medvedev's first annual address to the Federal Assembly on 5 November 2008.

nothing specified in the 1918 and 1924 Constitutions). However, the political reality of the Soviet era, at least before *perestroika*, ensured that by the time draft legislation reached the Supreme Soviet, debate was over and the text presented was passed unanimously, so the requirement for qualified majorities was of symbolic value not practical limitation.[110] Medvedev's painless amendment of the 1993 Constitution led parallels to be drawn to that previous position.

IV. CONCLUSION

Commentators, including the current author, who considered the 1993 Constitution when it first appeared, had grave doubts about its balance and durability, whilst welcoming the first Russian Constitution to take itself seriously as an applicable legal document. Passing time has quelled those doubts, although it has also allowed scope for political shifts which have altered the impact of the Constitution. These are explored in relation to the three main agencies of State power in the following three chapters.

FURTHER READING

RB Ahdeih, *Russia's Constitutional Revolution: Legal Consciousness and the Transition to Democracy 1985–1996* (University Park, PA, University of Pennsylvania Press, 1997).

B Bowring, 'The Russian Constitutional System: Complexity and Asymmetry' in M Weller and K Nobbs (eds), *Asymmetric Autonomy and the Settlement of Ethnic Conflicts* (Philadelphia, PA, University of Pennsylvana, 2010) 48.

G M Danilenko, 'The New Russian Constitution and International Law' (1994) 88 *American Journal of International Law* 451.

J Kahn, *Federalism, Democratization, and the Rule of Law in Russia* (Oxford, Oxford University Press, 2002).

R Moore, 'The path to the new Russian Constitution: a comparison of executive–legislative relations in the major drafts' (1995) 3 *Demokratizatsiya* 44.

---

[110] The first open legislative debate was during passage of the 30 June 1987 Law of the USSR 'On the procedure for appealing to a court unlawful actions of officials which impinge upon the rights of citizens'.

W Pomeranz, 'The Russian Constitutional Court's interpretation of federalism: balancing center-regional relations' (1997) 4 *Parker School Journal of East European Law* 414.

C Ross and A Campbell (eds), *Federalism and Local Politics in Russia* (London, BASEES/Routledge, 2009).

R Sakwa, *Russian Politics and Society*, 4th edn (Abingdon, Routledge, 2008).

R Sharlet, 'Russian constitutional crisis: law & politics under Yel'tsin' (1993) 9 *Post-Soviet Affairs* 314.

PJ Söderlund, 'The significance of structural power resources in the Russian Bilateral treaty process 1994–1998' (2003) 36 *Communist and Post-Communist Studies* 311.

4

Executive Power, the President and the Government

Introduction – The Presidency – The Government – Accountability – Para-Constitutional Institutions – Executive Power in the Federal Subjects – Conclusion – Further Reading

I. INTRODUCTION

THIS CHAPTER DEALS with the exercise of executive power in Russia. In the 1993 Russian Constitution the President is designated as Head of State, but not as head of the Executive (as he was in the previous Constitution), nor even as head of the Government. According to the Constitution, executive power is exercised by the Government, headed by the Government Chairman (sometimes translated as Prime Minister). Nevertheless, the Constitution, with its provisions finalised during a period of presidential rule in Russia, gives very wide powers to the President, and it is convenient to discuss them under the heading of executive power.

The office of President is a comparatively recent innovation in Russia, but the principle of a single individual having the major leadership role is not. Looking back both to the Russian Empire and the Soviet period, despite some rare occasions when shared authority was the stated intention, for example immediately after the death of Stalin and following the ouster of Khrushchev as Party leader, there has been a consistent 'strong hand on the tiller' exercised by a named individual; as Tsar, Emperor or Empress, Party First (or General) Secretary. The novelty of the post of President, and the comparative lack of a strict legal framework defining his role, has created a dynamic system which is still developing. So far only three individuals have held the post of Russian President, and the character of each has set its stamp on its development.

The exercise of executive power in Russia raises the central issue of how the President relates to the Government Chairman and the Government over which he presides. This is still evolving, and there is ample scope for the personal and political relationships between the individual officeholders to impact the practical working of this 'dual Executive'. The interrelation between the President and the Prime Minister gained particular attention following the March 2008 presidential elections. The outgoing incumbent, Vladimir Putin, was not able to stand as he had just served two terms as President, and the Constitution prohibits serving more than two terms in succession. Putin gave his 'seal of approval' as his heir to fellow Petersburger Dmitrii Medvedev, a Deputy Government Chairman and also Chairman of the Board of the immense Russian natural gas company Gazprom. One of Medvedev's campaign promises was that he would appoint Putin to be his Government Chairman. Medvedev won the presidency with a large majority (which indeed may have been artificially enhanced: see 'Accountability' in section IV. below). Since then, Medvedev and Putin claim to work in tandem. Political pundits view this 'tandemocracy' with some suspicion, wondering whether Putin may actually have remained in overall charge, perhaps as a prelude to being re-elected as President. The Russian Constitution does not forbid a return to presidential office after a gap, unlike the USSR Constitution which imposed an absolute restriction on serving more than two presidential terms, whether or not consecutive. Evidence so far as to the real balance of power between Medvedev and Putin is inconclusive. As President, Medvedev holds more formal power, but at the time of writing, half way through his term of office, he has not yet strongly stamped his individual authority on the role.

Another important characteristic of the Russian constitutional settlement is the lack of effective accountability. This is discussed in more detail in section IV. below.

This chapter also assesses three institutions which are not mentioned in the 1993 Constitution but which have been introduced either by or at the behest of Putin when he was President. These are the Presidential Representatives in federal districts, the State Council and the Public Chamber. All three give the President additional tools to promote his policies and enhance his already very broad powers.

Finally the Executive in the broader federal context will be considered, that is, the relationship between the President and those holding executive power in the federal subjects. This has changed under all three Presidents, altering the realities of Russia's federative structure. Before that, however, is an overview of the presidency and the scope of presidential power.

II. THE PRESIDENCY

A. The President and his role

There is currently no federal law, or federal constitutional law, on the President. Initially there was. The law of 24 April 1991 'On the President of the RSFSR' established the first Russian presidency, following the result of a referendum on 17 March 1991. Now the legal definition of presidential power is set out solely in the Constitution, which does not require that there should be a law on the President. This contrasts with the Government's position, where the Constitution specifically requires a federal constitutional law to determine the 'procedure for the activity of the Government' (Article 114(2)). The Constitution does demand a federal law on presidential elections; the current one dates from December 1999, replacing a law from 1995.

The only other law which relates directly to the President is the February 2001 federal law 'On the Guarantees for a President of the Russian Federation, who has Ceased his Powers, and for the Members of his Family'. This was preceded by a presidential edict, the first act of newly-installed Acting President Putin when he took up office on Yel'tsin's sudden voluntary retirement on 31 December 1999. The edict gave unqualified immunity to any former President, as well as generous pension provisions for him and the members of his family. Clearly it had Yel'tsin and family in mind, as there was no other former President. The current law is not quite so open-handed. It contains a procedure allowing immunity to be overturned, so that a former President could be prosecuted for serious crimes committed during his period of office (see section IV. below, 'Accountability').

What, then, does the 1993 Constitution say about the President? A candidate for office must be a citizen of the Russian Federation of at least 35 years old, who has 'permanently resided' in Russia for at least 10 years. There is no upper age limit, as there was when the presidency was introduced in 1991. Then there was no residency requirement but a maximum age of 65. Boris Yel'tsin, the first Russian President, was born in 1931, and would have already reached 65 at the latest date for his possible re-election, which was July 1996. No surprise, then, that the upper age limit was eliminated with the reorganisation of the conditions for candidacy for the presidency under the 1993 Constitution.

The first Russian Presidency had a five-year term. The 1993 Constitution reduced the term to four years, although other periods had been discussed during the drafting process. In December 2008 the first major amendment to the Constitution was passed, increasing the term of office to six years, to come into effect from the next presidential election in 2012. The need for the increase was not clearly articulated in the media, but informed commentators wondered if it might be part of a longer-term strategy for Putin to return to office with enhanced control. The term for the lower legislative chamber, the Duma, was increased at the same time to five years, so that there would be elections for President and Duma in the same year only once every 30 years.

The fact that the President is not defined as a member of the Executive but that he exercises powers which cover a number of functions which include executive, control and coordination activities, has led Russian commentators to suggest that his office stands in a category of its own, above the classic triad of executive, legislative and judicial State powers.[1] Such an approach of treating the presidency as a separate category neatly sidesteps the problem that the extent of his powers otherwise might subvert the principle of autonomy of the three branches set out in Article 10 of the Constitution. This special position of the President is supported by the reference, in both Article 80 and the presidential oath, to the President's role as the guarantor of the Constitution, and the fact that he 'coordinates' the functioning and interaction of the agencies of State power and conciliates between them, so therefore must stand separate from them.

It has also been the consistent practice so far that the Russian President does not belong to a political party or faction while in office. The law initially setting up the presidency in 1991 specifically allowed in Article 1 for membership of a political party or social organisation to be

---

[1] TIa Khabrieba, 'Pravitel'stvo RF – vysshuu ispolnitel'nyi organ gosudarstvennoi vlasti Rossiiskoi Federatsii' in TIa Khabrieba (ed), *Pravitel'stvo Rossiiskoi Federatsii* (Moscow, Norma, 2005) 104.

suspended during the period of office. Yel'tsin, as Russia's first President, took a deliberate stand in favour of independence from the existing political parties, saying that he was President of all the Russians not just a particular grouping. Of course, such independence also left him more scope for playing off the different factions against each other in the early days of the development of multi-party democracy in Russia. The current Constitution does not have an equivalent provision, but the federal law 'On Political Parties' of 2001 does.[2] Article 10(4) provides that the President 'shall have the right to suspend his membership in a political party for the term of effectuation of his powers', although this is clearly permissive not mandatory.

Interestingly, a President's apparent independence from party politics does not stop any party openly supporting a particular presidential candidate. Whilst he was President, Vladimir Putin was strongly supported by Unified (or United) Russia (*Edinaia Rossiia*), which was created not long after he first took office. It campaigned during the Duma elections of 2003 on the policy of unwavering support for President Putin without feeling the need to elaborate on content.[3] Putin was happy to lend his name and image to Unified Russia's December 2007 Duma election campaign based on an unspecified 'Putin's Plan'.[4] In the last presidential election in 2008, four political parties endorsed the candidacy of Dmitrii Medvedev: Unified Russia, A Fair Russia, the Agrarian Party and Citizens' Power (Civilian Force), yet he did not become a member of any of them. Since leaving the presidency Putin agreed to be party chairman of Unified Russia, while still not becoming a member. The party's rules had to be especially amended to allow this possibility.

It is not forbidden for members of a particular party to campaign as presidential candidates. A candidate on behalf of the Communist Party of the Russian Federation (CPRF) has stood and come second in each of the presidential elections. The founder and head of the Liberal Democratic Party of Russia, Vladimir Zhirinovskii, has also stood repeatedly, coming fifth in 2000 with under 3 per cent, similarly fifth in

[2] English translation in WE Butler, *Russian Public Law*, 2nd edn (London, Wildy, Simmonds & Hill, 2009) 75.

[3] See B Whitmore, 'Running on a Unified Platform of Power' (2003) 46 *RFE/RL Political Weekly*, 19 November, and L Belin, 'Unified Russia's Winning Non-message' (2003) 229 *Radio Free Europe/Radio Liberty Newsline End Note*, 8 December.

[4] R Coalson, 'Russia's President "Unifies" a Party System on Life Support' (2007) 185 *Radio Free Europe/Radio Liberty Newsline End Note*, 5 October.

the first-round elections in 1996 with just under 6 per cent and third in 2008 with nearly 9.5 per cent. He did not run in 2004. Whether the current practice of the President remaining an independent will carry on beyond Medvedev may depend as much on the development of party politics as on the personality of the individual winning candidate.

The fact that there is no Vice-President in Russia may also elevate the President above the general fray, as he stands as sole 'sovereign' with no obvious deputy. This was not always so. The first President of the Soviet Union, Gorbachev, and Yel'tsin, as first President of Russia, each had a Vice-President, Gennadii Ianaev (Yanaev) and Aleksandr Rutskoi respectively. In both cases the Vice-President ended up in pitched battle against his President: Ianaev as one of the Committee for the State of Emergency in August 1991, and Rutskoi in the siege in the Russian Legislature building, the White House, in October 1993 (see chapters two and three). It was therefore unsurprising that no provision was made for a Vice-President when the position and powers of the Russian President were revised in the 1993 Constitution. It specifies that if a President leaves office prematurely (voluntarily, or through incapacity or impeachment) the Government Chairman at the time becomes Acting President. This happened at the end of 1999, when Yel'tsin voluntarily stood down and his Government Chairman Putin took up the temporary post of Acting President, in which role he successfully campaigned for election to full office in March 2000. New presidential elections must follow not later than three months from an early termination of the President's powers, and during the interim the Acting President may not dissolve the Duma, call a referendum or propose any amendments to the Constitution. Otherwise he exercises full presidential powers.

The role of the President is summarised in Article 80 of the Constitution. It states that the President is Head of State and his main duties are: to be the guarantor of the Constitution and the rights and freedoms of man and citizen; to take measures in the procedure established by the Constitution to protect Russia's sovereignty and independence and State integrity; and to 'ensure the coordinated functioning and interaction of the agencies of State power'. He 'determines the basic orientations of internal and foreign policy of the State' (Article 80(3)), and as Head of State he represents the Russian Federation internally and in international relations.

Article 80 is not just window dressing. The Russian President was never intended to be a mere figurehead; with few exceptions the alternative draft Constitutions planned that his was to be a position of real power. Yel'tsin defended the considerable presidential power in his draft Constitution, 'but what do you expect in a country that is used to tsars and strong leaders?'[5] Nikolai Ryzhkov, USSR Government Chairman from 1985 to January 1991, remarked that 'neither Gorbachev nor Boris Yeltsin . . . liked the idea of "reigning like the Queen of England"'.[6] The main purpose of introducing the USSR presidency in 1990 was to create a strong Executive to push through economic reforms regarded as absolutely necessary. The same was true for Russia. It too felt the need for a *khoziain* (a protective leader), although there may have been an added element of power play and personal animosity between Yel'tsin and Gorbachev in the introduction of the Russian presidency in 1991.

The presidential oath (Article 82) contains almost all the elements listed in Article 80 (the exception is 'to ensure the coordinated functioning and interaction of the agencies of State power'), although in a slightly changed order. The Constitution stipulates that administering the oath when the new President takes up office should be a 'solemn ceremony'. Recent inaugurations have shown off the rich panoply of Russian ceremonial. Medvedev's inauguration on 7 May 2008 followed the pattern set by Putin of a lavish affair in the Grand Kremlin Palace, which Yel'tsin had had restored. Both Yel'tsin himself and Soviet President Mikhail Gorbachev had been inaugurated 'elsewhere on the Kremlin grounds – in the boxy modern building where Soviet-era Communist Party congresses were held'.[7] The hundreds of guests at Medvedev's inauguration included Patriarch Aleksii II, then head of the Russian Orthodox Church (who later led a separate prayer service in honour of the new President), politicians, foreign ambassadors and Russian media chiefs, as well as members of the Legislature and senior Judiciary. The swearing-in ceremony was in the Andreievskii Hall, a former tsarist-era throne room. An estimated 1,700 had attended Putin's inauguration four years previously. One media report pointed up the contrast between Medvedev taking the role of President following an active and popular Putin, and Putin's succession to an 'ailing and unpopular' Yel'tsin:

---

[5] S White, *Russia's New Politics* (Cambridge, Cambridge University Press, 1999) 70.
[6] *Ibid.*
[7] 'Russia Swears in Putin Protégé as New Leader', available at <http://www.msnbc.msn.com/id/24485967/#storyContinued>, accessed 6 August 2010.

> The departing Yeltsin left Putin a pen with which he used to sign laws as a symbol of a handover of power. Putin said in a newspaper interview last month [April 2008], he would take the historic pen with him rather than leave it to Medvedev.[8]

The implication was that Putin would as Government Chairman still have a major role to play and would wield his 'presidential pen' in fulfilment of his Chairman's duties.

The presidential oath has legal significance. It was on the basis of the President's sworn duty to preserve the integrity of the State that the Constitutional Court found to be lawful Yel'tsin's order to send troops into the breakaway republic of Chechnya in 1994 during the first Chechen war.[9]

B. Presidential power

Presidential power under the 1993 Constitution is extensive. Analysts labelled it 'super-presidentialism'[10] and likened the President's role to that of the Tsar.[11] As Head of State he can bestow citizenship, grant political asylum and pardon an individual. He confers State awards and titles of honour, and the highest military ranks. In relation to executive power, the powers he exercises can conveniently be classified under four main heads:

a) formation of the agencies of executive power;
b) exercising leadership over them and defining their fundamental direction of activity;
c) supervision and oversight of executive agencies; and
d) mediating between agencies of executive power.[12]

---

[8]   *Ibid.*

[9]   GP van den Berg, 'Chechnia_ruling_310795 No. 10-P' (2001) 27 *Review of Central and East European Law* 230; WE Pomeranz, 'Judicial Review and the Russian Constitutional Court: the Chechen case' (1997) 23 *Review of Central and East European Law* 9.

[10]   Eg, S Holmes, 'Superpresidentialism and its Problems' (1993-94) 2/3 *East European Constitutional Review* 123.

[11]   A Korkeakivi, 'A Modern Day Czar? Presidential Power and Human Rights in the Russian Federation' (1995) 2 *Journal of Constitutional Law in Eastern and Central Europe* 76.

[12]   IuL Shul'zhenko, 'Kompetentsiia Presidenta RF v otnoshenii ispolnitel'nykh organov gosudarstvennoi vlasti' in AA Bondarenko (ed), *Ispolitel'naia vlast' v Rossii. Istoriia i sovremennost' problemy i perspektivy razvitiia* (Moscow, Novaia Pravovaia Kultura, 2004) 63.

i. Formation of the executive branch

1. Appointment and dismissal of the Government Chairman

The President appoints the Government Chairman, although with the consent of the Duma. Such procedure, where one agency nominates a candidate for another to approve, was common during the Soviet period, and is the nearest thing to 'checks-and-balances' in the post-Soviet Russian constitutional system.

However, other constitutional provisions undermine the Duma's autonomy to reject the candidate. Article 109 gives the President the power to dissolve the Duma in 'instances provided for by Articles 111 and 117'. Article 111 relates to the Government Chairman, and the fourth paragraph provides that

> After triple rejection by the State Duma of the candidacies submitted for Chairman of the Government of the Russian Federation, the President of the Russian Federation appoints the Chairman of the Government of the Russian Federation, dissolves the State Duma, and calls new elections.[13]

In 1998 this provision was put to the test by President Yel'tsin. He presented three times to the Duma the same candidate for Government Chairman, 'young reformer' Sergei Kirienko. The Duma at that time was dominated by the Communist Party of the Russian Federation, and the majority believed Kirienko to be too young and inexperienced to hold the office of Chairman and rejected him twice. His candidacy reportedly was presented to the Duma within one hour, and then 10 minutes, of his previous rejections.[14] The third time Kirienko was proposed the majority of deputies decided that their main imperative was to preserve the Duma's existing composition. It was strategically more important to avoid an immediate re-election campaign than for the Duma to express its clearly-felt disapproval for a third time. It therefore approved Kirienko as Government Chairman, on 23 April 1998.

Five months later, Yel'tsin sacked Kirienko and proposed to the Duma a return of Viktor Chernomyrdin, who had been the immediately previous Chairman. The Duma rejected Chernomyrdin. Yel'tsin immediately proposed him a second time. He was yet again rejected. However, this time

---

[13] Y Luryi, 'The Appointment of a Government Chairman in Russia: the President. The Duma. The Constitutional Court'(1999) 25 *Review of Central and East European Law* 585 at 588.

[14] *Ibid* at 593.

Yel'tsin forbore to present the same candidate a third time. Instead he proposed Evgenii Primakov, an acceptable compromise candidate whom the
Duma readily appointed. At that stage, after the very serious economic
crisis in the late summer of 1998, Yel'tsin did not want to trigger off elections for the Duma which would most probably result in a new composition even more antagonistic to his policies than the existing one.

That was not quite the end of the story. The Duma exercised its right
to appeal to the Constitutional Court for a ruling on the constitutionality of the President's actions (see chapter six for the Court's powers). By
a majority of 14, with three strong dissents by Justices Luchin, Vitruk
and Oleinik, the Court decided that the literal interpretation of the
Constitution did not give a clear answer to the issue, but that the
President's overall duty to form, direct and control the Government,
and his constitutional responsibility for its activity, gave him the prerogative to decide on the candidate for Government Chairman. The
Constitution did not restrict his right, so that it followed that the
President could propose 'one candidate three times, or two or three different candidates'.[15] By this decision, the Constitutional Court majority
ruling handed the President a tool giving him disproportionate leverage
over the Duma. As Luryi points out, an unscrupulous President could
propose on three occasions an obviously unsuitable candidate as a
means of triggering off the dissolution of the Duma.[16] The wisdom of
allowing the Duma to be dissolved if it did not agree with the President's
choice of candidate was questioned when the Constitution was at the
draft stage,[17] but in the overall circumstances of its adoption the
President was not going to relinquish such a useful means of ensuring
his choice would prevail. The theoretical justification is the President's
right to determine internal policy and his duty to ensure the coordinated
functioning of the agencies of State power. As Head of State he needs
a Government Chairman in whom he has confidence. If the Duma
decides it cannot work with such a person, it should stand down.
However, this has not been an issue for Presidents Putin or Medvedev.

Article 83 of the Constitution allows the President to dismiss the
Government Chairman at will. In 1998 Yel'tsin sacked his Government

---

[15] GP van den Berg, 'appointing_Premier_Article_111_interpretation_111298
No. 28-P' (2001) 27 *Review of Central and East European Law* 337 at 338.

[16] Luryi, above n 13, at 588.

[17] *Ibid*, citing IG Shablinskii, *Predely vlasti. Bor'ba za Rossiidkuiu Kontitutsionnuiu
Reformu (1089–1995)* (Moscow, 1997, publisher not given).

Chairman on three different occasions. This presidential power impacts the accountability of the Government Chairman; see section IV.B. below.

2. Formation of the Government

On the basis of proposals from the Government Chairman, the President appoints deputy Chairmen and federal ministers, and relieves them of office (Article 83(e)). Three weeks before the 14 March 2004 presidential elections in which Vladimir Putin was standing for his second presidential term, he dismissed the entire Government, chaired by Mikhail Kas'ianov.[18] Putin asserted that this was not because of any dissatisfaction with its activities over the previous three years, but in order to install a new Government before the election.[19] The new Government Chairman was Mikhail Fradkov, and Putin made it clear in a speech to him on 9 March, when he was presenting his proposed ministers, that their reinstatement after mandatory dissolution of the Government five days later because of the presidential election would be a formality.[20] From the tenor of the discussions, it seemed very likely that the President had made prior suggestions to Fradkov as to whom to propose. The extent to which this happens will of course depend very much on the personality of the two officeholders.[21]

If a Government as a whole tenders its resignation, the President decides the outcome, including the possibility of its continuing to serve. So far neither event has happened.

3. Governmental structure

Not only does the President have the final decision on who holds ministerial office, he is also in charge of deciding the overall structure of the Government. He will do this within the framework of the Federal

[18] Kas'ianov did not disappear from public life. In 2005 he was successfully prosecuted over the illegal sale of an official residence. He applied to stand as a candidate in the 2008 presidential elections, but his application was rejected on the basis of too high a proportion of invalid signatures.

[19] R Coalson, 'Putin Dismisses Government' (2004) 8 *Radio Free Europe/Radio Liberty Newsline*, 24 February.

[20] V Putin, 'Transcript of a Meeting with New Cabinet Members', 9 March 2004, on President's website <http://www.kremlin.ru/eng/text/speeches/2004/03/09/2103_type82913_61669.shtml>, accessed 6 August 2010.

[21] On the various Chairmen, see R Sakwa, *Russian Politics and Society*, 4th edn (Abingdon, Routledge, 2008) 116.

Constitutional Law on the Government,[22] but that imposes few restrictions. Article 112 of the Constitution says that the Government Chairman, within a week of his appointment, will submit to the President proposals on the structure of the federal agencies of State power, but as with the Government Chairman's proposal of candidates for ministerial posts, the President takes the final decision.

Two days before the March 2004 election, incumbent President Putin announced his plan for reform of the governmental structure. This followed two years' work on administrative reform. One of the authors of the reform was the able public servant and friend of Putin, Dmitrii Kozak (originally a St Petersburg-trained lawyer who had worked in the city administration with Putin). It consisted of a clear three-tier hierarchy. At the top level are the ministries, which have the task of elaborating policy, drafting laws and enacting ministerial legislation. At the middle level are the federal services, which monitor implementation of such legislation, and compliance with it by citizens and organisations. Unlike the ministries, federal services have no power to adopt acts or draft legislation. At the lowest level are the federal agencies, which perform State services for citizens.

> The official goal of the new structure is to improve manageability. An unarticulated goal of the shake-up is to rid the Government of the holdovers from the era of former President Boris Yel'tsin.[23]

The new Government Chairman Mikhail Fradkov was seen as someone without an independent power base, and so entirely dependent on Putin and therefore unquestioningly loyal. Although many of the personnel in the new Government had previously held ministerial office, analysts at the time saw Putin's reorganisation as a way of building a consensus Government which would readily follow his direction.[24]

When Medvedev took up office as President, there was intense speculation as to the extent to which in his Government he would maintain continuity with the 'Putin regime'. There was considerable retention of personnel, but various promotions, demotions and sideways shifts, with the result that, on the whole, commentators felt that the personnel arrangements in his new Government team kept an appropriate balance

---

[22]   Butler, above n 2, at 188.
[23]   JA Corwin, 'Putin Unveils a Pyramid Scheme' (2004) 4 *Radio Free Europe/Radio Liberty Russian Political Weekly*, 12 March.
[24]   *Ibid*, P Rutland giving his expert opinion.

between different rival factions.[25] As time has gone on, he has been increasingly bringing in his 'own men', and, so it appears, reducing the influence of people with a military or similar background, while keeping up the trend of appointing personnel from St Petersburg.

4. *The Presidential Administration*

As well as setting up the Government, the President forms his own Presidential Administration, directly responsible to him. This is a huge bureaucracy, with a number of subdivisions which act almost as parallel government departments. Such duplication is very reminiscent of the structure of the Communist Party paralleling the Soviet Government,[26] but the modern Presidential Administration is already several times the size of the old Communist Party Central Committee apparatus. It does carry out many of the same oversight, law-drafting and appointment functions as the Central Committee, and the constitutional language about the functions of the President is quite similar to that relating to the Party in the 1977 Constitution.[27]

It is not clear in law whether the Presidential Administration is a State body, but given the President's broad powers, the answer is probably yes.[28] The Presidential Administration currently works under a statute confirmed by presidential edict on 6 April 2004; there are also presidential edicts establishing separate statutes on specialist subdivisions within the Presidential Administration, for example for Foreign Policy, and the State-Legal Administration.[29]

In Huskey's meticulous study of presidential power in Russia[30] he says that this 'is an institution unique to Russia'. One 'undisputed

---

[25] See, eg, 'A Lineup Aimed at Taming Siloviki' (2008) *Moscow Times*, 15 May, available via Westlaw, and G Hahn, 'The Siloviki Downgraded in Russia's New Configuration of Power', 21 July 2008, available at <http://www.russiaotherpointsofview.com/2008/07/the-siloviki-do.html>, accessed 13 August 2010.

[26] E Huskey, 'The State-Legal Administration and the Politics of Redundancy' (1994) 11 *Post-Soviet Affairs* 115.

[27] Thanks to Professor Huskey for pointing out these parallels; personal correspondence, 7 May 2009.

[28] W Burnham and P Maggs, *Law and Legal System in the Russian Federation*, 4th edn (Huntington, New York, Juris Publishing Inc, 2009) at 191.

[29] The three statutes in Butler, above n 2, at 174, 183, 185.

[30] E Huskey, *Presidential Power in Russia* (Armonk, NY, ME Sharpe, 1999) at 58.

feature' is its 'mammoth size and complexity'. At the time he was writing in 1999, the Presidential Administration (translated by Huskey as 'Executive Office of the President') had 'forty-three bureaux and two thousand professional staff members'. Huskey notes that:

> In a purely presidential system, such as that of the United States, a presidential apparatus of this size would appear large, though unremarkable. The current White House staff in Washington, for example, includes more than fifteen hundred officials. But in the United States, there is not a separate executive leader – the Chairman of the Government – with his own extensive apparatus. The more fitting comparison, then, is France, where the Élysée Palace – home to the President – employs fewer than a hundred officials.[31]

On 25 March 2004, shortly after resuming office as President for his second term, Putin announced that he was streamlining the Presidential Administration.[32] Sakwa suggests a common theme of the reorganisation plans was to reduce competition between the Presidential Administration and the Government, by the former focusing on political matters and the latter on economic.[33] The Administration was reorganised to have three tiers, coincidentally the pattern of the governmental restructuring announced a couple of weeks earlier (see section II.B.i.3. above). Amongst other things, as a result of the changes, the then head of the Presidential Administration, Dmitrii Medvedev, would have only two deputy heads rather than the previous seven, as well as a first deputy. (The same day, Government Chairman Fradkov also announced that each minister in the Government would have only two deputies rather than many.[34]) Nevertheless, the Presidential Administration remains a large and extremely influential body, currently with 15 specialist subdivisions.[35]

As part of his Presidential Administration, the President may appoint and dismiss presidential plenipotentiary[36] representatives. These are

[31] *Ibid* at 59.

[32] JA Corwin, 'Putin Reshuffles the Presidential Administration' (2004) 8 *Radio Free Europe/Radio Liberty Newsline*, 26 March.

[33] Sakwa, above n 21, at 109.

[34] JA Corwin, 'Government Chairman Slashes Number of Deputy Ministers' (2004) 8 *Radio Free Europe/Radio Liberty Newsline*, 26 March.

[35] 'Presidential Executive Office/Subdivisions', available at <http://kremlin.ru/eng/articles/podr_eng.shtml>, accessed 7 August 2010.

[36] From the Latin for having full power, the word is equivalent to the Russian *polnomochnye* used to describe these presidential representatives.

listed on the President's website along with other aides and advisers. Apart from the federal representatives discussed in section V.A. below, there is a presidential representative in each of the two legislative chambers, and at the Constitutional Court.[37] These ensure that the President's perspective is borne in mind, and views can be reported back directly to him. Appointment may be a reward for exemplary service. For example, having tried but failed to get Valerii Savitskii appointed as a Constitutional Court judge, Yel'tsin assigned Savitskii as his Constitutional Court representative. This was probably in return for the support that Savitskii, as a renowned academic jurist, had given Yel'tsin during the autumn of 1993.

5. *Appointment of other important personnel*

The President nominates to the Duma (lower chamber of the Legislature) the candidate for appointment to the post of Central Bank Chairman. Whether the Central Bank is part of the Executive is unclear, but its role puts it close to it, even if it is not formally included.[38] The President also asks the Duma to consider the question of the Central Bank Chairman's dismissal. Whether the Bank's role is regarded as so fundamental to good order that both the President and the Duma need a hand in appointing its Chairman, or whether the process may merely spread the blame if he proves to be incompetent, is unclear. The Duma debates the annual budget presented by the Government, and the regular reports on its implementation, so it may have been felt appropriate for it be involved in appointing and dismissing this non-governmental yet key economic player.

The President nominates to the upper chamber of the Legislature, the Federation Council, candidates for appointment to other high offices. These include judges to the Constitutional Court, the Supreme Court and the Highest *Arbitrazh* Court, and the Court Chairmen. This last power was a recent innovation in respect to the Constitutional Court, and is discussed in relation to judicial independence in chapter six. Appointment of presidential nominees was not a foregone conclusion in Yel'tsin's day. In 1994–95 he nominated candidates to bring the Constitutional Court up to its new quorum of 19, but the Federation

---

[37] See 'Presidential Executive Office' available at <http://kremlin.ru/eng/administration.shtml>, accessed 7 August 2010.

[38] Shul'zhenko, above n 12, at 63.

Council rejected a number of them, seriously delaying the recommencement of Court activity after its suspension in autumn 1993. The Federation Council has been content to accept all nominations to high judicial office by Yel'tsin's successors.

The President appoints all the other federal judges. In the Constitution this right is completely unqualified, but other legislation ensures that the candidates he appoints are subject to professional vetting (see chapter six).

The Procurator-General is appointed and dismissed by the Federation Council, but in both instances following a proposal by the President (see chapter six for an outline of the Procurator's role). This is another area where Yel'tsin came to be at loggerheads with the Legislature. In 1999–2000 the Federation Council three times refused to vote Procurator-General Skuratov out of office. Skuratov had been overseeing investigations of corruption within the circle of those close to Yel'tsin when, on 17 March 1999, extracts from a video of 'a man resembling Skuratov' in bed with two naked women were broadcast on the State-owned television channel. The timing was suspicious. It was immediately after the Federation Council had first refused by 142 to 6 votes to dismiss Skuratov. Interestingly, at the time Vladimir Putin was in charge of the Federal Security Service, known by its Russian acronym as the FSB and successor to the infamous Soviet security force, the KGB (Committee for State Security).[39] He claimed the FSB had proved the man in the video was Skuratov.[40] In April, hours after receiving Skuratov's report on corruption, Yel'tsin suspended him from office, on the justification of a criminal case resulting from the video. The Duma showed its disapproval by inviting Skuratov to address its deputies. Then the Federation Council rejected Skuratov's dismissal a second time. It was not until April 2000, by which time Yel'tsin was no longer President, that the Federation Council eventually voted to dismiss Skuratov.[41] In the course of this complex episode both chambers of the Legislature demonstrated their opposition to Yel'tsin, suspecting that he

[39] Thanks to Professor Bill Bowing for alerting the author to Putin's role in procuring the video.

[40] A Jack, *Inside Putin's Russia: Can There Be Reform Without Democracy?* (London, Granta Books, 2005) at 83.

[41] See, eg, T Muradova, 'The Skuratov Affair' (1999) *Arena Magazine* 5, available at <http://findarticles.com/p/articles/mi_hb6469/is_1999_Oct/ai_n28743321/pg_1?tag=artBody;col1>, accessed 8 August 2010.

was using Skuratov as a scapegoat to protect himself, his family and friends. By the time Skuratov was dismissed, Yel'tsin was out of office, but with the former President's immunity.

ii. Defining the fundamental direction of activity

The President directs the policies to be executed by his Government, the Presidential Administration and other key post-holders. He does this both directly and through legislation.

1. Setting policy directions

The President 'determines the basic direction of the State's internal and foreign policy' (Article 80). He may be 'hands-on' in his direction of the Government as he has the right to 'preside at [its] sessions' (Article 83(b)). President Putin reportedly presided at about half of the weekly meetings.

The President can declare policy direction through set-piece speeches, for example annual addresses to members of the full Legislature, the Federal Assembly. President Medvedev made his first such presidential address in the Marble Hall of the Kremlin on 5 November 2008, coincidentally the day after Barack Obama won the American presidential election. Invited dignitaries included members of the Government, Chairmen of the Constitutional Court, Supreme Court and Highest *Arbitrazh* Court, the Procurator-General, Chairmen of the Central Electoral Commission and of the Audit Chamber, members of the State Council (discussed in section V.B. below) and leaders of Russia's main religions, as well as a horde of media reporters, both Russian and foreign. The address was also broadcast by all the federal TV channels. It laid down a number of important policy objectives.[42] These included: the change of term for President and Duma; 'developing a new legal system and independent courts'; 'combating corruption and legal nihilism'; 'reduction of State bureaucracy'; 'parties that have received from 5–7 per cent of the vote could be given a guaranteed one or two seats in the Duma'; 'nominations of heads of the executive authorities in the regions could be made only by the parties that have won the biggest

---

[42] D Medvedev, 'Address to the Federal Assembly of the Russian Federation', available at <http://archive.kremlin.ru/eng/speeches/2008/11/05/2144_type70029type82917type127286_208836.shtml>, accessed 8 August 2010.

number of votes in the regional elections, and by no one else'; 'gradual reduction of the minimum number of members required for registering a new political party' and more. The President's annual address is taken very seriously as a fundamental policy directive.

The President also makes regular budget addresses, and other 'set-piece' speeches. He can also declare policy extemporaneously. For example, on 11 January 2009, President Medvedev declared an agreement signed the previous day by the heads of the Ukrainian, Russian and Czech Governments to renew the supply of natural gas to the Ukraine by Gazprom to be 'null and void'.[43] Gazprom is an open joint stock society (OAO) under Russian law, but the Russian State owns a 50.002 per cent controlling interest of its shares.[44] The news item continued, saying that Medvedev had told his Foreign Minister Sergei Lavrov that 'we will not be bound by it'.[45]

In this example the President exercised his power as Head of State to set Russia's internal and foreign policy, while leaving the Government – here in particular Government Chairman Putin and the Foreign Minister Lavrov – to take the appropriate steps to put his decision into effect. In fact supplies were restored; Medvedev's comments were part of an ongoing dispute about gas supply, and importantly gas pricing, as Russia simultaneously sought to exploit her natural reserves while rebalancing her relationship with the 'near abroad' of former USSR States. Nevertheless, the incident neatly illustrates the division of labour between President and Government. Medvedev was well placed to comment on gas supply policy: from June 2000 he was chairman of the Gazprom board of directors, combining it with the post of first deputy Government Chairman from November 2005. He was still chairman of Gazprom when he was inaugurated as President on 7 May 2008, and did not relinquish the position until 27 June 2008.

---

[43] See 0709 item on 'Today: Monday 12 January 2009', available at <http://news.bbc.co.uk/today/hi/today/newsid_7823000/7823430.stm>, accessed 8 August 2010.

[44] 'Gazprom in Questions and Answers', available at <http://www.gazprom.com/eng/articles/article8511.shtml>, accessed 8 August 2010.

[45] *Ibid.*

2. *Setting policy through legislation*

The President has the right of legislative initiative, and increasingly draft bills brought to the Duma originate from either the Government or the Presidential Administration.[46] Thus, and especially in recent years with a cooperative Legislature, the President's influence on the content of laws (*zakony*) has been significant.

All federal legislation must be signed by the President to go into force. Legislative procedure is discussed in chapter five, but in relation to presidential power it should be noted that he has a right to veto federal law, although his veto may be overridden by a qualified majority vote of two-thirds in both legislative chambers. Then he must sign the law within seven days. He has no right to veto federal constitutional law.

Aside from potential input into the content of *zakony*, the President also has independent power to issue edicts (*ukazy*) and regulations (*rasporiazhenii*), binding throughout Russia. The only restriction is that they should not be contrary to the Constitution and existing federal law. The broad extent of the President's legislative powers contrasts with that of the Government. The Government can issue decrees (*postanovleniia*) and regulations (and ensure their execution), but only 'on the basis of and in execution of the Constitution, federal laws, and normative edicts of the President' (Article 115). In practice, much of the legislation developing the economic sphere during President Yel'tsin's time was by presidential edict, as the Legislature was reluctant to bring in the necessary reforms quickly enough for Yel'tsin's taste. Yel'tsin reportedly said that a true *muzhik*[47] enacted 'an edict a day'. Sakwa estimates that he issued 'over 1,500 policy-relevant *ukazy* during his term in office'.[48]

Occasionally Yel'tsin's edicts did more than fill gaps where federal law had not been passed. For example, in 1993 he decriminalised consensual male homosexual activity by presidential edict, in direct contradiction to the 1960 Criminal Code then in force, but the newer presidential legislation was applied. Putin and Medvedev have enjoyed compliant Legislatures and so have relied less on presidential edicts than Yel'tsin.

---

[46] P Chaisty, 'Majority Control and Executive Dominance: Parliament-President Relations in Putin's Russia' in *Leading Russia: Putin in Perspective - Essays in Honour of Archie Brown* (Oxford, Oxford University Press, 2005) 119 at 134.

[47] Real man, from the Russian for a male peasant worker; Yel'tsin described himself as a Siberian peasant.

[48] Sakwa, above n 21, at 108.

3. Defence, security and foreign relations

As protector of Russia's sovereignty, independence and State integrity (Article 80) the President has overall control of defence and security, and foreign affairs. He is Supreme Commander-in-Chief of the Armed Forces, and appoints and dismisses their High Command. He also forms and heads the Security Council, and confirms the Russian military doctrine. In the event of aggression against Russia or direct threat of aggression, he can introduce a 'military situation' (martial law) in the whole or part of Russia, the only restriction being that he must immediately inform the Legislature. The Constitution specifies that the details for establishing a 'military situation' must be determined by a federal constitutional law (Article 87(3)). The appropriate law was signed on 30 January 2002. The President is further empowered to declare an 'extraordinary situation' (state of emergency), with a similar requirement that he notify the Legislature. This also required a federal constitutional law; it was passed on 30 May 2001, and requires approval from the upper legislative chamber within three days or the presidential declaration loses effect.[49] This replaced a 1991 law which was evoked in November 1991 for the incursion into Chechnya in the first Chechen war mentioned above.[50] (Of course, officially there were never any emergencies during Soviet times, so there was no need for any emergency powers legislation.[51])

As Head of State exercising leadership over foreign affairs, the President has the appropriate duty, after consultation with the respective committees or commissions of the Legislature, to appoint and recall diplomatic representatives to foreign States and international organisations (Article 83(l)). He conducts negotiations and signs international treaties.

4. Direct control of the Presidential Bloc

One very interesting characteristic of the Russian distribution of executive power is the fact that key federal ministries and other executive agencies relating to defence and security, and foreign affairs, are directly

---

[49] See AN Domrin, *The Limits of Russian Democratisation. Emergency Powers and States of Emergency* (Oxford, Routledge, 2006) at 127.

[50] *Ibid* at 101 and 124.

[51] *Ibid* at 29.

answerable to the President. This group of agencies is referred to collectively as the Presidential Bloc, with the Security Bloc as a subset. According to the English language section of the President's official website, the terms Presidential Bloc and Security Bloc 'have firmly established themselves in the political lexicon, but they have no official basis in law.'[52] The terms may have no basis in law, but presidential control of the ministries in these important areas does. Article 32 of the Federal Constitutional Law on the Government of the Russian Federation, on 'Specific features of the leadership of some federal organs of executive power', lists the areas over which the President shall 'direct the activity'.[53] These are defence, security, internal affairs, justice, foreign affairs, preventing extraordinary situations and 'liquidation of the consequences of natural disasters'. The Ministry of Justice did not used to be in this special group, but was included as result of reforms in 2004. It may be coincidental that by then the Ministry of Justice had taken charge of the whole penitentiary system. Russia undertook to transfer this from the Ministry of Internal Affairs to the Ministry of Justice as a condition of joining the Council of Europe in 1996. The formal reassignment of jurisdiction occurred in August 1998.

Within a week of his 2008 inauguration, President Medvedev issued an edict on the structure of the federal executive agencies, which included in an appendix the full list of Russian Federation agencies whose activities he directly effectuates. The array is extremely impressive: the Ministry of Internal Affairs (MVD), which controls the police, and its subsidiary Federal Migration Service; the Ministry of Civil Defence, Emergencies and Natural Disasters; the Ministry of Foreign Affairs (MID) and the Federal Agency for Affairs of the Commonwealth of Independent States; the Ministry of Defence, which is in charge of the Armed Forces, with associated Federal Services for Military-Technical Cooperation, Defence Order, Technical and Export Control, and the Special Construction Agency; the Ministry of Justice, with its Federal Service for Execution of Punishments, and the Federal Court Bailiff Service; the State Courier Service; the Foreign Intelligence Service; the Federal Security Service (FSB); the Service for Control of Narcotics Trafficking; the Federal Protection Service (FSO); as well as the Chief Administration

---

[52] 'Institutions: Federal Government' at <http://kremlin.ru/eng/articles/institut02.shtml>, accessed 13 August 2010.

[53] Butler, above n 2, at 199.

of Special Programs of the President and the Administrative Office of the President.[54] New additions were the Federal Service on Migration and the agency dealing with the Commonwealth of Independent States, which used to be a separate ministry not within the Presidential Bloc but is now included as a federal agency under the Ministry of Foreign Affairs.

Thus, not only is the President the Supreme Commander-in-Chief of the Armed Forces, but in his Security Bloc he has direct hands-on control of those agencies known in Russian as the 'power ministries' (in Russian *silovie ministerstva*) of State security (FSB), internal affairs (MVD), defence, the Foreign Intelligence Service (SVR), the Ministry of Civil Defence and Emergency Situations (MChS), and others.

> Simply put, power ministries are those state agencies in which the personnel generally wear uniforms and in which some people carry guns. More precisely, these bodies are military, security, or law enforcement bodies that possess armed units or formations.[55]

These are the State agencies which would be needed to maintain control by force, if such occasion arose (and as noted, the President is empowered to declare martial law or a state of emergency). Individuals with power ministry backgrounds are collectively known as *siloviki*.

The extent to which Putin, a former KBG officer, has surrounded himself with former *silovik*, and their potential impact, has been a perennial topic of discussion by political pundits.[56] The most balanced view is that as President Putin promoted individuals whom he felt he could trust, it was therefore not surprising that many of them had worked either directly with him, or in associated professions. A similar phenomenon has encouraged Medvedev to appoint lawyers from St Petersburg, who share his professional background.

---

[54] The previous list of federal agencies of executive power as amended up to 2004 is in WE Butler, *Russian Public Law* (London, Wildy, Simmonds & Hill, 2005) at 227. The list from September 1998 is in Huskey, above n 30, at 113.

[55] BD Taylor, 'Russia's Power Ministries: Coercion and Commerce', October 2007, *Monograph of The Institute for National Security and Counterterrorism*, available at <http://insct.syr.edu/uploadedFiles/insct/uploadedfiles/PDFs/Taylor_Russia%20Power%20Ministries.pdf>, at vii, accessed 9 October 2010. Taylor gives approximate manpower of listed agencies *ibid* at 2.

[56] *Ibid*; also B Renz, 'The Russian Force Structures' (2007) 17 *Russian Analytical Digest* 5, available at <http://www.res.ethz.ch/analysis/rad/details.cfm?lng=en&id=29428>, accessed 13 August 2010; and Hahn, above n 25.

The Government is not completely excluded from dealings with the Presidential Bloc. By law it 'coordinates' their activity. The Presidential Bloc agencies are answerable to the Government for fulfilling their assigned objectives, as well as to the President, a system reminiscent of the 'dual subordination' of Soviet times.

iii. Supervision and oversight

1. Cancelling or suspending governmental legislation

The President may cancel any central governmental decrees and regulations which he regards as inconsistent with the Constitution, federal laws and his own edicts (Constitution, Article 115(3)). There is no requirement for any judicial consideration, although the Government could appeal to the Constitutional Court. In practice, exercise of this rather unique Presidential power of cancellation is rare.

The President also may suspend the operation of legislative acts issued by governments of the federal subjects (Article 85(2)). The grounds for this are that the President judges them to be contrary to the Constitution or federal laws, or to Russia's international obligations, or that they violate the rights and freedoms of man and citizen. The effect is that the acts are not repealed but merely suspended, 'until this question is decided by the respective court'. Clearly, if there is no court hearing, the suspension could be permanent. As with cancellation of federal governmental legislation, the federal subject may challenge suspension at the Constitutional Court. Putin made a point of exercising this presidential power shortly after coming into office as part of his policy to impose a 'dictatorship of law' and achieve consistency throughout the federated legal system.[57] He suspended eight pieces of local legislation in short order, and the Constitutional Court gave him its backing. Along with the changes made to the formation of the Federation Council discussed in chapter five, and the new federal presidential representatives discussed in section V.A. below, this was part of Putin's campaign to strengthen central control over Russia's wayward periphery, creating what he called a *vertikal* (vertical hierarchy) of power.

---

[57] See J Kahn, *Federalism, Democratization, and the Rule of Law in Russia* (Oxford, Oxford University Press, 2002) 245, and R Sakwa, *Putin: Russia's Choice* (New York, Routledge, 2004) 139.

2. *Dismissing regional executives and legislatures*

This has profound implications for the federal dynamic of Russia. Originally, the President had the right to appoint and dismiss the executive heads in federal subjects, with the exception of the republics. The introduction of the federal law 'On the basis of the organisation of power in subjects of the Federation' of 6 October 1999 changed this by establishing that there should be elections for such heads. However, this has since been changed back to presidential nomination, as is discussed below in connection with the interrelation between the central executive powers and those of the federal subjects (see section VI.)

Part of Putin's *vertikal* of power campaign was the passage of a federal law on 29 July 2000, 'On Procedures for the Dismissal of Regional Executives and Legislatures'.[58] This laid out a strict timetable for regional executives and legislatures to bring their legislation into conformity with federal law, on pain of dismissal or dissolution if a second warning was ignored. The President can initially suspend the legislation, as seen in the previous section. If within two months it has not been replaced by compliant rules, he can issue a warning. If this is ignored, he may dismiss the regional executive within six months of the initial suspension of the legislation. The dismissal could be appealed to the Supreme Court, but no recourse to a court is needed for any of the earlier stages. In November 2003 Putin commented that 'No-one has been dismissed so far'.[59] Medvedev has been more active in this area; see section VI. below.

The President may also suspend a regional executive from office following an accusation by the Procurator-General that the regional executive committed a grave or especially grave crime. In this case suspension can be immediate, without warning, and clearly without recourse to a court. In the circumstances of Russian political life it would not be difficult for the Procurator-General to find grounds for accusation, so the mere existence of this power ensures that most regional executives respect central policy.

---

[58] See Kahn, above n 57, at 326, for Table 8.4 setting out detailed procedure.

[59] JA Corwin, 'Putin Expresses Openness to Improving Law on Ousting Governors' (2003) 214 *Radio Free Europe/Radio Liberty Newsline*, 12 November.

iv. Conciliation

The final set of powers is exercised by the President more by way of an open hand than a fist. It is fundamental to his role that he 'ensures the coordinated functioning and interaction of the agencies of State power' (Constitution, Article 80(2)). One important way he achieves this is by setting up conciliation commissions to resolve disputes (Article 85), for example to settle disagreements between the Executive at federal level and the executive agencies of federal subjects, and also between the executive agencies of different federal subjects. Yel'tsin set up conciliation commissions to deal with centre-periphery issues in 1997 and 1999, in relation to Ingushetiia and Bashkortostan respectively, although these were not well received in these fiercely independent republics.

In instigating conciliation, the President is standing above the Executive at different levels within the federal State, and taking a fatherly role. The emphasis is supposedly on reaching consensus and a mutually acceptable solution; however, if no agreement is reached, the dispute may be appealed to the Constitutional Court, and lying behind the conciliation process are of course the President's other considerable powers of 'persuasion'.

v. Implied powers

As if the express powers described above were insufficient, the provisions of Article 80 on the role of President have been used to justify the extension of presidential powers by implication. The Constitutional Court has developed, or possibly imported, a doctrine of implied powers. Under this, the President may exercise authority even though it has not been explicitly delegated to him, so long as it fits within the overall spirit of the constitutional provisions defining his role. The President's implied powers have even extended to a situation where the Constitution designates that the Legislature pass a specific federal law on a particular legal regime. The Constitutional Court affirmed that in the absence of such a law the President may adopt an edict as an interim solution. The only proviso is that the presidential edict must lose force when the appropriate federal law is eventually passed. In 1995 the Constitutional Court also held that the President had by implication a power to amend the Constitution, incorporating by presidential edict an amendment to

Article 65 listing the federal subjects, when a new subject had been created by voluntary amalgamation in the proper procedure.[60]

Overall, the President's powers are impressive, and when the 1993 Constitution was first examined by Western scholars there was serious disquiet that it set up the possibility of a presidential dictatorship. Certainly, there are few ways in which the President can be held to account (see section IV.A. below). However, in practice much has depended on the characteristics of the individual officeholder as to how strongly the hand of the President has been felt. Particularly during his second term, an unwell Boris Yel'tsin was content to leave much day-to-day activity to his successive Government Chairmen, interfering for political reasons only if he felt that a Chairman was becoming either too popular (and hence a rival, as for example Chernomyrdin in early 1998[61]) or too unpopular and therefore could be an appropriate sacrificial lamb (as Kirienko five months later).[62] Under the current regime, it is still a matter of debate to what extent Medvedev is a smooth-talking puppet in the hands of a scheming Putin, and to what extent he really has mastery as President of Russia.

III. THE GOVERNMENT

It is time to consider more closely the body defined by the Constitution as exercising executive power: the Government (Article 110). Duma deputies may not simultaneously be in the Government (Article 97(3)). Recalling the discussion in chapter three, the Constitution's Transitional Provisions allowed 'compatibility' during the first Duma from 1993–95. (See chapter five for formation of the Duma.)

The requirement to focus the mind on one post was broadened in November 2004 by an amendment to Article 11 of the Federal Constitutional Law on the Government, forbidding Government members from 'holding other office in agencies of State power and agencies

---

[60]   M Lomovtseva and J Henderson, 'Constitutional Justice in Russia' (2009) 34 *Review of Central and East European Law* 37 at 59.
[61]   L Shevstova, *Yeltin's Russia: Myths and Reality* (Washington, DC, Carnegie Endowment for International Peace, 1999) 239, cited in DD Barry, *Russian Politics: The Post-Soviet Phase* (New York, Peter Lang, 2002) 138.
[62]   Barry, above n 61, at 139.

of local self-government'; so simultaneously holding two federal posts or a federal position and a local position was also proscribed.

It is unusual, compared to some other systems, that there is no necessary relationship between the political affiliation of individual members of the Government and the majority party in the Duma. The Government is appointed by the President, who does not belong to any party. The President may appoint on whatever basis he likes. Suggestions have been floated that the majority Duma party might nominate an appropriate person to be appointed as Government Chairman, but so far these ideas have been soundly rejected. Similarly, there have been no demands that government ministers should belong to the party in power in the Duma. In April 2008, for example, it was noted that only three out of the Government Chairman's cabinet of 22 were members of Unified Russia, despite that party's large majority in the Duma and its strong support for both Putin as Chairman and Medvedev as President. In fact, before October 2004 it was not clear whether ministers were allowed to be members of a political party, and at least one, Deputy Chairman Aleksandr Zhukov, was reported as suspending his membership of Unified Russia whilst holding ministerial office.[63] The Russian President's website section on Federal Government links the President's power to dismiss the Government at will with

> the way governments are formed in Russia. The Constitution does not tie the government's formation to the distribution of seats among the different parties and factions in the parliament. In other words, the party that holds the majority in parliament can be asked to form a Government, but this is not automatically the case. Either way is permitted by the Constitution.[64]

It suggests that the President's prerogatives, including summary dismissal, are necessary to 'influence the Government's work' otherwise

> problems in various areas, including law-making, can arise within the executive power system's work. The result would be to make the executive power system less effective and less able to deal with the tasks at hand.[65]

This is an interesting justification for the President having power to behave capriciously, if he wishes.

---

[63] JA Corwin, 'Duma Lifts Ban on Cabinet Ministers' Political Affiliations' (2004) 8 *Radio Free Europe/Radio Liberty Newsline*, 14 October 2004.

[64] 'Federal Government', above n 52.

[65] *Ibid.*

A. The Government Chairman's role and powers

As noted above, the Government Chairman is head of the Government, and therefore, formally speaking, the head of the Executive. However, he does not have any specific executive powers, apart from the right to have the casting vote when he chairs Government meetings (Article 188, Federal Constitutional Law on the Government). The Constitution says that he shall 'in accordance with the Constitution and federal laws and edicts of the President determine the basic orientation of activity of the Government and organise its work' (Article 113). However, in doing this he will be carrying out policies determined by the President.

Within a week of taking office, the Government Chairman should make proposals to the President on the structure of the federal agencies of State power, and put forward candidates to fill the offices of his dep-uties and to be the federal ministers (Constitution, Article 112), but, as noted above, the President makes all the final decisions. The Government Chairman does have the power to distribute duties between members of the Government. This power was instituted as one of the features of the governmental reforms of June 2004, with the aim to increase effi-ciency. Compared to the President, the Chairman has very few formal powers. His main source of leverage is through allocation of personnel, but even here he can be trumped by a President with contrary views.

B. The Government's role and powers

The Government consists of an apparatus of ministries and State agen-cies. In 2004 the structure of the Government was reorganised by President Putin on the basis of plans worked out by Dmitrii Kozak (see section II.B.i.3. above). As a result of this, the number of ministers was reduced from 30 to 17,[66] with seven federal services and over 30 federal agencies. The size of the Government has since grown again to 18 min-istries, 35 federal services and 31 federal agencies.

The Government, although not its Chairman as individual officeholder, has the right to 'issue decrees and regulations and ensure their execution',

---

[66] Putin, above n 20.

but these are to be 'on the basis of an execution of the Constitution, federal laws, and normative edicts of the President' (Constitution, Article 115(1)). As noted in section II.B.iii.1. above, the President has unfettered power to repeal governmental legislation which he feels fails to conform to the Constitution, federal laws or his own edicts.

The Constitution lists the main areas of government competence in Article 114, and unsurprisingly these focus mainly on financial and social matters: the federal budget; financial, credit and monetary policy; culture, science, education, public health, social security and ecology; the administration of federal ownership; ensuring defence, State security and the realisation of foreign policy; ensuring legality, the rights and freedoms of citizens, protection of ownership and public order, and the struggle against criminality. The list is open-ended, as additional powers could be given to the Government under the Constitution, by federal law or presidential edict.

Medvedev's May 2008 reform of the governmental structure created a new Ministry of Sports, Tourism and Youth Policy, and a Ministry of Energy, both under the direction of the Government. These are not completely *de novo* creations but were formed by amalgamation of existing agencies. Nevertheless, through this reorganisation President Medvedev was giving an indication that he attached particular priority to those fields, thus indicating an important policy direction.

The Government is in direct charge of the federal ministries which are not in the Presidential Bloc (see section II.B.ii.4. above). These deal with economic and social affairs, so, for example, health and social development, culture, education and science, natural resources and ecology, industry and trade, regional development, communications and media, agriculture, transport, finance and economic development. However, even in respect of these ministries, the President has important input. For example, he gives an annual budget address which sets out both short-term and strategic budget policy, and forms an integral part of the procedures for drafting the federal budget.[67] The Government is therefore literally the Executive, as it executes the policies defined by the Head of State.

---

[67] 'Federal Government' above n 52.

IV. ACCOUNTABILITY

Although the Russian Constitution asserts that the different agencies of
State power are autonomous, it makes no claims to have a system of
checks-and-balances. This section will highlight the lack of practical
accountability of the President, and of the Government Chairman and
his Government.

A. Presidential accountability

i. Election

From the next presidential elections in 2012, the President will be
directly elected for a term of six years by a nationwide popular vote
under conditions of a secret ballot. When the presidency was first introduced, the term of office was five years, and Yel'tsin's first term was for
that period. He was then re-elected under the new conditions of the
1993 Constitution for a four-year term in July 1996; after an inconclusive first round of voting, he beat Gennadii Zhiuganov in a second
round run-off between the two leading contenders. He voluntarily
stood down from the presidency at the end of 1999. Amendments to
the Constitution and the electoral law in late 2008 extended the term of
office to six years. Direct accountability of the President to his electorate will therefore be exercised only after six years, if and when a future
president seeks re-election for a second term. A President cannot serve
more than two terms in succession, although he could return after a
break. Some observers expect Putin to do this.[68]

Direct popular accountability through elections works only if the
elections are free and fair. The presidential elections for Yel'tsin's second
term in 1996 were less than transparently even-handed. A group of

---

[68] See, eg, J Bransten, 'Putin Says He May Run Again in 2012' (2007) 11(106)
RFE/RL Newsline, 11 June; M Tsvetkova, N Ivanitskaia, I Reznik and N Kostenko,
'*Shest' let Putinu* [Six Years for Putin]', *Vedomosti*, 6 November 2008, available via
Westlaw as 'Putin may return to Kremlin in 2009 – Russian newspaper', *BBC Newsfile*,
7 November 2008; and a cartoon making play of the fact that Soviet and Russian
leaders have alternated between being bald and hairy, showing Medvedev and Putin
taking turns to be President, available at <http://static.oper.ru/data/gallery/
11048752602.jpg>, accessed 9 October 2010.

oligarchs used their control of the media to turn public opinion round from a mere 2–3 per cent in favour of Yel'tsin to over 35 per cent at the first ballot. Yel'tsin's state of health was kept secret; a video of him voting was doctored to eliminate any clues of his recent massive heart attack, and it was only once he was safely elected after the run-off ballot that his health issues were made public as he underwent a quintuple heart bypass operation.[69]

More recently, in 2008 there were doubts about the last set of Russian presidential elections. International observers from the Office of Democratic Institutions and Human Rights (ODIHR), one of the institutions of the Organisation for Security and Cooperation in Europe (OSCE), decided to not proceed with their planned mission of observation because of what they saw as unreasonable restrictions imposed on them at very short notice by the Russian Central Elections Commission, although a 22-member delegation from the Parliamentary Assembly of the Council of Europe (PACE) did observe and report, albeit negatively.[70] The results themselves overwhelmingly supported Medvedev, who received 70.2 per cent of the popular vote. However, they also showed some unlikely statistical characteristics. Statistician Sergei Shpilkin noticed that the official returns revealed a disproportionate number of polling stations nationwide reporting percentages ending in either a zero or a five for both voter turnout and for Medvedev's percentage of the vote. One would expect a normal distribution curve, but statistical analysis of the results looked normal only up to the 60 per cent level:

> After that, [the results] look like sharks' teeth. The spikes on multiples of five indicate a much greater number of polling stations reporting a specific turnout than a normal distribution would predict. A suspicious voter might say polling officials stuffed ballot boxes to achieve nice, clean percentages like 65, 70, 75, 80 and so on.[71]

[69] See DE Hoffman, *The Oligarchs: Wealth and Power in the New Russia* (New York, PublicAffairs, 2003) ch 13, 'Saving Boris Yel'tsin'.

[70] 'Russian Presidential Election: for an election to be good it takes a good process, not just a good election day', available at <http://assembly.coe.int/ASP/Press/StopPressView.asp?ID=2013>, accessed 13 August 2010.

[71] N Abdullaev, 'Medvedev Won by Curious Numbers', *Moscow Times*, 14 April 2008, available at <http://www.moscowtimes.ru/article/1010/42/361890.htm>, accessed 20 January 2009. See also R Coalson, 'End Note: How The Kremlin Manages to Get the Right Results' (2008) 12 *Radio Free Europe/Radio Liberty*, 7 March.

When Shpilkin explained the anomalies he suggested that the spikes on those exact numbers not only revealed manipulation, they also demonstrated 'an administrative demand' for a specific turnout to be reported to superiors. He also noticed that the higher the turnout, the higher was Medvedev's percentage of the returns; a correlation not seen in the returns for any of the other three candidates. Shpilkin also noticed statistical anomalies in the December 2007 Duma elections. Arranging a suitable electoral outcome was not an uncommon phenomenon in Russia in the past, and it seems that the old skills may have been exercised again.

ii. Immunity

Once in office, the President is inviolable (apart from possible impeachment, discussed in section IV.A.iii. below). Constitution Article 91 asserts that the President possesses inviolability, but does not spell out what this means. There is no procedure for depriving the President of this protection. These two factors contrast with the situation for Duma deputies or Federation Council members, who enjoy only qualified inviolability during their period in office. Their immunity is that they

> may not be detained, arrested, [or] subject to search, except in instances of detention at the site of a crime, and also subjected to personal inspection, except in instances when this has been provided for by a federal law in order to ensure the safety of other people. (Constitution, Article 98)[72]

As noted in section II. above, Acting President Putin's first edict, signed on 31 December 1999, gave unqualified immunity to any former President from 'being brought to criminal or administrative responsibility, detained, arrested, subject to search, [or] subjected to personal inspection'. Also noted above in relation to the dispute over the dismissal of Procurator-General Skuratov was the fact that he was responsible for investigations of dubious or corrupt practices by members of Yel'tsin's inner circle, but these investigations were not taken further. Putin's edict also gave generous pension provisions to Yel'tsin and the members of his family. Under the terms of the edict, the only qualification to former Presidents' immunity was that the edict could be replaced by federal law (but could not be repealed). In due course, on 12 February

---

[72] Butler, above n 2, at 27.

2001 the federal law was passed, which contained the equivalent immunity guarantee, but tempered by the possibility of withdrawal in the event of commission of treason or another grave crime (Article 3(2)). A grave crime is defined in the Criminal Code as one for which a perpetrator might receive 10 years' or more deprivation of freedom. Under the procedure laid down in the law, the Procurator-General would send a recommendation to the Duma, which would then decide whether or not to remove the presidential immunity. Thus far, this procedure has not been used.

iii. Impeachment

The main mechanism for accountability of a President is expulsion from office as a result of impeachment. In 1991, when the RSFSR presidency was introduced, a President could be impeached 'in the event of a violation of the Constitution of the RSFSR or laws of the RSFSR, and also of the oath sworn by him'.[73] The procedure would be initiated by the full Legislature as it existed at that time, the Congress of People's Deputies (CPD); its smaller permanently functioning chamber, the Supreme Soviet; or one of the Supreme Soviet's two chambers, the Soviet of the Republic or the Soviet of Nationalities. The Constitutional Court would give an opinion about the alleged breach. (The Court was not yet in operation, but at the time of these constitutional reforms legislation to set it up was already in process, and reference to it was included in the constitutional amendment.) The decision to impeach would be made by the CPD through a two-thirds majority vote. Impeachment proceedings were commenced against Boris Yel'tsin, in March 1993 and May 1999, but neither attempt was successful. The same procedure would apply for impeachment of the Vice-President, but on the grounds of violation of the RSFSR Constitution or laws.

When the 1993 Constitution was adopted, the requirements for impeachment were made distinctly narrower. Acting in violation of the Constitution or presidential oath was not enough. Under Article 93, the President may be impeached only on the basis of an accusation of treason or commission of another grave crime. The procedure has also been made more stringent. The initial accusation is put forward by the Duma, by a two-thirds vote of the total number of deputies, at the initiative of

---

[73] Article 121-10 of the 1978 RSFSR Constitution, as amended in 1991.

not less than one-third of the deputies, with the added requirement of the existence of an opinion from a special commission formed by the Duma. The President cannot dissolve the Duma once an accusation against him has been put forward, until a decision is reached on the outcome (Article 109). After the Duma has made the accusation, the Supreme Court needs to confirm the existence in the actions of the President of the necessary elements of the alleged crime. The Constitutional Court has to give an opinion that the requisite procedure for putting forward the accusation has been followed. Following this complex process, the actual decision of whether or not to impeach is taken by the Federation Council. It requires a two-thirds vote of the total number of members of the Federation Council, which must be held within three months of the initial accusation. The effect of successful impeachment is that the President's powers terminate immediately, which would also remove his presidential immunity. Elections for a new President should take place within three months, and in the meantime the Government Chairman is Acting President (as he is in the case of early voluntary retirement).

Clearly, under these provisions, it is theoretically possible for a President to be impeached. However, realistically, if more than a third of the members of either the Duma or the Federation Council are unswervingly loyal to the President, the procedure to impeach will never be successful. In the current Russian situation, the proportion of deputies in the Duma who belong to political groups which have pledged support to the current President is well over 78 per cent (Unified Russia: 315 seats and Fair Russia: 38 seats out of a total of 444). The current rules for formation of the Federation Council mean that up to half of its members will be nominees of governors who themselves are selected by the President (see section VI. below). The other half are the Chairs of the federal subjects' legislatures, increasingly filled with Unified Russia supporters. Also, attendance at the Federation Council has been problematic. So there could be serious practical difficulties in getting a decision from it within three months of an initial accusation, when during that time two high courts also have to fulfil their part of the process. The practical implementation of impeachment procedure has yet to be tested, but it seems likely to be ineffective to hold a President to account in all but the most extreme (and unlikely) circumstances. Otherwise the President is untouchable, and the fact that whilst in office the President has been independent of any political party removes opportunities for pressure on him to behave in a manner which might optimise that particular party's chances of electoral success.[74] Under current conditions, the Russian President is virtually unaccountable.

B. Government accountability

The President appoints the Government Chairman only with the consent of the Duma but has a completely free hand in dismissing him. One serious consequence of this is that there is no necessary relationship between the quality of the Government Chairman's performance of his office and his retention of that post. The President can dismiss him at will, irrespective of his success in office. Alternatively, the President may decide for his own political reasons to retain a Government Chairman despite evidence of incompetence. A career-minded Government Chairman would therefore pay more attention to pleasing the President than to the organisation of effective Government, cooperation with the Legislature or indeed striving to do the best for the general population.

An analogous principle applies also to the ministers. Each is appointed by the President, after proposal by the Government Chairman. To optimise the chance of remaining as minister, or even advancing to take over a more exciting ministry, an individual would strive to put on a good show for the President (and to lesser extent the Government Chairman) rather than cooperating with other government ministers. 'Survival of the fittest' trumps any altruistic principle, and development of a well-functioning cabinet willing and able to take collective decisions is impaired. There is a resonance here with the situation in Russia in the 19th century, when the Emperor appointed ministers to form his government but would then deal with each individually. Communication and cooperation between the ministers was severely discouraged, as that might detract from the hierarchy of power headed by the Emperor as supreme autocrat. Particularly in a political system such as Russia's, where personality tends to more important than bureaucratic efficiency, and 'departmentalism' has a strong tradition, the incentive to cooperate with other ministers may be diminished, and indeed infighting between different groups or 'clans' may undermine good governance.[75]

[74] This could change if Unified Russia develops into a hegemonic party; see E Huskey, '*Nomenklatura* lite? The Cadres Reserve in Russian Public Administration' (2004) 51 *Problems of Post-Communism* 2.
[75] See above n 25 and Huskey, above n 74.

i. Motion of no confidence

The Duma has the right to pass a decree of no confidence in the Government. This requires a simple majority vote of the total number of Duma deputies (Constitution, Article 117). However, the effect is not necessarily what those deputies would desire. After the Duma adopts such a decree, the President may dismiss the Government but is not obliged to. He may decide to keep his Government. At that stage all that the Duma majority would have achieved would be an ineffective expression of disapproval. There is more. Article 117(3) says that if the Duma expresses its lack of confidence a second time within three months, the President at that point has the choice either to dismiss the Government or to dissolve the Duma. As with the issue of appointment of the Government Chairman, the Duma is powerless to dissuade a determined President from having his own way, and the end result could be that the Duma deputies are forced to seek re-election, rather than an untrustworthy Government being removed.

The Government Chairman can initiate consideration by the Duma of its confidence in his Government (Article 117(4)). If the Duma declines to give its confidence, the President has the right within a week to dismiss the Government or, alternatively, dissolve the Duma and call new elections. It is easy to see that this procedure could be manipulated by a Government Chairman to force an unhappy Duma to back him, or risk itself being dissolved. This particular provision does not require any repeated action on the part of the Duma; one refusal of confidence will be sufficient to give the President scope to call for new Duma elections.

The Duma is protected against dissolution following a confidence issue (raised by its own deputies or by the Government Chairman) for one year after its election, once impeachment proceedings have been initiated (see section IV.A.iii. above), during a period of martial law or state of emergency, or in the six months before a presidential election (Article 109(3)-(5)). As Sakwa points out, in its first year or within six months of a presidential election, 'the Duma can dismiss one government after another with impunity'.[76] This has not yet happened.

President Medvedev set his sights on increased government efficiency. He prompted amendments on 30 December 2008 to the Constitution and the federal constitutional law on the Government, mandating the Government to make annual reports to the Duma (Article 40). But as the

---

[76] Sakwa, above n 21, at 115.

newspaper *Nezavisimaia Gazeta* pointed out, there is no obligation on the Government Chairman to report personally, and the wording of the amendment suggests that the report will be oral, not written, making detailed assessment and criticism more difficult.[77] Nevertheless, it may become a useful added opportunity for communication, or could trigger further questioning, through the parliamentary queries and inquiries systems discussed in chapter five, section II.C.i. Alternatively, it could be a piece of theatre devoid of real political import.

V. PARA-CONSTITUTIONAL INSTITUTIONS[78]

There are three institutions, none of which is directly mentioned in the Constitution, but all of which may give additional leverage to the President. Their collective significance is that they show that the President can orchestrate important changes to the organisation of the State, bypassing the Constitution. This reinforces the potential rift between 'law in the books' and 'law in action'; a long-standing issue in Russia. The three are the presidential representatives in federal districts, the State Council and the Public Chamber.

A. Federal plenipotentiary presidential representatives[79]

The President has general power to appoint presidential representatives, as seen in section II.B.i.4. above. Federal presidential representatives had existed under Yel'tsin, but at the level of the federal subjects (although not all subjects had one), but these had had difficulty challenging the authority of the governors. In the late 1990s, as a member of the

---

[77] I Rodin, 'Deputies do not want to listen to the premier', available at <http://www.ng.ru/politics/2008-12-26/1_duma.html>, accessed 10 February 2009.

[78] Sakwa, above n 21, at 341, categorises these under the heading 'para-constitutionalism'.

[79] See E Huskey, 'Political Leadership and the Centre-Periphery Struggle: Putin's Administrative Reforms' in A Brown and L Shevtsova (eds), *Gorbachev, Yel'tsin, Putin: Political Leadership in Russia's Transition* (Washington, DC, Carnegie Endowment for International Peace, 2001) 113; J Kahn, above n 57, at 240; C Ross, *Federalism and Democratisation in Russia* (Manchester, Manchester University Press, 2002) 137; C Ross, 'Putin's federal reforms and the consolidation of federalism in Russia: one step forward, two steps back!' (2003) 36 *Communist and Post-Communist Studies* 29 at 33; Sakwa, above n 57, at 141.

Presidential Administration, Putin investigated reorganisation of the presidential representatives.[80] Within a week of his inauguration as President in May 2000, he adopted an edict amending the system to create federal presidential plenipotentiary representatives, *polpredy*.[81] Putin's innovation was to create seven new federal districts, with the existing federal subjects divided between them, and set up a new *polpred* in each. When on 18 May Putin appointed his seven *polpredy*, it could be seen that all but two were generals, either military or from the security services, with quite fierce reputations.[82] The exceptions comprised a politician[83] and a former rowing champion who had become a career diplomat. The choice of mainly *siloviki* – former military or 'power ministry' personnel – added weight to Putin's reform. Ross noted that the new federal districts also closely matched Russia's military districts, 'thus giving the envoys . . . direct access to the command and control networks of the military garrisons situated in their districts'.[84]

The *polpredy* can attend the weekly meetings of the federal Government, and are members of the Russian Security Council.[85] They each have deputies and a sizeable support team (around 100 staff), luxurious offices and an impressive salary.[86] Putin made it clear that their role was not to supplant the governors but to 'coordinate' with them, although this could include gathering information about their behaviour and compliance.

Six days after the first appointments, the recently-installed Procurator-General Vladimir Ustinov announced that the Procuracy would also establish an office with a deputy Procurator-General in each of the seven districts. Within two days the Minister of Justice Yurii Chaika said

[80] Huskey, above n 79, at 118.

[81] Contraction of their name in Russian: *Polnomochnye predstaviteli Presidenta.*

[82] See J Henderson, 'Redefining Russia's Federal Structure?' (2000) 6 *European Public Law* 496.

[83] Former Government Chairman Sergei Kirienko, appointed to his former base of Nizhnii Novgorod, centre of the Volga federal district (and the only centre which is not simultaneously the headquarters of a military district). (2000) 5 *EastWest Institute Russian Regional Report* 25 noted that 'Putin could appoint a politician rather than a general in the Volga region, because unlike all the other federal districts, it is not located on a border.'

[84] Ross, above n 79, at 34; Huskey, above n 79, at 123.

[85] Ross, above n 79, at 35, says that edict to set up the federal districts was drafted by the Security Council.

[86] On their pay, see Kahn, above n 57, at 244; Huskey, above n 79, at 131.

his ministry would follow suit. The Audit Chamber, FSB, Ministry of Internal Affairs, Ministry of Defence, the Federal Tax Police and others were also quick to add the new federal level to their hierarchies. Putin thus effectively added a layer to Russia's federal system, without the need for discussion, primary legislation or constitutional reform.

On 19 January 2010, President Medvedev created an eighth federal district, the North Caucasian, taking federal subjects from the Southern Federal District. The new district includes the troubled Chechen Republic, and other potential conflict areas of Dagestan and Ingushetia.

The current office holders as listed on the presidential website are also predominately *siloviki* or equivalent.[87] As of August 2010 they comprise former members of the Armed Forces, the State Tax Police, Security Services, two former Procurators (including former Procurator-General Ustinov himself), one who was deputy Minister for Industry, Science and Technology after nearly 30 years in the KGB (Committee for State Security) and an engineer who moved into State service, a former banker and a shipbuilder who became governor of a territory. The last two were Medvedev appointments, as were the two former Procurators. The banker got the new North Caucasus district; his appointment was seen as a clever move:

> 'Khloponin is a man who has never had anything to do with the Caucasus or with men from the Caucasus,' a presidential administration official explained. 'Hence the reasoning behind his promotion.' It is reasonable indeed. Without close ties to any clan or tribe, Khloponin will be able to retain impartiality. The presidential administration also counts on Khloponin's other assets, namely on his being smart and wealthy (meaning that buying him is going to be a chore).[88]

B. The State Council

The State Council in its current form was established by Putin by presidential edict on 1 September 2000, to be an advisory body to the

[87] 'Presidential Executive Office', at < http://archive.kremlin.ru/eng/administration.shtml>, accessed 12 August 2010. It is debatable whether the Procuracy should be regarded as one of the power ministries, but it has a military-style uniform and hierarchy, and acts as the State prosecutor, so is at least analogous to them.

[88] N Kostenko, Yu Fedorinova, A Nikolsky, 'Smart, Wealthy, and Expendable' (2010) *Vedomosti* online, 20 January, available via Westlaw in 'What The Papers Say (Russia)'.

President. It was not quite an innovation. Its section on the official Presidential website reminds us that the 'first State Council was formed as part of the liberal reforms undertaken by Tsar Alexander I' as an advisory body, although in 1906 it was transformed into the upper chamber of the new bicameral Legislature:

> From this moment, the State Council became a semi-representative organ. The Tsar appointed the Council's Chairman, deputy chairman and half of its members, but the other half were elected from among the clergy, the nobility, the provincial *zemstvo* organizations (a form of local Government), the Academy of Sciences, university professors and large industrialists' and merchants' associations.[89]

The current State Council is not as directly representative as that one. Its establishment went hand-in-hand with the 2000 reforms to the composition of the upper legislative chamber, the Federation Council (see chapter five), and was part of a deal Putin made with the executive heads of federal subjects. They make up its composition, although other people may be appointed at the President's discretion. In February 2007 Putin widened its membership to include a number of former governors who supported the Government.[90]

The full State Council meets four times a year, under the chairmanship of the President. It discusses policy matters, on an agenda set by the Presidential Administration. At its inaugural meeting it discussed the Russian State symbols – flag, coat of arms and anthem – and a plan for State development up to 2010 (despite the fact that the Presidential Administration already had one).[91] Current practice is that each session focuses on a single issue. Occasionally meetings might be held jointly with the Security Council, which the President also appoints and chairs.

There are monthly meetings of a smaller Presidium. By both name and function this recalls Soviet practice in State and Party organisations of having a smaller executive group which met more frequently and wielded extensive power. However the State Council's Presidium can have only limited influence. It has no specific powers, and its composition changes every six months. The President chairs its meetings, and personally selects one executive head of a federal subject from each of

[89] 'State Council', at <http://kremlin.ru/eng/articles/council.shtml>, accessed 12 August 2010.
[90] C Ross, 'Federalism and Inter-governmental Relations in Russia' (2010) 26(2) *Journal of Communist Studies and Transition Politics* 165 at 176.
[91] J Henderson, 'Signs and Portents' (2002) 8 *European Public Law* 321 at 324.

the federal districts described above. The Presidium considers the State Council's work plans, and analyses their implementation. It meets the day before a full State Council meeting to discuss and set its agenda.

Both the State Council and its Presidium are purely consultative bodies. They have no firm basis in law; created by presidential edict, they could be dissolved at the stroke of a presidential pen. By colluding with the President to allow themselves to be removed from sitting in the Federation Council, governors of federation subjects showed their preference for regular personal contact with the President rather than a direct role in the Legislature. They clearly prefer a lobbying forum to legislating. Personal relationships, and what is said rather than what is written, have traditionally had an important role in Russia's polity. Alena Ledeneva explained the situation:

> As it tended to be in the Soviet Union, the party boss's word was most conclusive when it was spoken, not written. If the two ever deviated, the verbal held. . . . The primacy of the informal oral commands and handshake agreements reflected the weakness of the law, insidious secrecy and mistrust, and the need for authority figures to cut through the thicket of often conflicting administrative requirements.[92]

At the State Council and its Presidium, governors feel that they can speak directly to the President and so have a hand in creating policy, even if in fact their input may have no impact. The President is happy to allow them a sense of involvement, as one way of forestalling overt opposition.

C. The Public Chamber[93]

The most recent of the three institutions established by President Putin is the Public Chamber. As with the other two, this was not an innovation. Yel'tsin had created a body with the same name and similar functions in the early 1990s as 'a ready-made alternate leg of legitimacy on

---

[92] A Ledeneva, 'Telephone Justice in Russia' (2008) 24 *Post-Soviet Affairs* 324 at 329, citing Timothy Colton, *Yel'tsin: A Life* (New York, Basic Books, 2007) 82. In a comment to her, Colton also tells a story about an official who reproached his subordinate for implementing his written instruction: 'If I wanted you to do something, I would have called you.'

[93] *Obshchestvennaia Palata*, translated on its website as 'Civic Chamber'; see <http://www.oprf.ru/en/>, accessed 12 August 2010.

which to stand in the event of a dissolution of parliament',[94] although in the event he did not use it in that role.

The Public Chamber differs from the other two institutions discussed in this section in a number of respects. It was established on the basis of federal law, not presidential edict. The idea was presented by President Putin as one of his reforms following the tragic siege of the school in Beslan in September 2004. A draft law was produced by the Presidential Administration. It was enthusiastically received by the Duma and the Federation Council, and signed into law on 4 April 2005.[95] The aim of the Public Chamber is that it should be a consultative body to 'facilitate coordination between the socially significant interests of citizens of Russia, NGOs, and national and local authorities.'[96]

The composition of the Public Chamber is by selection. Of its 126 members, 42 are selected by the President and another 42 are representatives of social organisations. The final 42 are chosen by the other 84 members. Individuals serve for two years. The Chamber holds four to five plenary meetings a year, as well as 'over 100 public events'. It has 17 commissions, with sub-commissions focusing on various areas. It has involved itself with a wide range of sensitive issues: the rights of conscripts, elections, child abuse, health care, media restrictions, draft laws' impact on rights. Its website lists an extensive time-line of initiatives, although not all met with success.[97]

One of the principal authors of the law, Duma Deputy Valerii Galchenko of Unified Russia, reportedly said: 'The country must have at least one moral-ethical organ that can stand on the same level with the president in the eyes of society.'[98] Putin required prospective members to be non-politicians and 'distinguished people who have made contributions to the state and society'.[99] Not everyone welcomed this collection of worthies. Some critics drew parallels with a body that existed in Italy under Benito Mussolini's Fascist regime, and a number of promi-

---

[94] Huskey, above n 30, at 174.

[95] JA Corwin, 'Duma Gives Initial Approval to Creation of New Federal Organ' (2004) 8 *Radio Free Europe/Radio Liberty*, 23 December.

[96] 'About', at <http://www.oprf.ru/en/about/>, accessed 12 August 2010.

[97] 'Chronology of Events', at <http://www.oprf.ru/en/about/1217/>, accessed 12 August 2010.

[98] R Coalson, 'As Bill's Author Defends the Initiative' (2005) 9 *Radio Free Europe/Radio Liberty Newsline*, 18 February, citing strana.ru 17 February 2005.

[99] 'VY Putin Forges Ahead on "Public Chamber" Project' (2005) 9 *Radio Free Europe/Radio Liberty Newsline*, 4 August.

nent human rights organisations refused to be involved in the initial selection process.[100] The Public Chamber met for the first time on 1 October 2005. When the composition of the Public Chamber was renewed two years after its establishment, twenty-five of the original members appointed by the President were kept on, with 17 incomers, a number of whom had ties to Putin. Some more well-known human rights campaigners were newly included as appointees of the social organisations, evidencing a greater acceptance of the new consultative body by active non-governmental organisations (NGOs). Its current members represent the educated intelligentsia: all members have completed, or are completing, higher education. They include 60 with higher degrees; 21 members have the academic title of reader or professor; eight are corresponding members or academicians of the Russian Academy of Sciences or the Russian Academy of Medical Sciences. Twenty-two members are academics; 16 are political scientists or economic analysts; 15 work in the arts and culture; 14 are lawyers; 12 are journalists or literary figures; eight are religious leaders; seven are entrepreneurs; five are doctors; four are education experts; and the remaining 23 have other occupations. A quarter of the members (32) are women. Sixty per cent of the members are aged over 50, 40 per cent are between 30 and 50, and 3 per cent are under 30.[101]

In March 2008, then President-elect Medvedev spoke at a meeting of the Public Chamber and gave his support to draft legislation receiving more 'expert examination'.[102] The Public Chamber seemed to be an ideal forum. As a result, its scope was expanded in December 2008, giving it the right to receive all draft legislation for consideration, not just selected bills. It also was empowered to demand views from State agencies on any draft measures which would restrict individual freedoms in respect of arrest, detention or seizure of property. It had previously made a strike for rights by complaining that the procedure for registering an NGO with the Federal Registration Service was too complex and poorly understood by regional officials of the Service.[103] The Public

---

[100] J Bransten, 'Public Chamber Criticized As "Smokescreen"' (2005) 5 *RFE/RL Russian Political Weekly*, 1 April.

[101] Above n 96.

[102] 'Bills should undergo public scrutiny before adoption – Medvedev', *Itar-Tass*, 19 March 2008.

[103] R Coalson, 'Public Chamber Criticizes Application of NGO Registration Law' (2008) 12 *Radio Free Europe/Radio Liberty Newsline*, 10 April.

Chamber criticised proposals to reduce access to jury trial for those accused of treason. Its comments were ignored by the Federation Council, but induced President Medvedev to order a review of the proposed amendments (although to no avail).

D. Conclusions on the Para-Constitutional Institutions

What conclusions should be drawn about these para-constitutional institutions? All three are 'children' of the President and are therefore unlikely to act as fora for opinions too strongly distinct from those of their founder, although the Public Chamber has taken the opportunity to voice legitimate concerns, and is not always ignored. It was established to express informed public opinion, and conceivably this compensates for the Legislature, which increasingly fails to reflect more than a narrow range of views (see chapter five). The Public Chamber at least has the security of being based on federal law, not presidential edict like the State Council. The President could easily decide that it serves only as a vanity project for Governors and abolish it. The presidential federal representatives are very useful as channels of communication, but the extent to which the communication is two-way will depend on the personality of the President and his political needs. All three are examples of the President manipulating his considerable constitutional powers to gain additional means to influence Russian public life.

VI. EXECUTIVE POWER IN THE FEDERAL SUBJECTS

This section deals with an important federal dimension: the changes to how the executive heads in the federal subjects are put in post, and their relationship with the Russian President. There is a tension between local democracy and federal accountability; the current outcome unsurprisingly favours the latter.

The executive heads in the federal subjects have a variety of different names, such as President (of a republic within Russia), Head of Government, Government Chairman or Governor, but for convenience they will be collectively referred to as 'governors'. Under the Federation Treaty of 1992, the republics within Russia were given power to write their own constitutions and elect their governors. The other federal subjects had charters, not constitutions, and their governors were appointed by the Russian President.[104] The effect of this on the composition of the Federation Council is discussed in chapter five. Part of that story was the establishment by legislation in December 1995 that by December 1996 all governors should be elected by local suffrage. A law of 6 October 1999, to come into effect on 19 October 2001, restricted elected governors to two terms consecutively. An amendment in January 2001 set the start date for this restriction as the time the law was adopted; this allowed 69 governors to run for a third term and 17 for a fourth.[105]

Putin changed all this. Ostensibly in response to the tragic school siege in 2004 in Beslan, Putin sought to strengthen the 'unified system of executive power' ('power *vertikal*') by having governors nominated by the President to the federal subject legislature for approval for a five-year term. Amendment to existing federal legislation was required, but Putin's proposal was agreed with comparatively little opposition in either the Duma or the Federation Council, resulting in the federal law of 11 December 2004. In fact the existing governors seemed to welcome the new policy with surprising alacrity.[106] A considerable number arranged a personal meeting with Putin, then voluntarily stood down early, to be reappointed under the new procedure. As an earlier commentator succinctly phrased it, 'it is much easier to lick one boot than to clean 400,000'.[107] Apart from saving themselves the expense of a re-election campaign, these newly-appointed governors bypassed the restriction on the number of successive terms they could serve. The new appointment procedure would also give governors more immunity from

> local dependence on their pre-election supporters . . . They used to be 'people with large sums of money who provide[d] for the elections and then [went] to the governor to solve various problems'.[108]

[104] Ross (2002), above n 79, at 24.
[105] Sakwa, above n 57, at 153.
[106] See JP Goode, 'The Puzzle of Putin's Gubernatorial Appointments' (2007) 59 *Europe-Asia Studies* 365.
[107] Said by an unidentified Federation Council member to former presidential adviser L Smirnyagin in March 2001, cited in J A Corwin, 'Why are So Many Elected Leaders in Russia Ready to Give Up on Elections?' (2004) 36 *Radio Free Europe/Radio Liberty Political Weekly*, 16 September.
[108] AV Ledeneva, *How Russia Really Works: The Informal Practices that Shaped Post-Soviet Politics and Business* (Ithaca, NY, Cornell University Press, 2006) 56.

It was easier for the governors to owe a favour to the President than to a range of local power-brokers.

Disquiet amongst some Western commentators that Putin's reform was an attack on democracy failed to take into account that election of governors had been far from 'free and fair'. At least the new system would build in a measure of real accountability, even if only to the President. The last gubernatorial election was on 23 January 2005 in the oil-rich Nenets Autonomous Area:

> The elections were noteworthy not because they were the last, but because they included all of the usual political tricks that have become so popular in recent years.[109]

The exact appointment procedure was set by a presidential edict of 27 December 2004.[110] The presidential federal representative (*polpred*) would submit a shortlist to the head of the Presidential Administration, who would in turn put two names forward to the President. This was amended in June 2005, cutting out the input of the Presidential Administration and allowing the *polpred* to suggest a single name to the President.[111] The candidate would then be presented to the appropriate legislative assembly for confirmation. On 21 December 2005 the Constitutional Court reversed a previous ruling that governors should be popularly elected, now acquiescing to the constitutionality of appointment (see chapter six).

Under both Yel'tsin and Putin there had been quite remarkable tenacity amongst existing governors, under whichever method of gaining office.

> Russia's regional elite has always been 'adroit in the ways of the tsar's court' and that it is no accident that Communist Party *Obkom* [regional committee] secretaries often held their jobs for 15 years or longer at a time.[112]

As of early 2007, 'not a single regional assembly has openly challenged a presidential nomination for governor'.[113]

---

[109] Y Shabaev, 'Russia's Last Governor's Election'(2005) 3 *Russian Regional Report*, 2 February.

[110] Sakwa, above n 21, at 277.

[111] L Belin, 'Putin Changes Procedure for Selecting Regional Leaders' (2005) 125 *Radio Free Europe/Radio Liberty Newsline*, 1 July.

[112] Smirnyagin, cited in Corwin, above n 107.

[113] Goode, above n 106, at 382.

Under President Medvedev there may be change. He has highlighted
the need to avoid stagnation in personnel (a problem of the Brezhnev
Soviet era), expanding the system of a list of suitable candidates – a so-
called cadre list – begun under Putin.[114] In 2008 Medvedev announced
plans to draw up and publish a list of a 'Golden 1,000' of top management personnel as part of a recruitment drive for fresh talent in government service. This contrasts with Putin's rather secretive appointments
policy. On 17 February 2009 the first 100 names were published.[115] The
previous day Medvedev had dismissed four governors, an unprecedented act.[116] He also proposed that the party that holds most seats in a
regional legislature should have the right to nominate the candidate for
governor. This move does not necessarily take control away from the
current centre, given that Government Chairman Putin chairs the
Unified Russia Party which holds the majority in most legislatures.
However, it is a change of style, and may signal a more open and diversi-
fied approach. As well as transparency, Medvedev's appointment procedure is more efficient, taking one and a half months instead of three,
and is more orderly; governors are replaced only if their term is up, or if
they have been ineffective.[117] Medvedev is also bringing in 'fresh blood'.
In 2010 the terms of 30 regional heads expire, including some impressive survivors, such as Mintimer Shaimiev, who had been President of
Tatarstan since 12 June 1991. On the basis of the 17 governors
appointed under Medvedev by early 2010, his ideal candidate profile is:

> A man aged 35–50; not involved in local elite disputes; a member of United
> Russia; understands the region; an economist, or better a lawyer, by training;
> prepared to implement the federal centre's policy; experience of working at
> the federal level; knows how to be flexible, find compromises.[118]

Nine of the 17 appointees were from Moscow and eight were regionally
based (although not always where they became governor). A balance must

[114] Huskey, above n 74.
[115] A Malpas, 'Medvedev Names Top 100 Candidates for Senior Posts' (2009)
Moscow Times, 17 February, available online at <http://www.moscowtimes.ru/article/
1010/42/374625.htm>, accessed 17 February 2009.
[116] B Whitmore, 'The Kremlin Gets Hyperactive' (2009) *Radio Free Europe/Radio
Liberty Russia Report*, 17 February.
[117] A Beluza, 'Gubernatorial Callup 2010' (2010) *Moscow Izvestiya Online* (Moscow
Edition), in Russian, 19 January, available in translation via Westlaw under the title
'Russian: Experts Eye Medvedev's Personnel Policy, Gubernatorial Appointments'.
[118] *Ibid.*

be struck between knowing the area, yet not being involved with local elite disputes. Almost all appointees have been part of the federal bureaucratic establishment. 'Men dominate candidate lists for governorships . . . in the realm of decision-making . . . women remain in second place.'[119]

Medvedev's replacement policy has not always run smoothly. There was public unrest and a local media campaign in Khanty-Mansiisk when the popular Governor Aleksandr Filipenko was replaced in February 2010, and protests in Kaliningrad in the same month when approximately 10,000 demanded the resignation of their unpopular governor.[120] In the development of centre-regional executive relations there has been an oscillation in relative power between centre and periphery. Yel'tsin was content to allow regional autonomy, but Putin (with considerable public support) used a range of means to restore order and claim power back to the centre. Medvedev has been reaping the result of Putin's reforms:

> Analysts say an unintended consequence of having appointed governors was that the Kremlin lost a crucial line of defence in the regions when things go bad. Under the old system, troubles in any given region were the responsibility of elected governors. But now, with appointed governors, the Kremlin owns any problems that arise.[121]

One possible consequence may be the return to elected governors; certainly public opinion polls show the majority of Russians would support that.[122]

VII. CONCLUSION

The 1993 Russian Constitution awards impressive powers to the President, which have been extended both by implication and by presi-

---

[119] *Ibid.*

[120] B Whitmore, 'Kremlin Stumbles In Regions As Unrest Mounts' (2010) *Radio Free Europe/Radio Liberty Feature*, 16 February, available at <http://www.rferl.org/content/Kremlin_Stumbles_In_Regions_As_Unrest_Mounts/1959861.html>, accessed 13 August 2010. See also T Stanovaya, 'Kremlin's New Personnel Policy and Priorities' (2010) *Politkom.ru*, 15 February, available via Westlaw as 'Russian pundit analyses changes to Kremlin's regional personnel policy' (2010) *BBC Monitoring Former Soviet Union*, 20 February.

[121] Whitmore, above n 116.

[122] Whitmore, above n 120.

dential edict. Also, as in prior periods and under quite different political regimes, the accountability of the Head of State is weak under the current Russian constitutional regime. The Government is only really answerable to the President, although it is also subject to legislative inquiry, discussed in the next chapter.

Practical implementation of presidential power has varied according to the *modus operandi* of the particular President. During Boris Yel'tsin's first term he took an active role and regularly legislated by edict. During his second term health issues and economic problems induced him to leave day-to-day running of the State to whichever Government Chairman was in post. Throughout, there was a marked degree of negotiation with both the federal Legislature and the governors of the federal subjects to gain him necessary support for his policies. Central executive power was not strongly imposed.

This changed when Vladimir Putin took up office as President. He set himself to rein in the centrifugal forces and create a unified legal space. He instituted a series of reforms which bypassed the existing constitutional framework, and created new tools for the central Executive to influence regional government.

Under Dmitrii Medvedev the change has been more nuanced. A high-profile Government Chairman in the shape of Vladimir Putin led to discussion of a 'tandemocracy' as the two carefully emphasised their coordinated efforts. It is difficult to assess whether Medvedev acts as a puppet under Putin's direction, is self-directed but generally agrees with his predecessor's policies, or is more subtly building up his own support, to take a more individualised approach to the presidency in the future. As things stand, Medvedev has been cultivating excellent public relations. His presidential website seems designed as much for overseas consumption as for consumption at home; its English-language section is impressive, in stark contrast to the Government's site which is in Russian only. He has also been saying all the 'right things' as he speaks out against corruption and in favour of humanisation of the criminal justice system, and balances his potentially fractious government ministers at the centre and regional governors on the periphery.

Political analysts have suggested that a presidential-parliamentary system, such as that in Russia, is likely to be unstable.[123] However, in Russia

---

[123] See MS Shugart, 'Of Presidents and Parliament' (1993) 2 *East European Constitutional Review* 30.

there seems to be more risk of stagnation with the current trend towards an almost Soviet-style cadre policy, one-party rule (under Unified Russia) and Russia's traditional tendency towards personalist politics.[124] Putin's legacy is that the direction of the exercise of executive power is towards strength and stability. Medvedev's rhetoric is rather more towards developing a broader-based democracy. At the time of writing, the build-up to the 2012 presidential elections has begun, and the outcome of that contest will set the conditions for the next phase of exercise of executive power in Russia.

FURTHER READING

WA Clark 'The presidential transition in Russia, March 2008' (2008) 28(2) *Electoral Studies* 342.

GM Hahn, 'The Past, Present, and Future of the Russian Federal State' (2003) 11 *Demokratizatsiya* 343.

JP Goode, 'The Puzzle of Putin's Gubernatorial Appointments' (2007) 59 *Europe-Asia Studies* 365.

E Huskey, 'The State-Legal Administration and the Politics of Redundancy' (1994) 11 *Post-Soviet Affairs* 115.

——, 'Political Leadership and the Centre-Periphery Struggle: Putin's Administrative Reforms' in A Brown and L Shevtsova (eds), *Gorbachev, Yel'tsin, Putin: Political Leadership in Russia's Transition* (Washington, DC, Carnegie Endowment for International Peace, 2001).

H Oversloot, 'Reordering the State (without Changing the Constitution): Russia under Putin's Rule, 2000–2008' (2007) 32 *Review of Central and East European Law* 41.

TF Remington, 'The Evolution of Executive-Legislative Relations in Russia since 1993' (2000) 59 *Slavic Review* 499.

C Ross, 'Federalism and Electoral Authoritarianism under Putin' (2007) 3 *Demokratizatsiya* 347.

——, 'Federalism and Inter-governmental Relations in Russia' (2010) 26(2) *Journal of Communist Studies and Transition Politics* 165.

JF Young and GN Wilson, 'The view from below: Local Government and Putin's reforms' (2007) 59 *Europe-Asia Studies* 1071.

---

[124] See Huskey, above n 74.

5

The Legislature and its Formation

———◆◆———

**Introduction – The Federal Assembly – The Legislative Council
– Conclusion – Further Reading**

I. INTRODUCTION

'THE FEDERAL ASSEMBLY – the parliament of the Russian
Federation – is the representative and legislative agency of the
Russian Federation' (Constitution, Article 94). This chapter
explores Russia's idiosyncratic representative system and its impact on
the Federal Assembly's overall role. The rules on formation of the
Federal Assembly have been amended with remarkable frequency, for
both its chambers, the Duma and the Federation Council. Political scientists with an interest in electoral systems follow these developments
with glee, as Russia presents an exemplary sandpit in which to study the
effects of electoral rule changes. The developments are important in the
context of Russia's stated aim to be a 'democratic federated rule-of-law
State with a republican form of government' (Constitution, Article 1).
The legislative process will also be considered, and the political importance of some of the other powers exercised by the Duma and the
Federation Council, for example the Duma's budgetary and audit oversight, and its other means, albeit rather limited, to monitor governmental performance.

II. THE FEDERAL ASSEMBLY

A. The structure of the Federal Assembly

The two chambers of the Federal Assembly are the Federation Council (also known as the Council of the Federation or the Soviet of the Federation; *soviet* being the Russian word for council) and the State Duma (or, more briefly, the Duma). The decision to reintroduce the name 'Duma' into the 1993 Constitution for the general representative assembly was interesting. The Russian verb *dumat'* means to think, and various Dumas existed in pre-revolutionary Russia to advise the autocratic monarch. One commentator remarked that the

> prerevolutionary name 'Duma' evokes a not very successful history, the first three Dumas having been elected and then summarily dismissed by Tsar Nicholas II.[1]

The basic premise of Russia's bicameral Legislature is that the Duma represents the general population, and the Federation Council is 'the collective voice of the regions',[2] representing the 83 federation subjects. It is possible for the two chambers to meet together to hear important addresses, for instance by the President, but all decision-making is made by each chamber separately, and they are housed in separate premises in Moscow. Both chambers hold two sessions each year, although of slightly different lengths, running from dates in January to June/July, and September to December. The Duma has plenary meetings on Wednesdays and Fridays, and committee meetings on Mondays, Tuesdays and Thursdays. The Federation Council is more part-time, meeting 'as necessary, but not less than twice a month' (Article 41(1) of its Reglament).[3]

---

[1] M Merritt, 'The Russian State Duma, On-stage and Off: Inquiry, Impeachment, and Opposition' (2000) 8 *Democratizatsiya* 165 at 175, fn 4.

[2] I Busygina, 'Federalism in Russia: outcomes of the decade 1993–2003 and the newest developments' in K Malfleit and R Laenen (eds), *Elusive Russia. Current Developments in Russian State Identity under President Putin* (Leuven, Leuven University Press, 2007) 52 at 57.

[3] 'Glava 5. Poriadok provedeniia sessii i zacedanii Soveta Federatsii', available at <http://www.council.gov.ru/about/agenda/ch1/item258.html>, accessed 14 August 2010.

The Constitution is surprisingly unspecific about how each chamber of the Federal Assembly should be made up. It does prescribe that the Duma has 450 deputies and 'shall be elected for a term of five years' (Article 96 as amended December 2008; previously four years), and stipulates that the 'procedure for the formation of the Federation Council and the procedure for elections of the Duma shall be established by federal laws'. Importantly, it leaves unclear whether members of the Federation Council should be elected or appointed. The choice between these two methods of selection has varied, as discussed below. The Constitution does specify in Article 95(2) that the Federation Council shall consist of two representatives from each federal subject, one from its representative agency (subject-level legislature) and one from the subject's executive branch. It follows that the number of Federation Council members is 166, that is twice the number of federal subjects. (The list on the Federation Council website of the composition as at 23 July 2010 shows that only eight of the 166 are women.)

Each of the two chambers elects a Chairman and Deputy Chairmen to preside over sessions. The Chairmen have appropriate powers to maintain discipline in their respective chamber. Each chamber also establishes committees which play an important role in preparing legislation and monitoring governmental activity. The Duma has 32 committees and five commissions listed on its website, and the Federation Council 16 committees and 11 commissions.[4] Generalising, committees' areas of interest correspond to government ministries and departments, and commissions to more general fields or internal issues such as the Duma Commission for Credentials and Deputy Ethics.

i. Formation of the Duma

The Duma must be elected but the rules for the elections have changed, arguably leading to a less representative set of deputies. Under the Soviet regime, democratic representation had a meaning different from standard Western usage. Successful election required that an absolute majority of the electorate voted for the candidate. It was immaterial that only one stood in each constituency after careful selection by the Communist Party.

---

[4] List of committees in Art 20 of the Duma Reglament in WE Butler, *Russian Public Law*, 2nd edn (London, Wildy, Simmonds & Hill, 2009) 290.

During the *perestroika* era, multi-candidate elections were introduced and there was experimentation with different representation. In 1989 the USSR Congress of People's Deputies bypassed the principle of 'one person, one vote' with its three separate sets of constituencies, but introduced for the first time more-or-less full-time, paid deputies. After amendments in March 1990 to the 1977 USSR Constitution, the Communist Party of the Soviet Union lost its monopoly as the only political party, and other groups began to form (the Liberal Democratic Party of Russia claims to be the first opposition party, registered earlier in 1989). The equivalent amendment of the RSFSR Constitution was on 15 June 1990.

Yel'tsin decreed on 21 September 1993 that the Russian Legislature should be dissolved and replaced (see chapter three). The new Constitution specified that, apart from the special transitional arrangements for the first two years, the Duma should be elected for a term of four years (since extended to five), but did not stipulate a particular system. Yel'tsin, however, did. In a compromise which combined familiar constituencies with a move to encourage formation of political parties, he decreed that half of the 450 seats in the Duma should be populated by first-past-the-post elections in single-member districts, and the other half by proportional representation, based on votes received nationwide by a registered party or electoral bloc. A threshold was set for the proportional representation seats. They were reserved for parties or blocs who received 5 per cent or over of valid votes. Voters indicated their preference under each of the two systems on two different ballot papers, including the possibility of voting 'against all' on the proportional representation ballot (which counted as valid votes in the overall total). A candidate could stand for a single-member district while also being on a party list, because of the different basis of representation. This, for example, allowed Vladimir Zhirinovskii to take up a proportional representation seat on behalf of his (so-called) Liberal Democratic Party of Russia list after his own single-member district election in Shchelkovo, 15 miles east of Moscow, was declared invalid because of irregularities on the ballot paper and all candidates had not had equal television time.[5] Any party list deputy could be replaced by his or her party by someone further down the list, and single-seat Duma deputies were not under any

---

[5] 'Local Court Annuls Zhirinovsky's Election' (1994) *Associated Press Online*, 26 February, available via Westlaw.

obligation to vote in line with the party for which they had stood, if there had been one (many were independents).

In the Duma the parties themselves would form factions or could form party groups. Factions are groups within the Duma, and any party who surmounts the proportional representational threshold automatically forms one, which may then be joined, for example, by independent single-seat deputies. A deputy group can be formed by others, provided at least 35 deputies wish to join (55 from January 2004). Occasionally members of parties forming factions might be 'lent' to other deputy groups.[6] Factions and deputy groups had important roles to play in the allocation of chair and membership of the various Duma committees (although after 2004 a majoritarian rather than proportional approach was taken, which favoured the Unified Russia party[7]).

In June 1995 the Law on Election of Deputies to the State Duma was passed, in preparation for the upcoming elections in December that year, at the end of the first Duma's two-year term.[8] There had been disputes about both the overall required turnout and the size of the proportional representation segment of the Duma. Yel'tsin wanted to keep the traditional 50 per cent turnout requirement for the election to be valid, but to minimise void elections acceded to the Duma's 25 per cent. A conciliation commission mediated between the Duma's desire to keep its current half-and-half ratio and the Yel'tsin's preference for an uneven split of 150 proportional representation seats and 300 single-member district seats, which he believed would reduce extremist parties' chances of controlling the Duma. The compromise was that the half-and-half ratio would remain, but no more than 12 per cent of any party list could be Moscow-based, to ensure a greater chance of inclusion of regional candidates. Parties had to register with the Ministry of Justice by October to be included in the proportional representation ballot, submitting nomination lists with 200,000 supporters' signatures (double the previous election's requirement; the other change was that party affiliation appeared on the single-member constituency ballots).

> Of the 43 parties and blocs which took part, only 4 succeeded in surmounting the 5% hurdle, taking just under 50% of all votes between them. Given that the official turnout was only 64.4% this means that the parties securing the proportional seats actually reflected the choices of only 32% of the

---

[6] R Sakwa, *Russian Politics and Society*, 4th edn (Abingdon, Routledge, 2008) 189.
[7] *Ibid* at 193.
[8] J Henderson, 'Election time in Russia' (1996) 2(1) *European Public Law* 63 at 65.

electorate. . . . While the Communists and their allies have remained just short of a controlling majority in the Duma, they normally have had sufficient support to win important votes. An early indication of this was the election of a member of the Communist Party, the former *Pravda* editor Gennady Seleznev, to the chairmanship on 17 January 1996.[9]

The effect was that for an important four years of Yel'tsin's presidency he had an oppositional Duma.

By the time of the next elections in December 1999, Putin was Government Chairman. Twenty-six parties and blocs competed for the proportional representational seats. Six succeeded in crossing the 5 per cent barrier, including the new pro-Government 'interregional bloc' Unity (*Edinstvo*) and the 'Zhirinovski Bloc' registered by Vladimir Zhirinovski after his Liberal Democratic Party's registration was rejected by the Election Commission because of irregularities in its candidate list.

Unity supported Putin's campaign for the March 2000 Presidential elections, and combined with another bloc to create a new party, Unified Russia (*Edinaia Rossiia*, sometimes translated as 'United Russia'), for the Duma elections in December 2003. It campaigned solely on its support for Putin, refusing televised debate and publicising no policies.[10] It won 222 seats, only four away from an absolute majority. There were 65 independents amongst the single-member district deputies, so it would not take much wheedling to persuade a handful of them to lend sufficient support to pass whatever federal laws it wanted, and allied with the Motherland-Patriotic Union bloc, the People's Party and the Zhirinovski Bloc, it had enough of a majority to pass federal constitutional laws. As one commentator concluded in respect to the 2003 Duma elections:

[President] Putin was not necessarily hampered from pursuing his political goals with the previous Duma, where he often managed to pull together a majority – and even passed several controversial laws in the final days before the election. Still, such efforts took time, persuasion, and delicate diplomacy – something the President may need far less of now.[11]

[9] R Ware, 'Democracy in Russia' (1998) 98/89 *House of Commons Research Library* 14, available at <http://www.parliament.uk/parliamentary_publications_and_archives/research_papers/library_research_papers_1998.cfm#81-100>, accessed 24 August 2010, at 11.

[10] See J Henderson, 'The Russian Constitutional Court to the Rescue: Freedom of Political Comment Reasserted' (2005) 11(1) *European Public Law* 17.

[11] S Lambroschini, 'Russia: How will Duma vote effect Putin's policy?' (2003) *Radio Free Europe/Radio Liberty*, 9 December.

The result in the December 2007 Duma elections was even more dramatic. Unified Russia, supporting not only Putin but also his chosen presidential heir, Medvedev, won 315 seats, 70 per cent of the Duma. This gives it an absolute controlling qualified majority, gifting the incoming President a very complaisant Duma. Major changes in 2005 came into effect for these elections. All the single member seats have been abolished so that the Duma is now constituted solely on the basis of proportional representation. The threshold has also been raised to 7 per cent. Only four parties from the 11 that were on the ballot managed to cross that barrier.

Parties are no longer allowed to unite to form an election bloc to improve their chance of passing the minimum threshold. The rules on the composition of the individual party lists are quite complex, to ensure both a federal spread and some local representation. Seats gained by a successful party are allocated to candidates in territorial groups on the party list in proportion to the votes in that territory. The 'against all' option was removed, although with special provisos for the extreme situations where only two parties succeeded, or where the total vote for the successful parties was less than 60 per cent of the overall vote.[12]

Putin's justification for the changes was that they would encourage a strong party system. However, this assessment may have been either over-optimistic or indeed mendacious. To be sure, the link between the electorate and their elected representative became more tenuous, as the party leaders effectively controlled which candidates were awarded seats by manipulation of placement on the list; 'favourites' would be put higher. But even if electors were encouraged to vote for headline delegates well placed on the list, their wishes could easily be thwarted:

> 105 candidates winning United [Unified] Russia seats in the 2007 [Duma] election resigned shortly after their election and their seats passed to names lower down the party's list.[13]

Some of this may have been as a result of household-name candidates who took places in the Government, or were governors, but the effect is that:

---

[12] For details see N Munro and R Rose, 'A Guide to Russian elections', *Study in Public Policy number 428* (Aberdeen, University of Aberdeen Centre for the Study of Public Policy, 2007) at 17.

[13] R Rose and W Mishler, 'A supply-demand model of party-system institutionalization: the Russian case', *Study in Public Policy number 445* (Aberdeen, University of Aberdeen Centre for the Study of Public Policy, 2008) at 11.

Duma members are not immediately accountable to the electorate but to the party leader who puts them high enough up the party list to receive seats allocated to the party by the PR system. Any Duma member who leaves his or her party is thereby deemed to have resigned their Duma seat. In the words of the United Russia's general secretary, 'The Duma's place is not for political discussion but technical issues'.[14]

Under current arrangements, with Unified Russia's overwhelming majority, the Duma has turned into a rubber stamp for executive policy, so that, for example, such major changes as the length of the President's term of office (which required constitutional amendment) and the procedure for establishing the Chairman of the Constitutional Court (which required change in a federal constitutional law) were passed with very little discussion and no effective opposition.

Whether the Duma with its current party list system can be described as representative may be in doubt. There were systemic inequalities with the previous single-member seats, which had very different-sized constituencies.[15] Disproportion between the number of votes for a particular party and the seats allocated to it are inevitable in any system with a threshold,[16] but the current 7 per cent threshold is

> higher than in any democratic European PR [proportional representation] system and well above the vote share that either of Russia's more liberal pro-market parties could expect to win.[17]

One consequence of such electoral defeat is that a party which gains less than 4 per cent of the overall vote forfeits its deposit; less than 3 per cent loses its annual State subsidy of 5 roubles per vote received; and less than 2 per cent, must pay at commercial rates for otherwise free airtime allocated on State-owned media during the election campaign.[18]

These disincentives may be one factor in President Medvedev's reforms to electoral rules in April 2010 to find ways to encourage

[14] *Ibid* at 14, citing A Jack, 'Critics see no room for dissent in new Duma' (2004) *Financial Times* 5 February.

[15] See H Oversloot, 'On the inequality of the vote in the Russian Federation's State Duma elections' in F Feldbrugge and WB Simons (eds), *Human Rights in Russia and Eastern Europe* (The Hague, Nijhoff, 2002) 205.

[16] See Munro and Rose, above n 12, at 14, for a table of 'wasted votes'; as high as 43% in the 1995 Duma elections.

[17] Rose and Mishler, above n 13, at 11.

[18] R Coalson, 'Russia: Moscow Shifts From "Managed Democracy" To "Manual Control"' (2007) *Radio Free Europe/Radio Liberty Russia Report*, 6 December.

smaller parties to have a voice in the Duma, and in subject-level legisla-tures. The number of signatures required for registration for Duma elections is reduced if a party has a widespread presence at subject-level, and in subject-level elections parties that fail to pass the 7 per cent threshold but gain more than 5 per cent will be allocated one seat. Some commentators have raised doubts whether Medvedev's motivation stems from concern about the state of Russia's democracy, or whether he is driven more by a desire to widen his support base away from the Putin-led Unified Russia party. Whichever, the rules for forming the Duma may be changed again before the next elections in December 2011.

ii. *Political parties in Russia*

The development of a successful multi-party system is an ongoing problem in Russia. There was no strong historical tradition of political parties in pre-revolutionary Russia, and during the 70-odd years of Soviet rule independent pressure groups of any kind were not tolerated by the Communist Party of the Soviet Union (CPSU). The Communist Party itself was not a political party in the sense that that expression is used in Western-style democracies.[19] Organised on principles laid down by Lenin to create an effective vanguard for the working class, it had a restricted membership; only the brightest and best were to take on the responsibility for speeding history towards its inevitable conclusion of the achievement of communism. Anyone aspiring to membership needed personal recommendations from at least three existing members of at least five years' standing, and the decisions on applications required a two-thirds majority at both the primary Party organisation and the dis-trict or city Party committee confirming the decision. Only after suc-cessfully showing themselves as worthy during a mandatory one-year probation as a 'candidate member' could full membership be attained.

In many respects membership of the CPSU was more like member-ship of a disciplined religion than a political party in the Western liberal sense. Not only was the ideology of primary importance, but the expected standard of behaviour of 'new Socialist man (or woman)' touched all aspects of the individual's life. Although membership did bring privileges in the shape of access to clinics, special shops and so

---

[19] WE Butler, *Soviet Law*, 2nd edn (London, Butterworths, 1988) 163.

on, it also brought extra responsibilities, as members were expected to set a shining example of good behaviour as well as following the Party rules. Lenin even took the view that any Party member who committed a crime should be punished more severely by the courts than a non-member because of the higher standard of conduct expected.[20] In the developed Soviet system this would have been against the equality provision in the 1977 USSR Constitution; nevertheless, after establishing identity the first question put to an accused in a criminal case was '*Partinost*'?' – that is, 'Party membership?' The Party Rules (Article 12) allowed for expulsion of a Party member who had committed a crime, and in practice a Party member would likely be stripped of his or her membership before trial to save the Party embarrassment (an overall conviction rate of around 99 per cent meant acquittal was unlikely). Expulsion would in fact be an additional form of punishment, as it would disallow previously-enjoyed privileges. The high behavioural expectation meant that a Party member might also have to make difficult life choices. For example, he or she could sue for divorce like anyone else, but 'may find either the fact of or the grounds for divorce disclose conduct incompatible with continued party membership'.[21] Likewise, the Party controlled personnel through the *nomenklatura* system, whereby it nominated or approved appointment to all key positions. If Party members wished to leave *nomenklatura* posts they risked Party disapproval; and if the Party refused permission for them to resign, they might be put in the invidious position of having to choose whether to exercise their legal right to leave that post or retain Party membership.

There were Party Rules and a Party Manifesto, and Party members worked under Party discipline. Some of the vocabulary normally associated with political parties became associated with the CPSU, which has made it difficult for newly-developing political parties in Russia even to contemplate elaborating a 'party manifesto' for themselves. Added to this,

> [t]he key trend in Russian party politics since 1999 is the emergence of parties that lack a clear ideological orientation, are able to rely on administrative resources and favorable media coverage, and whose overriding rationale is to provide support for the president.[22]

[20] *Ibid.*

[21] *Ibid.*

[22] D White, 'Victims of a managed democracy? Explaining the electoral decline of the Yabloko party' (2007) 15 *Demokatizatsiya* 209 at 221.

Rather than any ideological framework, there has been a very strong tendency for post-communist political groupings in Russia to be centred around particular lead individuals and their personal preferences. The *Yabloko* (meaning 'apple' in Russian) party even coined its name as an acronym of its original founders: Yavlinsky, Boldyrev and Lukin.

One resulting problem is highlighted by Alena Ledeneva as the

> [w]eakness of party politics: there are no stable party images in Russia because of the short party history and the specifics of the political party formation process. Due to the political instability of the 1990s, reputations of politicians in Russia are volatile: they are easy to create and easy to ruin.[23]

This approach to political parties is problematic. It does not give the electorate scope to choose candidates who approximate to the individual voter's viewpoint if the voter does not know what the candidate 'stands for', and it also undermines consistency in political life as the various personalist groups form and reform at the whim of the main 'names' to suit the leaders' personal ambitions. Also, until recently, there has also been a lack of any system of 'party discipline', with no requirement that a Duma deputy stay in the party that nominated him or her for election.

In recent times there appears to have been the cynical creation of a 'party of power', that is, a party whose main purpose is to support the Executive. The most recent is Unified Russia. To give a semblance of competitive party politics, a 'loyal opposition' in the form of A Just Russia (*Spravedlivaia Rossiia*, sometimes translated as 'Fair Russia') was created in October 2006 by a merger of three existing parties. Its role 'as Putin's left foot' meant that:

> Russia ... [has] become possibly the first country in history with a two-party system in which both parties share the same overriding principle, [namely] that the executive is always right.[24]

Its leader, Sergei Mironov, is the Chairman of the Federation Council. Any serious opposition parties, such as Yabloko, have found themselves unable to get media time:

---

[23] AV Ledeneva, *How Russia Really Works: The Informal Practices that Shaped Post-Soviet Politics and Business* (Ithaca, NY, Cornell University Press, 2006) 45.

[24] P Moore, 'As Part of 'Imitation Democracy'(2006) 10(200) *Radio Free Europe/ Radio Liberty Newsline*, 30 October, citing *Moscow Times*, 30 October 2006.

Without effective opposition parties there can be no real prospect of the alternation of power, a key requirement of a functioning democracy. The reality in Russia, however, is that opposition parties have increasingly found themselves frozen out of the political process, starved of access to the media, and competing against pro-presidential parties able to tap into massive administrative resources.[25]

There have also been serious and persistent suggestions of outright electoral fraud, as well as complaints about inequalities such as in access to media, highlighted in successive OSCE election monitoring reports. These factors, along with the reduction in the number of effective political parties, undermine democracy in Russia and public perception of its value:

> Instead of growing complexity in the political system, which would testify to the evolution of the democratic system, its *simplification* is observable in Russia. The majority of citizens, according to sociological surveys, think, first, that the State Duma and the Federation Council are engaged in unnecessary activities and, second, that the dominant position of the United Russia faction in the State Duma is legitimate, giving the President's [Putin's] popularity.
>
> The previously described situation is explained to a considerable degree by the *absence of a genuine multi-party system in Russia*. Indeed, almost all of the Russian parties are either pre-election projects or elite groupings known only in Moscow and lacking support structures in the region.[26]

In April 2010 Medvedev instigated reforms to encourage smaller parties, but the main focus is on subject-level legislatures. Russia has yet to develop a functioning political party system and this undermines any effective representative role played by Federal Assembly.

iii. Formation of the Federation Council

By definition, half of the Federation Council membership comprises representatives from the legislature of each federation subject, and the other half representatives from each federation subject's executive.

---

[25] White, above n 22, at 210. See also M Bader, 'Understanding Party Politics in the Former Soviet Union: Authoritarianism, Volatility, and Incentive Structures' (2009) 17 *Democratizatsiya* 100.

[26] A Zakharov, 'The Russian Parliament and Vladimir Putin's Presidency' in K Malfleit and R Laenen (eds), *Elusive Russia. Current Developments in Russian State Identity under President Putin* (Leuven, Leuven University Press, 2007) 73 at 82–83 (emphasis in original).

Exceptionally, the first Federation Council was put in place entirely by first-past-the-post elections held on 12 December 1993, on the same day that the Constitution was adopted. Electing all the Council members at this point got over the problem that many of the subject-level legislatures had been disbanded followed Yel'tsin's attack on the Russian Supreme Soviet, so could not have nominated members.[27]

The new Constitution established special transitional arrangements, one of which was that the both the Duma and the Federation Council would sit initially for a term of two years (Constitution, Section II, Concluding and Transitional Provisions, provision 7). That period was within a week of coming to an end before the procedure was agreed to re-form the Federation Council. President Yel'tsin advocated a system of appointment, whilst the incumbent members were happy to try their chances at re-election.[28] The political compromise reached in December 1995 was that from the beginning of 1996 the Federation Council would consist of the executive head of each federation subject (governor or equivalent) *ex officio*, and the chairman of each subject-level legislature. Part of the package was that governors should be elected, rather than appointed by the President, to give effect to the principle of democracy. Following this reform, it was observed that membership of the Federation Council acted as a 'kind of political school for regional leaders and a means through which they move to the national level of politics'.[29] The governors tended to dominate in discussions over the chairmen of the legislatures, but because of governors' interests elsewhere, achieving a quorum was problematic even though the Federation Council sat for only one week in four.[30] At some points this difficulty of mustering the required quorum was so acute – particularly for federal constitutional laws, which require approval by three-quarters of the Federation Council members – that there was resort to postal voting. This was necessary, for instance, for the passage of the federal constitutional law on the Judicial System in 1996. The quorum issue was exacerbated by the fact that, unlike in the Duma, there is no mechanism in the Federation Council for a proxy vote for absent members.

---

[27] See R Ortung, 'New, but transitional, Federation Council starts working' (2002) 7(5) *EastWest Institute Russian Regional Report*, 6 February.

[28] J Henderson, 'Election time in Russia' (1996) 2 *European Public Law* 63 at 65.

[29] Busygina, above n 2, at 58.

[30] Ware, above n 9.

Under Yel'tsin's presidency, the Federation Council initially served as a buffer between the Duma and President, as the Duma was dominated by the Communist Party of the Russian Federation (CPRF), which tended to act as an opposition to governmental plans. The Federation Council

> often rejected leftist bills approved by the lower chamber, saving the president from having to veto them. In fulfilling this task, the Federation Council was seen as generally supporting Yeltsin, who had been willing to make extensive concessions to the regional leaders to preserve his own power. However, as Yeltsin's health deteriorated and the most powerful governors began jockeying for position in the post-Yeltsin era, the Federation Council began to oppose the president on important issues.[31]

As part of his package of centralising reforms, in 2000 newly-elected President Putin negotiated new rules for forming the Federation Council.[32] A new federal law on its formation was passed.[33] It established that half the members of the Federation Council would be elected by secret ballot by subject-level legislatures (and could be similarly recalled). The other seats on the Council would be filled not by the governors *ex officio*, as previously, but by their nominees. The chosen nominees would be appointed by gubernatorial decree, provided that the local legislature did not veto them by a two-thirds qualified majority. Recall was at the whim of the governor.

> The response to Putin's proposals were a little mixed. Members of the Duma's federation affairs committee had earlier complained that a likely result was regions being represented by the 'lovers and nephews' of incumbent Governors. A number of Governors and legislative council chairmen were clearly prepared to bow to the inevitable, but wanted to retain a satisfactory degree of control over their replacements. As the chairman of Tomsk regional legislative council reportedly said, 'Our situation is like that of a bride on her wedding night. Whether she wears her underwear or not, what will happen will happen. We will no longer gather in our present form.'[34]

---

[31] Ortung, above n 27.

[32] See J Henderson, 'Redefining Russia's Federal Structure?' (2000) 6 *European Public Law* 496; C Ross, 'Putin's federal reforms and the consolidation of federalism in Russia: one step forward, two steps back!' (2003) 36 *Communist and Post-Communist Studies* 29 at 38.

[33] Butler, above n 4, at 248.

[34] Henderson, above n 32, at 502–03, citing (2000) 4 *RFE/RL Newsline* 126, from (2000) *Kommersant-Daily*, 29 June.

Putin's aim may have been to reduce the influence of regional governors in federal lawmaking, although practically speaking 'the Governors remain[ed] strong in their regions, allowing them to block the implementation of federal laws'.[35] Governors were content to relinquish their obligation to attend Federation Council meetings in Moscow in exchange for membership of the newly-established State Council (see chapter four), which had no constitutional position or executive power but was chaired by the President, so members were guaranteed easy access to the ear of the Head of State and thus a new lobbying opportunity.

As a result of the Putin reforms, the Federation Council's composition changed noticeably from 1 January 2002, when the reforms came into full effect and all the old members relinquished their seats. On average, the new members were younger and had a Moscow business background, because governors nominated representatives whom they felt would 'know the ropes' in Moscow in order to achieve the optimal results for their federal subject. There was also talk of an influx of oligarchs (powerful individuals with immense personal wealth based on natural resources, acquired during Russia's transition to a market economy). There was a corresponding reduction in personal links between the representative and the federation subject; opponents of the new formation procedure alleged that some Federation Council members had never even visited the place they purported to represent. There was also increased turnover. In the 32 months since the new system was introduced, '69 of the 89 regions have recalled or replaced one of their [Federation Council members and] . . . 131 of the [then] 178 members of the Federation Council have changed'.[36]

This rather alarming turnover rate was reduced by a change in November 2004 in the rules for formation of the Federation Council. A list of grounds for recall of representatives was introduced, reducing the scope for governors and subject-level legislatures to act on a whim.[37] The amended rules also required subject-level authorities to appoint their representatives within three months, 'a change inspired by the fact

---

[35] Ortung, above n 27.

[36] JA Corwin, 'House of Lords or House of Valets?' (2004) 31 *Radio Free Europe/ Radio Liberty Russian Political Weekly*, 6 August, citing *Kommersant-Daily*, 2 August 2004.

[37] L Belin, 'Federation council seeks to reduce turnover' (2004) 222 *Radio Free Europe/Radio Liberty Newsline*, 29 November, citing *Regions.ru*.

that Chukotka Autonomous Okrug has left one of its seats in the upper chamber vacant for nearly two years.'[38]

Lack of attendance remained an issue, although possibly for reasons different from those of the busy governors:

> Business trips also frequently take senators away from Moscow. France has been a popular destination with some 33 trips already logged. Some senators also traveled to Las Vegas, Nevada, for a congress of international youth organizations and to Portugal to look into 'security questions in the Western Mediterranean.'[39]

Some illicit steps were taken to cover up for absences. In 2003 there were media reports of 'voting' by two Federation Council members who were out of the country at the time of adoption by a narrow majority of amendments to the law on communications.[40]

One probably unintended effect of the Putin reform was increased central cost. Under the previous system, Federation Council members who were governors, or chairs of subject-level legislatures, received their salary from their locality. Under the reformed system, not only were there relocation and increased housing costs, but pay rates proposed to give parity with Duma members would double the bill to the central budget.[41] There were also allegations of manipulation of membership:

> Accusations of the buying and selling of seats in the council have been rife since the very beginning of the chamber's transition to the new rules. In January 2001, then Federation Council Chairman Yegor Stroev said during an open session, 'I'm afraid that it's not apartments [that are] being bought but seats in the Federation Council' during a heated discussion over whether the latest batch of representatives even knew the location of the regions that they were representing.[42]

The last issue was addressed by an amendment to the Federation Council law in 2007, imposing on new members a 10-year residency requirement in the region that they represent, although existing mem-

[38] *Ibid.*

[39] JA Corwin, 'Is the upper chamber plagued by absenteeism?' (2002) 237 *Radio Free Europe/Radio Liberty Newsline*, 19 December, citing *Komsomolskaya Pravda* of 17 December 2002.

[40] JA Corwin, 'Vote rigging charged in upper legislative chamber' (2003) 123 *Radio Free Europe/Radio Liberty Newsline*, 1 July.

[41] JA Corwin, 'New federation council to be costly' (2001) 7 *Radio Free Europe/ Radio Liberty Newsline*, 11 January.

[42] Corwin, above n 36.

bers are exempt, as are military officers and prosecutors of at least 10 years' standing.

The change in membership brought about by Putin's reforms resulted in a change in the role for the Federation Council. It became difficult to assert that it represented federal interests when half its members were career negotiators with

> no political weight and their names are new on Russia's political scene . . . We observe not only atomisation of the Federation Council, but its transformation into a lobbying body. The deputies have turned into political managers employed by the regional executive and legislative bodies: the Governor can easily dismiss his political employees.[43]

Putin's reforms made the Federation Council 'boring'.[44] Its very *raison d'être* was questioned by Samara Oblast Governor Konstantin Titov in May 2004. Because of the huge majority of the Unified Russia party in the Duma, particularly after the 2007 elections but even before, the role of the Federation Council in debating legislation was nullified. Any dissent could easily be overridden in the Duma, 'leaving the Federation Council little to do besides appoint judges and prosecutors and declare war'.[45] Certainly its rate of passing legislation increased dramatically:

> On the last day of its first spring session in July 2002, it broke all previous records for productivity and passed 26 bills during a 6½-hour session. Among the more than two dozen bills were landmark legislation, including laws on selling agricultural land, bankruptcy, and alternative civil service [alternative service for conscientious objectors to military conscription].[46]

As a second chamber, the Federation Council has thus become ineffective as a major check on legislation. That is not to say that it is completely ineffectual, but under current conditions members tend to influence policy more by individual conciliation and negotiation rather than opposing legislative bills proposed by other State agencies.

---

[43]   Busygina, above n 2, at 58.
[44]   *Nezavisimaia gazeta*, 24 July 2001, as cited in JA Corwin, 'Has the Federation Council finally been tamed?' (2001) 22 *Radio Free Europe/Radio Liberty Russian Federation Report*, 25 July.
[45]   JA Corwin, 'Governor says Federation Council, State Council no longer needed' (2004) 8 *Radio Free Europe/Radio Newsline*, 14 May, citing an interview with utro.ru on 13 May 2004.
[46]   Corwin, above n 36.

Under President Medvedev there have been further developments.[47] According to *Radio Free Europe/Radio Liberty* reporter Mikhail Sokolov, writing in February 2009:

> Over the last three months, a law has been passed under which the Federation Council will be formed exclusively from deputies of regional and local legislatures. From now on, Governors must either plan far enough ahead to get their preferred candidates onto the party lists for regional elections in advance, or else hastily organize a vacancy in the legislature (perhaps through a convenient resignation) and a rigged by-election to install their chosen ones.[48]

This will be the fourth change since its establishment in 1993 in the procedure for determining the membership of the Federation Council, to take effect from 1 January 2011.[49]

However, there are some elements of continuity, at least as regards the Federation Council after 1995. First, it does not run to fixed terms. Each member's individual but renewable term will correspond to the term set by the agency that elected or appointed that member. Put another way, the Russian Federation Council has a 'rolling membership'. The whole Council is not subject to a periodic election prompting an assessment of all members. Any member might lose his or her Federation Council seat through early recall (though on limited grounds, as noted above) by the local governor or legislature that put him or her into office.

Secondly, there has been considerable continuity in the post of Chairman. The first Chairman, Vladimir Shumeiko, stood down at the end of the transitional two years of the Federation Council's first convocation, but after that there was no limit on the length of time a Chairman might serve. When the Federation Council was formed again for an unlimited term on 23 January 1996, it elected as Chairman Egor [Yegor] Stroev, the leftist governor of the Orel region south of Moscow. The terms of office of the Chairman and his deputies (and the chair-

---

[47] See WE Pomeranz, 'Medvedev and the Contested Constitutional Underpinnings of Russia's Power Vertical' (2009) 17 *Democratizatsiya* 179.

[48] M Sokolov, 'The Words And Deeds Of Dmitry Medvedev' (2009) *Radio Free Europe/Radio Liberty Commentary*, 3 February, available at <http://www.rferl.org/Content/Commentary_Words_Deeds_Dmitry_Medvedev/1378486.html>, accessed 14 August 2010.

[49] '*Istoriia*', at <http://www.council.gov.ru/about/history/index.html>, accessed 14 August 2010.

men of the committees and their deputies) were linked to regional elections in accordance with amendments to the Rules of the Federation Council adopted on 11 November 1999. Before that, there were no restrictions on their terms of office. Stroev stayed in post until voluntarily standing down towards the end of 2001, following Putin's reforms removing governors from the Federation Council by the beginning of 2002.[50] However, he was elected to the lifetime appointment of 'Honour[able] Chairman of the Council of Federation' and he and

> VF Shumeiko, Chairman of the Council of Federation of the first convocation, are granted personal seats in the session hall and cabinets inside the chamber's building. They received special identification cards and breastplates. They both enter the Council of Federation with deliberative functions and enjoy some other privileges.[51]

The third Chairman, Sergei Mironov, first sat in the Federation Council on 13 June 2001 as a representative of the St Petersburg Legislative Assembly. Six months later, he was elected Chairman of the Federation Council, and was re-elected at the end of January 2003 (after re-election by the St Petersburg Legislative Assembly as its Federation Council representative).[52] Despite being the head of A Just Russia, the political party established to be the 'loyal opposition' (see section II.A.ii. above), Mironov has been seen as being close to Putin as one of the 'St Petersburg clan', and under his chairmanship the Federation Council has had amicable relations with both the Executive and the Duma.

Thirdly, in contrast to the Duma, the rules of the Federation Council do not allow its members to form factions. Individual members are not forbidden to be members of political parties, but they are expected to refrain from pushing party agendas in the chamber. The ban on parties in the Council did not stop the formation, on 12 March 2001 at the instigation of Chairman Mironov, of a 'group' calling itself 'Federation', with the aim of supporting President Putin.[53] However, the influence of

---

[50] 'Yegor Stroyev quits under Putin reforms' (2001) *The Russia Journal*, 4 December.

[51] 'Status and Powers of the Council of Federation of the Federal Assembly of the Russian Federation', at <http://www.council.gov.ru/eng/about/status/index.html>, accessed 14 August 2010.

[52] 'Biography', at <http://mironov.info/Biography>, accessed 25 May 2009.

[53] 'Federation Council: if you can't beat 'em, join 'em' (2001) 7(55) *Centre for Defence Information Monitor*, 20 March.

party politics has generally been much more attenuated in the Federation Council than in the Duma, not only because of this rule against factions but also because until recently most Russian political parties had little influence outside Moscow and the Duma elections. Local elections tended to based more on local personality contests than on rivalry between political parties. Recently some moves have been made to encourage political party formation in the regions, but so far the influence back to the Federation Council has not been great.

B. Legislative activity of the Federal Assembly

The Federal Assembly passes legislation on matters within the jurisdiction of the federation as a whole (Article 71), or within the joint jurisdiction of the federation and the federation subjects (Article 72). Such legislation comprises either constitutional amendment, or federal constitutional law or federal law, and there are slightly different procedures for the adoption of each, outlined below. (Federal constitutional law was an innovation of the 1993 Constitution, outlined in chapter three.) No legislation may contradict the Constitution (Article 15(1)), although in the case of conflict between any law (even the Constitution) and an international treaty to which Russia is a party, the treaty provisions take precedence (Article 16(4), see chapter three). Federal laws may not be contrary to federal constitutional laws (Article 76(3)) and all have direct effect throughout the territory (Article 76), at least in theory.

i. Constitutional amendment

In chapter three, attention was drawn to the novel provisions for constitutional amendment, particularly in relation to the three entrenched chapters of the Constitution which cannot be amended by the Federal Assembly but require a specially convened Constitutional Assembly. Even the non-entrenched chapters can be amended only by a complex procedure, also outlined in chapter three. The one exception to these stringent requirements is the procedure to change the name of a federation subject in the list in Article 65. If the requisite process for voluntary amalgamation based on the December 2001 federal constitutional law has been followed, the change can be recorded by a simple federal law or, in its absence, a presidential edict.

ii. Federal constitutional law

The Constitution defines a number of areas to be regulated by a federal constitutional law.[54] These are: the conditions for an 'extraordinary situation' which limits individual rights and freedoms, or a military situation (martial law); the procedure for admission to the Russian Federation and formation within it of a new federal subject, or change of status of an existing subject; the description and use of the State flag, arms and anthem; the procedure for a referendum; the Plenipotentiary for Human Rights; the Government; the judicial system; the Constitutional Court; Supreme Court; Highest *Arbitrazh* Court; and other federal courts; and the procedure for invoking a Constitutional Assembly.

Federal constitutional law requires qualified majorities for adoption (two-thirds and three-quarters in the Duma and Federation Council respectively) but then cannot be vetoed by the President. The successful passage of all these important laws has been a prolonged affair. While Yel'tsin was President, with a largely oppositional Duma, federal constitutional laws were passed on the Constitutional Court in June 1994, on the Highest *Arbitrazh* Court in April 1995 and in October on the procedure for a referendum; on the judicial system in December 1996, on the Plenipotentiary for Human Rights in February 1997[55] and in December on the Government, and then in June 1999 on Military Courts. Thus within about three years of the adoption of Constitution, the main provisions for the judicial system were in place, although notably not the Federal Constitutional Law on the Supreme Court, which at the time of writing in August 2010 has still not yet been adopted. The federal constitutional law on the Government was passed three and a half years into Russia's new constitutional regime.

In December 2000, under President Putin, federal constitutional laws on the State arms, flag and national anthem were passed.[56] More substantively, the laws defining the conditions for an 'extraordinary situation' and a 'military situation' were passed in May 2001 and January 2002 respectively. In December 2001, the law 'On the procedure for admission to the Russian Federation and formation within it of a new federation subject' was adopted, and there have since been five federal

---

[54]   Arts 56, 65(2), 66(5), 70, 84, 87(3), 88, 103(1)(e), 114(2), 118(3), 128 and 135.

[55]   See J Henderson, 'The Russian Ombudsman' (1998) 4 *European Public Law* 184 at 187, 'two years and seven months after its first reading'.

[56]   J Henderson, 'Signs and Portents' (2002) 8 *European Public Law* 321.

constitutional laws changing the status of a federal subject as a result of voluntary amalgamations (plus three amending those).

The set of all federal constitutional laws specified to be passed is almost complete. The exceptions, as mentioned, are the law on the Supreme Court and a law on the procedure for invoking a Constitutional Assembly. Constitutional amendment within Chapters 3 to 8 is through federal constitutional law plus approval by at least two-thirds of the subject-level legislatures. As noted in chapter three, in December 2008 President Medvedev easily triggered this procedure to extend the presidential and Duma terms, and to make minor changes to the Duma's powers.

The system of adopting federal constitutional laws on important topics is designed to allow an opportunity for more thoughtful debate on their details. This certainly occurred in the 1990s, although there may be doubt as to whether the same careful scrutiny has been given since 2000 to federal constitutional laws, or the quite numerous amendments to them, or whether the 'will of the tsar' has easily prevailed in an overwhelmingly supportive Legislature.

iii. Federal law

Federal law is passed to cover the main fields over which the federation has jurisdiction. These include the main branches of law in Russia, which are codified. There are currently 28 codes of law listed in the legal document bank on the Presidential website: Civil Law (in four parts); Civil Procedure; Criminal Procedure; Criminal Law; Criminal Enforcement; Administrative Violations; Labour Law; Family Law; Customs; Air Law; Internal Water Transport; Merchant Marine; Land; Housing; and Budgetary Laws. The Codes for *Arbitrazh* Procedure; Water; City Planning; Tax; and Forest Law are in their second generation (the reduction in the number of fire rangers following the 2006 Forest Code was a factor in the devastating forest fires in central Russia in summer 2010). Codes are passed using the same procedure as any other federal law, and do not have any special place in the hierarchy of laws. Nevertheless, it is generally expected that other legislation will conform to the codes, and in particular the Civil Code on its own terms requires this.

In some branches of law that are in joint federal and subject-level jurisdiction, legislation defining the 'Fundamental Principles' will be passed at federal level which subject-level legislation must incorporate but can augment.[57]

iv. The legislative process

The outline of procedure for the passage of federal law by the Federal Assembly is set in the Constitution, with much added detail in the Reglaments of the Duma[58] and the Federation Council.[59] All federal legislation begins as a bill in the Duma. The right of legislative initiative in Russia is quite broad, although not as broad as it was in Soviet times. It belongs not only to the President, the Federation Council and its members, Duma deputies, the Government and the legislative agencies of federation subjects, but also 'with regard to questions of their jurisdiction' to the Constitutional Court, the Supreme Court and the Highest *Arbitrazh* Court (Article 104(1)). By contrast, under the 1977 USSR Constitution, Article 113, the right of legislative initiative belonged not only to all such equivalent agencies as existed, but also to the Procurator-General and 'social organisations through their all-union agencies'. This latter formula covered the trades unions and the CPSU. Important social legislation might well be jointly presented by Party and Government, and labour law traditionally had trade union involvement.

In practice, in modern Russia an increasing amount of draft legislation emanates from the Executive:

> Before 2001 the Duma deputies initiated more than half of all bills, but in 2001 a symbolic boundary was crossed: the President and the Government outstripped the members of Parliament in lawmaking by raising more than 60 percent of all bills for consideration in the lower house.[60]

A report 'On the State of Legislation in the Russian Federation', published in 2006 by the Federation Council, included figures on the sources

---

[57] See eg Fundamental Principles of Legislation on the Notariat of 11 February 1993 (as amended) in Butler, above n 4, at 813.

[58] Adopted by Duma decree, 22 January 1998, and amended, particularly in December 2003 and July 2004. English translation as amended to April 2009 in Butler, above n 4, at 280. The Reglament in translation is over 100 pages long.

[59] Section II of Federation Council's Reglament, '*Reglament: chast' II*', at <http://council.gov.ru/about/agenda/ch2/index.html>, accessed 18 August 2010.

[60] Zakharov, above n 26, at 81.

of bills and their success rates in 2004–06.[61] Over that period, the number of laws approved which had been proposed by the President each year and their percentage of all laws was 30 (13.16 per cent of the 2004 laws), 35 (14.83 per cent of the 2005 laws) and 26 (9.39 per cent of the 2006 laws). Furthermore, from 1996 to 2006, 'every draft law from the President' considered by the Federal Assembly was approved.[62] The equivalent figures for Government-drafted laws were for 2004, 67 (28.07 per cent); for 2005, 84 (35.59 per cent); and for 2006, 106 (28.27 per cent).[63] Consistently for each of the three years, 22 laws passed had been put forward by a single Duma deputy, whereas one Federation Council member successfully initiated a law in 2004, three in 2005 and none in 2006. The Federation Council as a whole did little more, with tallies of two, one and zero respectively for each of the years covered. The Report notes that nearly two-thirds of laws passed were amending existing legislation.[64]

Submission of a draft law entails a good deal of paperwork, although since November 1999 it is accepted in electronic format. The text submitted must be accompanied by an explanatory memorandum, a list of other laws which would be affected, a 'financial-economic substantiation' if the law will entail financial expenditure, and an opinion of the Government if the legislation would have an impact on the federal budget (Constitution, Article 104(3)). This collection is sent to the Duma Chairman who delegates to the 'profile committee' to register receipt and check for conformity with the set requirements. The Council of the Duma then allocates each draft to an appropriate Duma committee to be responsible for it, includes the bill in the Duma's draft work plan and sends copies to interested State agencies for their reactions. The Reglament lists such interested agencies as Duma committees, commissions and factions, the President, Federation Council, Government, the Public Chamber and also the three top Courts with regard to questions of their jurisdiction.

---

[61] SM Mironov and GE Burbulis (eds), 'On the State of Legislation in the Russian Federation', available at <http://www.council.gov.ru/eng/rep/index.html>, accessed 18 August 2010.

[62] *Ibid* at 159.

[63] *Ibid* at 143.

[64] *Ibid* at 144.

There are 32 Duma committees listed on the Duma website.[65] As in many jurisdictions, it is in the committees where the most serious work is carried out. Some of them parallel the areas of responsibility of government ministries – for example, defence, security, international affairs, health protection and education – whilst some clearly are concerned with specific fields of legislation, such as for 'constitutional legislation and State construction', 'civil, criminal, *arbitrazh*, and procedural legislation'. Others deal with particular sectional interests, such as the Committee for Problems in the North and Far East, and the Committee for Affairs of Veterans. The committees have between 12 and 35 members, and composition is proportional representation of factions in the Duma. Every deputy (except the Chairman of the Duma) must have a place on one, but only one, of the committees. Committee chairmen, vice-chairmen and committee members are recommended by factions, and their positions and the overall committee composition confirmed by a majority vote of the whole Duma. In earlier times, when there was a wider range of political parties in the Duma, the start of each new Duma convocation saw complex horse-trading between the different groups as they jockeyed for positions on important committees.[66] Even now, membership of a strategic committee is an important factor for an aspiring politician in Russia, and particularly as chairman, when they can generate a high media profile.

When considering a draft bill, a particular committee may consult State agencies and other organisations, and get scholarly expert evaluations, such as from the Duma's own Legal Administration which can comment on the draft's correspondence with existing law, its internal consistency and so on. Sometimes the committee creates a special working group of deputies, representatives of the originating agency, experts and other interested bodies who can bring specialist knowledge to the task.

When it arrives at the plenary Duma meeting for its first reading, a draft law has been already considered and prepared by its Duma committee. A representative of the originating agency should be present. At the first reading the overall conception is discussed, as well as its

[65] '*Komitety i komissii*', at <http://www.duma.gov.ru/index.jsp?t=comitet/index. html>, accessed 18 August 2010.

[66] Merritt, above n 1, at 165, gives the example of 'a dramatic walkout of minority parties in early 2000 when the two largest legislative blocs, the Communists and Unity, found common ground in dividing committee chairperson positions'.

conformity with the Constitution, urgency and practical significance. Assuming the draft passes its first reading, a period of at least two weeks is set for submission of suggested amendments to the relevant committee. The committee considers these before presenting the original and a revised draft to the Duma for a second reading, along with recommendations for adoption or rejection of specific amendments. Then the committee gets the agreed draft back for a final polishing with participation of the Duma Legal Administration. That final draft goes for its third reading, where it is either adopted or rejected as a whole. Adoption is by a majority of the total number of deputies for a federal law; two-thirds for a federal constitutional law or amendment of the Constitution. There are special considerations for the annual budget law, which is regulated in greater detail and routinely goes through four readings.[67]

The draft is then sent within five days to the Federation Council. That has 27 committees, which do not exactly parallel those of the Duma but nevertheless span the fields of interest of potential legislation, and the appropriate committee may consider a draft in detail. Not all draft laws are actively considered by the Federation Council, but the Constitution specifies that it must consider a draft if it relates to the federal budget; taxes; 'financial, currency, credit, customs regulation, and monetary emission'; ratification and denunciation of international treaties; status and defence of the Russian State boundary; and war and peace (Constitution, Article 106). Otherwise the Federation Council can choose whether or not to consider a particular draft. If it does not reject a draft within 14 days of receipt, it is deemed to be approved (Constitution, Article 105(4)). Alternatively the Federation Council may actively approve a draft bill, by a straight majority for a federal law or by three-quarters for a federal constitutional law. If the draft is rejected, it returns to the Duma which may override the Federation Council decision by a qualified two-thirds majority. Alternatively, a conciliation commission may be established consisting of members of both chambers, tasked to produce a compromise bill for further Duma consideration. These conciliation commissions are a useful 'back-door' through which the Federation Council can influence legislation.

A federal law that has successfully made its way through both chambers of the Federal Assembly is then sent within five days to the President for signature. He has 14 days to sign and promulgate it, or to

---

[67] WE Butler, *Russian Law*, 3rd edn (Oxford, Oxford University Press, 2009) 357.

exercise his veto. In the latter case, the two chambers of the Federal Assembly reconsider, and may override the veto by a two-thirds majority in each chamber, at which point the President is obliged to sign within seven days and promulgate the law. There is no provision for presidential veto in the case of a federal constitutional law or constitutional amendment.

The Constitution requires laws to be published and 'unpublished laws shall not be applied' (Article 15(3)). This is an important statement of principle, given that during Soviet times there was no such restriction.[68] In November 1990 the USSR Constitutional Supervision Committee issued an opinion that unpublished legislation which affected individual rights and liberties would lose force, and as a result a number of hitherto secret legislative acts were published in the official *Vedomosti*. However, as noted in chapter three, the Constitutional article must be read carefully. It requires laws – *zakony* – to be published but, for example, governmental decrees, which do not affect 'man and citizen' but impact legal entities, need not be published in order to be applied.[69]

Procedure in the Federal Assembly, particularly in the plenary sessions of the legislative process, is quite formal, although debate can be lively and physical confrontation is not unknown.[70] Contributions from the floor are strictly timed. The timetabling procedure makes it difficult for the Federal Assembly to react quickly to emergencies such as the first Chechen war.

C. Other powers of the Federal Assembly

i. Oversight

The Constitution defines the Federal Assembly as the 'representative and legislative agency' (Article 94) and, apart from budgetary control and

---

[68] See Butler, above n 19, at 57.

[69] The Federal Law on the Procedure for Publication and Entry into Force of Legislation of the Federal Assembly is in Butler, above n 4, at 67; discussion of current publication issues is in Butler, above n 67, at 115.

[70] Famously on 30 March 2005 between Vladimir Zhirinovskii and Motherland faction deputies: R Coalson, 'Duma Looking at Ways of Preventing Deputies from Fighting' (2005) 9 *Radio Free Europe/Radio Liberty Newsline*, 7 April. The proposed new service would 'comprise three to five "intellectually and physically well-developed men" wearing "clothing that inspires respect"': Coalson, citing *RIA-Novosti*, 6 April.

impeachment, before Medvedev's amendments in 2009 made no explicit mention of oversight of the Government or executive bodies,[71] and did not directly grant the Federal Assembly any rights to oversee other government bodies or enforce federal and constitutional laws.[72] The Federal Assembly can exercise indirect methods of oversight, although the position of the 'power ministries' which are under the direct aegis of the President is unclear, and the Presidential Administration is outside its purview.[73]

The Duma monitors spending of federal funds by the Government and other organisations, including companies, by assigning the Accounting Chamber (*Chetnaia Palata*, also known as the Chamber of Accounts) to audit their accounts. The Accounting Chamber is set up jointly by the Duma and the Federation Council. The Duma appoints and relieves from office both the Chairman and half the auditors; while the Federation Council appoints and relieves from office the Deputy Chair and the other auditors. The Accounting Chamber reviews federal accounts, and as a result of its findings the Duma may issue decrees pointing out unsatisfactory situations. But the Duma has no power to take direct action and, for example, 'There was not a single response' to its efforts in 1998 to raise in various decrees the issue of serious mismanagement by Boris Brevnov, head of United Energy System, and others.[74] It is unlikely that matters would be different now. The Federation Council reviews the work of the Accounting Chamber, subjecting its annual report to detailed analysis and making recommendations for improvement, although it cannot force action on any recommendations.

Another indirect mechanism for financial oversight by the Duma is through its command of the Central Bank. It appoints and relieves from office the Chairman, and every May hears the Bank's annual report, which the Duma refers to the President but also reviews itself. The Duma receives the Bank's draft annual monetary and credit policy plans for discussion in plenary session, and can initiate a Bank audit. In prac-

[71] S Whitmore, 'Parliamentary Oversight in Putin's Neo-patrimonial State. Watchdogs or Show-dogs? (2010) 62(6) *Europe-Asia Studies* 99 at 1003. Whitmore points out (*ibid*, fn 8) that this is not unusual; there is no provision for a constitutional oversight role in the US or German Constitutions.

[72] I Grankin, 'The Special Powers of Russia's Parliament' (2001) 9 *Democratizatsiya* 26 at 36.

[73] Whitmore, above n 71, at 1004.

[74] Grankin, above n 72, at 36.

tice the degree to which any of these mechanisms currently have a practical impact on Russia's labyrinthine fiscal structure may be doubted; nevertheless it is something that could be developed in the future.

Apart from financial monitoring, the Duma is involved in appointment of the Government Chairman, although as seen in chapter four, the check-and-balance system for Duma consideration of the candidate selected by the President does not work well. The President's power to dissolve the Duma if it repeatedly rejects his candidate renders it impotent to take a sustained stand on this issue against a determined President. By contrast, a determined Federation Council could thwart a President over the appointment to and relief from office of the Procurator-General, although when this happened in relation Procurator-General Skuratov, Yel'tsin bypassed the impasse by installing his choice as acting Procurator-General and sidelining Skuratov during the stand-off period.

The main tools in the armoury of the Federal Assembly against the Executive are impeachment of the President and motions of no confidence in the Government (see also chapter four, section IV.). Impeachment proceedings are instigated by an accusation adopted by a majority in the Duma. The decision whether or not to impeach the President is taken by a two-thirds majority in the Federation Council, after stringent procedural hurdles have been crossed.[75] No Russian President has yet been impeached; proceedings were initiated against President Yel'tsin in April–May 1998 but not carried through.[76] Questions of confidence in the Government may be triggered in two different ways, as discussed in chapter four. On the one hand, the Duma may adopt a motion of no confidence. If the President opposes this and the Duma adopts a second motion within three months, the President can choose whether to dismiss the Government or dissolve the Duma. So far, no motion of no confidence in the Government has been adopted, although the Duma has recommended to the President that particular individuals holding ministerial office are unsatisfactory; at the present time the Duma has no power to enter a motion of no confidence against specific individuals. On the other hand, the Government Chairman may himself raise a question of confidence at the Duma. To do this, he issues a report that is circulated amongst the deputies for immediate consideration. If the report is rejected by a majority vote, the Duma deputies must immediately vote on

[75] *Ibid* at 33.
[76] See account in Merritt, above n 1, at 169.

the general issue of confidence in the Government. If the majority express no confidence, the matter goes to the President who, within seven days, either dismisses the Government or dissolves the Duma. Thus again, the Duma is hostage to the fact that a no confidence vote in the President's Government may trigger its own dissolution, but if the Government Chairman initiates the procedure, there is no need for a second motion before the risk of that result.

The December 2008 constitutional reforms added a new paragraph to Article 103, giving the Duma power to hear an annual Government report and ask questions; Article 114 imposes the complementary duty on the Government to submit the report. Not specified in the Constitution but set out in the Federal Law on the Status of a Member of the Federation Council and Deputy of the Duma[77] are other provisions which allow some oversight of the Government. Four different measures are listed in Article 7(1):

> (b) participation in . . . work of a parliamentary commission [*parlamentskoe rassledovanie*];
> (f) submission of a parliamentary query [*parlamentskii zapros*] (or query of the Federation Council or Duma), [or] query of a member of the Federation Council or Duma (deputy query [*deputatskii zapros*]);
> (g) recourse with questions [*obrashchenie c voprosami*] to members of the Government at a session of the respective chamber of the Federal Assembly; [and]
> (h) recourse to respective officials with a demand to take measures with regard to the immediate suppression of a violation discovered in the rights of citizens.

The ability to set up a Parliamentary Commission is a recent development for the Federal Assembly. A law of 27 December 2005 put forward by Putin established a complex procedure to allow both legislative chambers to set up a joint Commission. The law filled in a gap. The Plenipotentiary for Human Rights (see chapter six) has power, under Article 32(2) of the law governing his role, to request the Duma to establish a Parliamentary Commission to investigate violations of human rights and freedoms of citizens, but until then there was no law on how to set one up. The 2005 law specifies three bases for a Parliamentary Commission:

---

[77] Federal law of 8 May 1994, as amended to 2009, in Butler, above n 4, at 252.

a) blatant or mass violations of constitutionally guaranteed rights and freedoms;
b) manmade emergency situations and
c) manmade or natural disasters. (Article 4(1))

Specifically excluded is consideration of activities of the President, the courts or preliminary investigation agencies (Article 4(2)). The agreement of both chambers is required to establish a Commission, and no investigation should last longer than a year.

The law has been criticised as being too narrow in focus, and too cumbersome, so that

> in practice investigation could only be initiated if the president approved, and some deputies (for example D5, D11) called this a law banning parliamentary investigations . . . [they] were now legal, but almost impossible to conduct.[78]

No parliamentary investigations were initiated during 2006–08, although some attempts led to ad hoc deputy groups considering troubling events.[79]

More practically, the Federation Council and Duma may each send a parliamentary query (*zapros*) to a wide range of officials 'with regard to questions within their competence' and may expect a reply within 15 days. The decision to send a parliamentary query is adopted by a majority vote.

An individual Duma deputy or Federation Council member may send a general inquiry (*zapros*), or raise a query (*obrashcheniia*) on his or her own initiative without any need for debate. The reply must be made within 30 days (see Article 7(1)(g) and (h) and Article 14). A query is likely to concern a specific issue affecting a member of the public, often social or financial. Such resort to a deputy for practical help is a legacy from the communist era, when reliance on someone in the position to 'pull strings' was effectively the only way to achieve a positive result, although as Merritt comments:

> Even those who work on handling deputies' inquiries quote the informal norm that the more notable the deputy, the less likely he is to need to use an inquiry at all: 'He just picks up the telephone and gets it done.'[80]

---

[78] Whitmore, above n 71, at 1010.
[79] *Ibid.*
[80] Merritt, above n 1, at 168, citing a personal interview with Valery Smirnov, Protocol Section of the Duma, May 1999.

In 2000 the governmental representative at the Duma, Konstantin Lubenchenko, wrote to the Duma Chairmen with an analysis of deputy inquiries and queries. He said that during 1996–99 the Government received six parliamentary and 522 deputy inquiries and queries. He complained that it was hard to distinguish between a deputy's inquiry and a query, and requested further measures to regulate them.[81] He also suggested that deputies should be more precise as to whom they direct their inquiries and queries, and that it should be mandatory 'for the publication in *Rossiiskaia Gazeta* and *Parlamentskaia Gazeta* of not only the parliamentary *zaprosy* but also the Government's responses'.[82]

It is also possible for relevant officials to be invited to speak at either the Federation Council or the Duma, particularly during 'Government Hour' which is held on Wednesdays (sometimes every other Wednesday) during Duma sessions, less frequently in the Federation Council. From 2004 the particular topic to be covered in Duma Government Hours is planned ahead of time, with input from the presidential and government representatives, and listed in the Duma plan. 'The change limited the capacity of the Duma to respond to the burning issues of the day.'[83] Topics also now have to be within the Duma's jurisdiction, which excludes 'important aspects of internal and foreign policy such as the military doctrine'.[84] Potential topics are listed in Article 41(4) of the Duma Reglament and correspond more or less to the areas of competence of government ministries. The names of invited officials are posted on the Duma website, and deputies may propose appropriate questions. If a particular invited official is unavailable, he or she informs the Duma Chairman, giving reasons and suggesting a substitute, although the Duma Council may choose to postpone that Government Hour topic until the specific official is available. Once there, the official gives a short speech, and individual deputies may put brief questions and receive replies. Representatives of deputy factions are allowed the chance briefly to express opinions before the official is given the right of last word.

---

[81] 'V Gosudarstvennoi Dume RF', at <http://www.rg.ru/oficial/from_min/gd/archives.htm>, entry for 25 April 2000, 'Analiz deputatskikh zaprosov i predlozheniia po ulucheniiu protsedury ikh prokhozhennia', available at <http://www.rg.ru/oficial/from_min/gd/294.htm>, accessed 19 August 2010.

[82] *Ibid.*

[83] Whitmore, above n 71, at 1009.

[84] *Ibid.*

Government Hour is a useful tool both for obtaining information and for expressing views on important issues, although individual deputies have ceded control of topics covered to the Duma Council. On occasion, it might be held *in camera*; for example, at its first plenary session after the summer of 2008, Government Hour in the Duma was behind closed doors for an assessment by Defence Minister Anatolii Serdiukov of lessons to be learned from the situation in Abkhazia and South Ossetia, although some information was publicly released.[85] The previous year the same minister had announced at the Duma Government Hour that the ministry was prepared for a transition from 1 January 2008 to a reduced period of service for conscripts.[86] During the Government Hour in the Federation Council at its first meeting in 2009, Foreign Minister Sergei Lavrov gave his views about the possibility of Georgia joining NATO.[87] At a Duma Government Hour in February 2009, 'head of Rostekhnologii corporation Sergei Chemezov announced that one-third of enterprises of the national military industrial complex were on the brink of bankruptcy'.[88] Occasionally an official is caught out. For example, on 9 May 2009, *Nezavisimaia Gazeta* reported that Minister of Finance Kudrin gave incorrect information during Government Hour that the Russian economy had contracted by only 0 per cent during the economic crisis. The newspaper claimed that according to the Russian Statistical Department the economic decline was nearer 9.5 per cent.[89]

The system of queries and statements is a comparatively weak instrument but has seen rapid growth in its use. Merritt tracks developments in the 1990s from 37 inquiries on any subject in 1994 to 3,025 in 1998,

[85]   Y Gavrilov, 'Troops are ordered to group themselves' (2008) 102 *Defence & Security*, 15 September, available online via Westlaw, citing *Rossiyskaya Gazeta*, 12 September 2008.

[86]   'Russian Defence Ministry is Prepared for Transition to One-Year Conscript Service Term from January 1 2008' (2007) 111 *Defence & Security*, 5 October, available online via Westlaw, citing *Itar-Tass*, 3 October 2007.

[87]   Aleksei Il'in, 'Sergei Lavrov rasskazal senatoram o prioritetakh vneshei politiki Rossii' (2009) 4837 *Rossiiskaia Gazeta* 29 January available at <http://www.rg.ru/2009/01/29/lavrov.html> accessed 24 August 2010.

[88]   'Reconfiguration of Military Industrial Complex Brought One-Third of Defense Enterprises to the Verge of Bankruptcy' (2009) 20 *Defence & Security*, 2 March, available online via Westlaw, citing (2009) *Gudok*, 26 February, at 2.

[89]   M Sergeev, 'Kreml' opustil pravitel'stvo Putina s nebes na zemliu', available online at <http://www.ng.ru/politics/2009-05-26/1_kremlin.html>, accessed 24 August 2009.

although she also notes that compared with the equivalent in the USA the numbers are extremely low.[90] Her statistics also showed that individual deputies were overwhelmingly the source of inquiries, rather than the more formal parliamentary inquiry. Whitmore considers oversight activities from 2000–08, and her figures, which exclude deputy inquiries, show an overall fall in use of the other three oversight tools.[91] More worryingly, she cogently argues that the role of oversight methods has been subverted, so that they act more to legitimate governmental activities than question them; and even more disturbingly, use of formal oversight channels in various ways for private gain is well documented.[92]

The chambers of the Federal Assembly may initiate oversight of constitutionality by the Constitutional Court. Its scope is defined in Article 125 of the Constitution, with added detail in the Constitutional Court law. Article 125(2) lists legislation which may be reviewed at the request of, inter alia, the Duma or Federation Council, or a group of at least one-fifth of their respective members. The Duma or Federation Council can ask the Constitutional Court to settle jurisdictional disputes where they are a party (Article 125(3)), and each may request a definitive interpretation of a constitutional provision (Article 125(5)). There is further discussion in chapter six of the powers of the Constitutional Court. It is noteworthy, however, that, once established, recourse to the Court quickly became a first resort for resolving disputes between different branches and levels of State power in Russia.

ii. Other activities

Each chamber of the Legislature has some other functions. The Federation Council has an important role in the appointment of a number of leading officials, touched on in chapter four, for example the Procurator-General. On the nomination of the President, the Federation Council appoints to office the judges of the Constitutional Court, Supreme Court and Highest *Arbitrazh* Court (see section VI.B. in chapter six). The Duma appoints to and relieves from office the Plenipotentiary for Human Rights (also discussed in chapter six, in section VIII.C.iii.). Both chambers of the Federal Assembly have a hand in composing the Central Electoral Commission, although the procedure

---

[90] Merritt, above n 1, at 168.
[91] Whitmore, above n 71, at 1011–13.
[92] *Ibid* at 1018–19.

differs in each chamber as to how the individual members are put forward for election onto the Commission.

As the body set up to represent the federation subjects, it is appropriate that the Federation Council has the jurisdiction to confirm changes of boundaries between federation subjects. The President turns to the Federation Council for confirmation of his edicts where he has established martial law, in the form either of a 'military situation' or an 'extraordinary situation'. However, these are ex post facto confirmations and do not derogate from the President's power as guardian of Russian security to take the appropriate steps (see Constitution, Articles 87, 88 and 102). Use of the armed forces outside the Russian Federation does require the Federation Council to decide the issue (Article 102(1) (d)), as it has done, for example, for peacekeeping operations in Bosnia-Herzegovina. It is also within the Federation Council's remit to take the formal step of calling presidential elections.

The 'single fully independent authority reserved for the Duma'[93] is its power to declare an amnesty (Article 103(f)). An amnesty applies to a group or class of people, unlike a presidential pardon, which is given to an individual. In February 1994 the Duma amnestied all those involved in the August 1991 abortive putsch against Gorbachev (see section III.I. in chapter two), and those members of the Russian Government and Legislature who in late September–early October 1993 held out in the Russian White House against Yel'tsin – the events described in chapter three which form the background to the adoption of the 1993 Constitution.[94] Yel'tsin was furious at this Duma amnesty and summoned the Procurator-General (who heads the State prosecution system), ordering him to arrange for its beneficiaries to be rearrested. The Procurator-General had to inform the President that the Duma had merely acted within the powers given to it in the 1993 Constitution.[95] The President was thus thwarted by a provision in the Constitution he had effectively imposed on Russia.

---

[93] Grankin, above n 72, at 37.

[94] The Duma issued a much wider amnesty at the same time for prisoners who had previously served in active combat zones, participated in the clean-up after the Chernobyl nuclear disaster, were over 60, were disabled, or were female.

[95] T Foglesong, *Pardons and Amnesties in Russia: Clarifying the Difference* (New York, Vera Institute of Justice, May 2002), available at <http://www.vera.org/download?file=155/Pardons%2Bin%2BRussia.pdf >, accessed 24 August 2010.

III. THE LEGISLATIVE COUNCIL

A brief word should be said about a body set up by Putin in May 2002 to parallel the State Council but involving the legislative branch. The Legislative Council is another of Putin's para-constitutional institutions (see chapter four), in this case allowing 'heads of legislative assemblies to take part in discussion of national policies'.[96] It consists of the Chairman of the Federation Council, who acts as its Chairman, the First Deputy Chairman of the Duma, who is its Deputy Chairman, one other Federation Council Deputy Chairman and all the chairmen of the legislative (representative) agencies of the federation subjects. Its main tasks, as defined in its Statute, are to promote cooperation, make recommendations, give feedback, and discuss significant draft federal laws and other important issues connected with legislating. There is a smaller 10-man Presidium (Chair and Deputy, plus a member from each federal district), which meets monthly, plus eight specialised commissions.

The Legislative Council meeting in July 2010 was the twelfth in seven consecutive years, and at it Medvedev suggested changing the working arrangements:

> This Hall (Alexandrovsky Hall of the Grand Kremlin Palace) is picturesque, and the place is meaningful; but the hall is too large, only four people have spoken so far, and 70 others are just sitting and writing something down.[97]

Ross suggests that this lack of active input is more systemic. The Legislative Council

> is primarily a tool of the federal centre, a body that assists the centre in monitoring federal legislation in the regions, rather than a body that represents and promotes the adoption of regional legislation in the centre.[98]

Analogous to the State Council, the Legislative Council gives an appearance of consultation, but in reality so far has been ineffective. Clearly Medvedev has plans to turn Putin's sham forum into something of

[96] Sakwa, above n 6, at 202.

[97] 'No Kremlin meetings for legislators council – Medvedev' (2010) *Itar-Tass*, 14 July, available at < http://www.itar-tass.com/eng/level2.html?NewsID=15318747 &PageNum=0>, accessed 27 August 2010.

[98] C Ross, 'Federalism and Inter-governmental Relations in Russia' (2010) 26(2) *Journal of Communist Studies and Transition Politics* 165 at 176.

more practical value, but whether any of its members care enough to bother may be a serious question.

IV. CONCLUSION

The Federal Assembly is defined as the representative and legislative agency of the Russian Federation. However, under its current rules for formation, it is not clear what or who is represented by each of its two chambers. The current Duma proportional representation elections, with their 7 per cent threshold, mean that many votes cast have no impact, and the Duma's composition in terms of political parties does not match the range of public opinion. Neither does the current system of political parties function well to harness the views of the electorate. The link between the Federation Council members and the local population of the areas of Russia that they are supposed to represent is only indirect, and accountability back to the federal subjects is slight. The legislative process is quite cumbersome, and around 70 per cent of draft laws address shortcomings in existing legislation, which suggests that scrutiny of drafts during passage is not sufficiently rigorous.[99] Oversight by the Legislature of the executive branch is at best weak and at worst a diversionary sham.

> The Russian case illustrates how accountability channels can be marginalised and deactivated de facto in an electoral authoritarian regime, but at the same time are maintained and even extended de jure for legitimation purposes.[100]

Nevertheless, it should be remembered how profound the changes have been since the Soviet era. Public debate in the legislative chamber was unknown; the first recorded instance was during the passage in 1987 of the 'Law of the USSR on the procedure for appealing to a court unlawful actions of officials which impinge upon the rights of citizens', which is discussed in chapter six at section VII.C.ii. Such was the novelty of legislative debate that during the *perestroika* era industrial output fell by 20 per cent as people stayed off work to watch it on TV.[101] Multiparty activity has been legal for a bare two decades. It should therefore be no

---

[99] Mironov and Burbalis, above n 61, at 178.
[100] Whitmore, above n 71, at 1001.
[101] DD Barry, *Russian Politics. The Post-Soviet Phase* (New York, Peter Lang, 2002) 29.

surprise that under the new conditions political culture is still finding its shape in Russia, and the Federal Assembly feeling its way towards an appropriate role within an Executive-dominated polity.

FURTHER READING

DD Barry, *Russian Politics: the Post-Soviet Phase* (New York, Peter Lang, 2002).

I Grankin, 'The Special Powers of Russia's Parliament' (2001) 9 *Democratizatsiya* 26.

SM Mironov and GE Burbulis (eds), *Council of Federation of the Federal Assembly of the Russian Federation 2006 report 'On the State of Legislation in the Russian Federation'* (Moscow, Federation Council, 2008), available in English translation at <http://council.gov.ru/eng/rep/index.html>, accessed 18 August 2010.

M Merritt, 'The Russian State Duma, On-stage and Off: Inquiry, Impeachment, and Opposition' (2000) 8 *Democratizatsiya* 165.

N Munro and R Rose, 'A Guide to Russian elections', *Study in Public Policy number 428* (Aberdeen, University of Aberdeen Centre for the Study of Public Policy, 2007).

WE Pomeranz, 'Medvedev and the Contested Constitutional Underpinnings of Russia's Power Vertical' (2009) 17 *Democratizatsiya* 179.

R Rose and W Mishler, 'How Do Electors Respond to an Unfair Election? The Experience of Russians', *Study in Public Policy number 446* (Aberdeen, University of Aberdeen Centre for the Study of Public Policy, 2008).

R Sakwa, *Russian Politics and Society*, 4th edn (Abingdon, Routledge, 2008).

S Whitmore, 'Parliamentary Oversight in Putin's Neo-patrimonial State. Watchdogs or Show-dogs? (2010) 62(6) *Europe-Asia Studies* 99.

A Zakharov, 'The Russian Parliament and Vladimir Putin's Presidency' in K Malfleit and R Laenen (eds), *Elusive Russia. Current Developments in Russian State Identity under President Putin* (Leuven, Leuven University Press, 2007).

6

The Constitutional Role of the Courts

———⊷•⊷———

Introduction – The Court System: Overview of the Constitutional Provisions – The Development of Constitutional Supervision – The Domestic Courts and the Constitution – Turf Wars – Judicial Independence – Protection of Human Rights – Conclusion – Further Reading

I. INTRODUCTION

THE DEVELOPMENTS IN Russia's court system from the *perestroika* era to the present day have resembled a roller-coaster ride. In the early 1990s idealist reformers initiated moves away from the subservience of Soviet judges to develop a more independent Judiciary. During Yel'tsin's time as President, judges in Russia gained security of tenure and greater self-government. Fears that they were becoming unaccountable triggered off a retrenchment under President Putin, although there were important practical reforms. More recently, under President Medvedev, there have been mixed messages. He has spoken out against pressure being applied to judges, but changes, for example in the appointment procedure for the Constitutional Court Chairman, have reduced that Court's independence. In 2009 a Constitutional Court judge expressed concerns that 'judicial authority . . . has become a tool in the service of the Executive'[1] and there is fear of obsequious compliance with 'executive orders'. But Medvedev, the

---

[1] V Yaroslavtsev in his interview published in *El Pais*, 1 August 2009, as cited in A Pushkarskaia, '*Konstitutsionnyi sud teriaet osobye mneniia*' (2009) *Kommersant'*, 2 December, available online at <http://www.kommersant.ru/doc-y.aspx?DocsID= 1284828>, accessed 3 December 2009.

former law professor, has emphasised the need for an effective judicial system and has pledged to make improvements.

During the Soviet era, despite assurances in the 1936 and 1977 USSR Constitutions that 'judges are independent and subordinate only to law' (Articles 112 and 155 respectively), judges could not be independent. The court system was explicitly part of the machinery of State, and judges were expected to assist in the smooth development along the pre-ordained path to the communist utopia. In fulfilment of that aim, a judge had responsibility to educate those who came within his or her purview (frequently 'her'; a sign of the low status of the judiciary in Soviet times). The CPSU positively vetted judicial candidates to ensure that they had the requisite 'social consciousness'. *Perestroika* reforms required judges to have higher legal education and doubled the judicial term of office from five years to 10, but there were no systemic changes.

Modern Russia faced a clear need for reform of the judicial system. The economic transformation from the planned economy to a market-based system reinvigorated the role of law and necessitated a complete overhaul of legislation affecting the economic sphere. A market economy uses legal mechanisms – company law, contract, new forms of property, securities and so on – all of which needed to be developed, as did the courts and enforcement procedures.

A key challenge has been to increase trust in the courts and enhance judicial prestige. Unfortunately, the central role of judges in the new economy has put them in a pivotal position as a prime target for bribery or other untoward pressure. This issue is discussed in more detail below.

The courts' role in the protection of individuals against infringement by others, including the State, also expanded. The development of directly enforceable human rights has created a problem for courts struggling to cope with the rising number of complaints. The impact on Russia of joining the Council of Europe and acceding to the European Convention on Human Rights, which gave individuals the possibility of appealing to the European Court of Human Rights, generated a new range of problems, and not just within Russia. The flood of Russian applications to the Court in Strasbourg, and Russia's protracted refusal to ratify Protocol 14 to allow speedier consideration of admissibility, exacerbated the Court's backlog of cases. But Russia's membership of the Council of Europe created a two-way street. The jurisprudence of the European Court of Human Rights is beginning to have an impact on domestic cases.

A lack of clarity in jurisdictional boundaries has potential for problems. Unfortunately a 'turf war' exists between the Constitutional Court and the Supreme Court, which is unhelpful in a State with little tradition of voluntary use of court remedies. This dispute is summarised in section V. below. As well as courts, other domestic mechanisms exist in Russia for overseeing rights, for example the Procuracy, exercising its power of 'general supervision', and the Plenipotentiary for Human Rights (Ombudsman), discussed in section VII. below, creating an overlapping array of remedies.

II. THE COURT SYSTEM: OVERVIEW OF THE CONSTITUTIONAL PROVISIONS

To those used to separation of powers it was rather alarming to discover at a first reading of Chapter 7 in the 1993 Constitution 'On Judicial Power' that the President would nominate the senior Judiciary and appoint all other federal judges, without apparent qualification apart from the procedure being 'established by a federal law' (Article 128(2)). In fact, the President's discretion is tempered by other legislation, in particular the Federal Constitutional Law on the Judicial System of 31 December 1996, which sets out detailed provisions and is supplemented by the Law on the Status of Judges, originally passed in June 1992 but subsequently amended, and the Code of Judicial Ethics of December 2004.[2] But it remains disquieting that, for example, the unlimited term of office of a federal judge is not established in the 1993 Constitution (as it had been in amendments to the previous Constitution).

The constitutional chapter does articulate some important principles. The first is that 'justice [*pravosudie*] in the Russian Federation shall be effectuated only by a court' (Article 118(1)). This formulation was also present in 1977 USSR Constitution, but at that stage carried a different meaning, that anything not a court need not be interested in 'justice'. So, for example, *arbitrazh* tribunals set up to resolve disputes between entities working under the centralised State-planned economy were expected to focus on pragmatic results to keep the economic plan working, rather than paying attention to legal niceties. Now the constitutional provision signifies that courts have proper procedures for administering justice through the

---

[2] Texts in WE Butler, *Russian Public Law*, 2nd edn (London, Wildy, Simmonds & Hill, 2009) 392, 447, 491.

defence of rights and protection of legal interests of individuals, legal entities and other claimants. The former *arbitrazh* tribunals have successfully transformed into the *Arbitrazh* courts (commercial courts) and therefore now should 'administer justice'.

A second clear principle set out in the Constitution also has historical roots. It is the qualification that 'the creation of extraordinary courts shall not be permitted' (Article 118(3)). In 1934, special boards attached to the Soviet Ministry of Internal Affairs (MVD) were given jurisdiction to try especially dangerous crimes against the State. Much of the Stalinist terror was channelled through these three-person extrajudicial bodies, colloquially known '*troika*' after the Russian sleigh drawn by three horses. They were abolished in the post-Stalin reforms of the late 1950s, which also introduced the principle of *nulla poena sine lege*,[3] reversing the previous possibility of crime by analogy, which had allowed a court to create a new offence (analogous to an existing crime) which criminalised behaviour the court had decided was 'socially dangerous', even though the Criminal Code itself was silent on the matter. Revulsion against the excesses of the *troika* prompted inclusion in the Constitution of the prohibition on extraordinary courts.[4] In more recent times this restriction may have backfired. Some commentators feel it would be helpful to have special family courts, but these are not envisaged in the Federal Constitutional Law on the Judicial System and are therefore currently prohibited as extraordinary. Separate administrative courts are a possibility, as they are mentioned in that Law, although they are not yet an actuality despite pressure from the Supreme Court.

Other principles in the Constitution were rooted in the desire to get away from the Soviet past: that 'proceedings in all courts shall be open' (apart from instances provided for by federal law); 'hearing criminal cases *in absentia* shall not be allowed except in instances provided for by federal law'; and 'judicial proceedings shall be conducted on the basis of adversarial principles and equality of the parties' (Article 123). All these formal rules contrast with Soviet practice, if not formal procedure. There were closed trials, *in absentia* convictions and an inquisitorial criminal procedure that justified inequalities between prosecution and defence on the basis of the neutral search for an objective truth

---

[3] 'No punishment without [an enacted] law [establishing the crime].'

[4] The 1977 USSR Constitution, Art 160 contained a prohibition against convicting for crime other than in a court.

(although the 1958 procedural reforms established some important defendants' rights[5]).

Although the Constitution says nothing about the length of judicial tenure, it does deal with some fundamentals of judicial independence. Article 120 states that 'judges shall be independent and subordinate only to the Constitution . . . and to federal law'. Unfortunately, a similar form of words appeared in both the USSR Constitutions of 1977 (Article 155) and 1936 (Article 112), and this did not protect the Soviet Judiciary from the pressure to conform to the wishes of the Communist Party and the prerogative State.[6] Judges are now irremovable (Article 121(1)) and inviolable (Article 122(1)), with the proviso in both cases that the procedure to terminate or suspend judicial office, or institute criminal proceedings, shall be defined by federal law. The relevant law is the Law on the Status of Judges.

The Constitution says little about the courts themselves. It does specify that there shall be constitutional, civil, administrative and criminal court proceedings (Article 118 (2)), but apart from the first category does not allocate types of proceedings to particular courts. The exception, constitutional proceedings, are assigned to the Constitutional Court, and Article 125 details its jurisdiction. The Constitution was adopted after RSFSR Constitutional Court had been caught up in the political turmoil of the spring and autumn of 1993 (see sections II.F. and II.G. in chapter three). President Yel'tsin was minded to abolish it altogether and give the Supreme Court constitutional oversight. He was persuaded that this would be an unwise move, but was determined to confine the role of the Constitutional Court by specifying in the Constitution exactly what its powers should be, ahead of the passage of the Federal Constitutional Law on the Constitutional Court.

None of the other courts has its jurisdiction so explicitly set out at constitutional level. The Supreme Court is merely described as the highest judicial agency in respect to matters within the jurisdiction of the courts of general jurisdiction such as civil, criminal and administrative cases. In terms of its role and tasks, all Article 126 specifies is that it exercises judicial supervision over the courts of general jurisdiction, and renders explanations (*raz"iazneniia*) on questions of judicial practice.

---

[5] See HJ Berman and JW Spindler, *Soviet Criminal Law & Procedure* (Cambridge, Mass, Harvard University Press, 1972).

[6] See R Sakwa, *The Quality of Freedom. Khodorkovsky, Putin and the Yukos Affair* (Oxford, Oxford University Press, 2009) 14.

These explanations effectively act as a source of law despite in theory being interpretation of enacted legislation. Similarly, the Highest *Arbitrazh* Court is defined in Article 127 as the head of the courts dealing with economic disputes, and it also exercises supervision and renders explanations. The Constitution does not clarify the division in jurisdiction between these two courts and the hierarchies that they head. They both apply the same Civil Code, and have given joint explanations on important civil law matters.

The Constitution (Article 128(3)) says that the

> powers, procedure for formation, and activity of the Constitutional Court, Supreme Court, Highest *Arbitrazh* Court, and other federal courts shall be established by federal constitutional law.

As of the time of writing in mid-2010, federal constitutional laws exist for the Constitutional Court, Highest *Arbitrazh* Court and the judicial system, but passage of a Federal Constitutional Law on the Supreme Court has been resolutely hampered over the years. This has delayed the introduction of a separate administrative court branch under the overall jurisdiction of the Supreme Court. The lack of separate courts to deal with the burgeoning administrative law cases has been blamed for the overcrowding of the domestic courts' lists. The reason for the delay in getting this legislation passed is not clear. It may be that now that President Medvedev is taking an interest in improving the judicial system – one of the points in his inaugural address – any political factors inhibiting the law's adoption could be swept away.

As well as the federal courts mentioned so far, the Federal Constitutional Law on the Judicial System allows for two categories of non-federal court whose judges have different terms and procedure for appointment. These are the constitutional or charter courts of federal subjects (although only a minority of subjects have established them[7]) and the justice of the peace courts set up following legislation on 17 December 1998.[8] The latter are an interesting reintroduction of courts that existed in the late imperial era but were abolished by the Bolsheviks. They have been resurrected to siphon off low-level civil, administrative

---

[7] See A Trochev, 'Less Democracy, More Courts: A Puzzle of Judicial Review in Russia' (2004) 38 *Law and Society Review* 513.

[8] J Henderson, 'Justices of the Peace in Russia' (1999) 5 *European Public Law* 373; P Solomon, 'The New Justices of the Peace in the Russian Federation' (2003) 11 *Demokratizatsiya* 381.

and criminal cases from the ordinary courts, and they have succeeded. For example, in 2008 the justice of the peace courts dealt with 43.8 per cent of first-instance criminal cases and 75.7 per cent of first-instance civil cases.[9] It is intended that they should hear all administrative offences that require a court hearing.[10] The justice of the peace courts form the lowest tier of the federal hierarchy of courts, and although the judges are not federal judges and do not have unlimited tenure, they enjoy the same protections against unwarranted removal as federal judges. Their financing is currently divided between federal and local budgets. Justice of the peace courts have been generally welcomed. The federal subjects where they have been introduced like them as being 'their' courts, and the federal authorities are pleased to have a channel into which minor cases can be diverted comparatively cheaply to relieve the overworked district courts. Court users also generally favour their accessibility and comparative informality.

The chapter in the Constitution on 'Judicial Power' has an anachronistic inclusion – the one article in the Constitution on the Procuracy (Article 129). This does little more than establish that the Procuracy exists as a 'unified centralised system' in a hierarchy under the overall control of the Procurator-General. It says nothing specific about the role of this distinctive Russian institution, which is outlined in section VII.C.i. below. However, whatever function the Procuracy has, or should have, it undoubtedly is not a judicial body, and therefore its inclusion in this chapter is inappropriate. Its relationship with the courts is problematic, as it struggles to forget the superior power of Soviet procurators compared to the subservient and practically toothless Soviet courts.[11]

---

[9] W Burnham and PB Maggs, *Law and Legal System in the Russian Federation*, 4th edn (Huntington, New York, Juris Publishing Inc, 2009) 77.

[10] O Schwartz, 'The Creation of an Independent Judiciary and the Changing Nature of Courts and the Courtroom' in WA Pridemore (ed), *Ruling Russia: Law Crime and Justice in a Changing Society* (Lanham, Rowman and Littlefield, 2005) 59 at 70.

[11] On the Procuracy, see GB Smith, 'The struggle over the Procuracy' in PH Solomon (ed), *Reforming Justice in Russia 1864–1996* (Armonk, NY, ME Sharpe, 1997) 348 ; GB Smith, 'The Procuracy: Constitutional Questions Deferred' in GB Smith and R Sharlet (eds), *Russia and Its Constitution: Promise and Political Reality* (Leiden, Nijhoff, 2008) 105.

III. THE DEVELOPMENT OF CONSTITUTIONAL SUPERVISION

A. Introduction

One of the biggest changes to the Russian legal landscape in the last two decades is the institution of a Constitutional Court.[12] Although a Constitutional Court pre-dated the current Constitution by 18 months, it could be argued that its importance has been enhanced by the 1993 Constitution in two ways.

First, unlike the previous Constitution, this one has direct application and therefore issues arise over its enforcement. Soviet Constitutions delineated the tasks of the different State agencies, but Soviet State theory emphasised the unity of State power not its separation. In any event, except for a short time in the 1920s when the first USSR Supreme Court had the power to advise the Legislature on inconsistencies of laws with the Constitution, no court or other tribunal before the *perestroika* era had jurisdiction to question the constitutionality of legislation.[13]

Secondly, the difficulty of amending the Constitution gives particular significance to the Constitutional Court's power to give authoritative interpretations of constitutional provisions (Article 125(5)). This was an expansion of jurisdiction for the Court from its powers under the 1991 law on the RSFSR Constitutional Court. At a press conference on 10 November 1994 to mark the election of new judges to the expanded Court, the new chairman, Vladimir Tumanov, emphasised the importance of the new power. He believed it would free the Court from a slavish adherence to the literal words of the Constitution, which in his view had been a problem for the first Constitutional Court dealing with a much-amended and internally inconsistent constitutional text. Valerii Zor'kin, who chaired the first Court from November 1991 until October 1993, and who was again elected as Chairman by his fellow judges in February 2003, has also highlighted the importance of the Court's interpretative power to bring the 'living voice' of the Constitution out from its words.[14] Both these

---

[12] See A Trochev, *Judging Russia: Constitutional Court in Russian Politics, 1990–2006* (Cambridge, Cambridge University Press, 2008).

[13] See PH Solomon, 'The USSR Supreme Court: History, Role, and Future Prospects' (1990) 38 American Journal of Comparative Law 127.

[14] M Lomovsteva and J Henderson, 'Constitutional Justice in Russia' (2009) 34 *Review of Central and East European Law* 37 at 49.

leading justices recognise the limitation of the written word, and emphasise the Court's role interpreting the Constitution to be an effective legal safeguard against abuses of power, in whatever manifestation.

Unfortunately the Court can give an authoritative interpretation only at the request of a closed list of agencies: the President, the Federation Council, the Duma, the Government and the legislatures of the federal subjects.

B. The USSR Constitutional Supervision Committee

Constitutional supervision in the USSR was a *perestroika* innovation. In July 1988 the CPSU resolved at its policy-making 19th Conference that it 'would be useful to institute a Constitutional Supervision Committee [CSC]' (Resolution 3). As a direct result of Conference resolutions there were major amendments in December 1988 to the 1977 USSR Constitution (see chapter two section III.F.), followed a year later by the USSR law 'On Constitutional Supervision in the USSR'.[15] This set up a 'committee', not a court – a compromise body. Its members were to be 'specialists in the field of politics and law' (Article 5 of the law). In fact, all but two held higher law degrees (the exceptions had degrees in philosophy and history), and all were academics without previous judicial experience. This was a sign that the CSC was to be respected, as in the culture of the time academics, but not judges, were well regarded.

The CSC clearly acted as a precursor to the Russian Constitutional Court, although its powers were rather different. Amongst other things, the CSC could review the constitutionality of draft laws as well as enacted legislation, and also it was empowered to review the constitutionality of the 'guiding explanations' given by the USSR Supreme Court Plenum instructing lower courts on interpretation of legislation. At a colloquium held at University College London in March 1990, the spellbound audience witnessed, possibly for the first time in the United Kingdom, one Soviet legal academic, Valerii Savitskii, publicly challenging another, Aleksandr Larin, the lead draftsman of the CSC law, over the inclusion of the right to review guiding explanations. Savitskii rightly pointed out that, formally speaking, these explanations were merely

---

[15] WE Butler, *Basic Documents on the Soviet Legal System*, 2nd edn (New York, Oceana, 1991) 185.

interpretation of existing legislation, not sources of law. Larin equally correctly responded that, as the courts were expected to treat them as binding, the draftsmen decided they should be included within the CSC remit. The colloquium was held just after Gorbachev was appointed as the first Soviet President. Larin admitted that he did not know whether presidential legislation would be subject to CSC supervision, because the presidency was established after its law had been passed. As it turned out, the CSC could review Gorbachev's edicts and decrees because he was appointed to office by the Legislature, not elected by the general population. As an 'official' of the Legislature, his actions were subject to review. The CSC was supposed to have 25 members, although never achieved the full complement. The three Baltic republics, Latvia, Lithuania and Estonia, refused to send anyone.[16]

The CSC issued declaratory opinions of unconstitutionality. The effect depended on the nature of the legislation reviewed. If the CSC decided that it had violated 'basic human rights and freedoms consolidated in the USSR Constitution and international treaties to which USSR is a party' (Article 21, law on the CSC) then it would become void. Other legislation would be suspended from application, but could be resurrected if the full Legislature, the USSR CPD, voted by a two-thirds majority to overrule the CSC's opinion. During its short period of existence, from March 1990 to the end of 1991, this never happened. The CSC had power to take cases on its own initiative, and one of its landmark opinions resulted from such a case.[17] It heard a complaint about housing rights where it became apparent that the applicable legislation had never been published. Taking up the issue of such 'secret law', the CSC issued a binding opinion that legislation affecting the rights and interests of citizens that remained unpublished after a specified date would be void. As a result, a number of previously unpublished laws appeared in the Legislature's official *Vedomosti* (Herald). This assault on secret legislation was a major victory for the principle of openness (*glasnost'*), although it did not eliminate the practice of 'limited circulation' legislation.

[16] There was also some 'doubling up' for representation of the autonomous republics within Russia. See H Hausmaninger, 'From the Soviet Committee of Constitutional Supervision to the Russian Constitutional Court' (1992) 25 *Cornell International Law Journal* 305 at 307.

[17] See P Maggs, 'Enforcing the Bill of Rights in the Twilight of the Soviet Union' (1991) *University of Illinois Law Review* 1049.

The CSC's powers were severely circumscribed,[18] and it was under-mined by the fractiousness of federal relations at the time. A leading study of the CSC by Joseph Middleton concluded that it was doomed to failure because of the unresolved issue of federal imbalance.[19] Gorbachev had hoped that the CSC would solve this, but by that stage the Union republics would not accept adjudication from a federal body, even if a committee not a court. Political events overtook the path-breaking CSC and it disbanded with the dissolution of the USSR.

C. The RSFSR Constitutional Court – 1991 Law

i. *Establishing the Court*

In the meantime, Soviet Russia had taken the bold step of passing legisla-tion to establish a true Constitutional Court. The RSFSR 'Law on the Constitutional Court of the RSFSR' was initially debated at the smaller legislative body, the Supreme Soviet, before being adopted by the Russian Congress of People's Deputies (CPD) on 12 July 1991. The explicit moti-vation for creating the Court was explained by Sergei Shakhrai, the Chairman of the CPD Committee on Legislation. He linked it to the establishment that spring of the Russian Presidency. This created a need for an 'instrument' to ensure the balance between legislative, executive and judicial powers.[20] The Supreme Soviet adopted the draft law on 6 May. Presidential elections were held on 12 June; Boris Yel'tsin won. The following month the draft was considered by the CPD. In particular it had to decide whether to reintroduce a section rejected by the Supreme Soviet, which would allow the Court to consider 'cases of constitutionality of the practice of application of laws'.[21] By this unusual and contentious power

---

[18] B Bowring, 'Human Rights in Russia: Discourse on Emancipation or Only a Mirage?' in I Pogany (ed), *Human Rights in Eastern* (Aldershot, Edward Elgar, 1995) 87 at 101.

[19] J Middleton, 'The Soviet experiment with constitutional control: the predicta-ble failure of the USSR Constitutional Supervision Committee' in A Mullerson, M Fitzmaurice, and M Andenas (eds), *Constitutional Reform and International Law in Central and Eastern Europe* (The Hague, Kluwer, 1998) 133.

[20] *VS Biulleten'* (1991) 26 at 12, cited in J Henderson, 'The First Russian Constitutional Court: Hopes and Aspirations' in R Mullerson, M Fitzmaurice and M Andenas (eds), *Constitutional Reform and International Law in Central and Eastern Europe* (The Hague, Kluwer, 1998).

[21] Section III, ch 3.

the Court could look not only at the text of a relevant law, but also at the practical impact of its 'customary application'. The CPD took the hint of the presenter, leading reformer Boris Zolotukhin, and passed the law with the enhanced power. Cases could be brought by individual litigants – citizens, foreigners, stateless persons and legal persons – with no special gateway provisions, apart from the requirement that other procedures had been exhausted. The Court could refuse to hear a case on a number of grounds, the broadest of which was that the court 'finds the consideration of the individual appeal to be inexpedient (*netseleoobraznoe*)' (Article 69(14)).

Two long-time analysts of the Russian legal scene, Bill Burnham and Alexei Trochev, date the ill-will discussed in section V. below between the Supreme Court and the Constitutional Court to the battle over this unusual jurisdiction.[22] The Supreme Court (and other bodies) thought that this 'intrusion' into the application of civil and criminal law would trump legislation with judge-made law – made by the Constitutional Court – and would also overburden the Court. In fact the latter fear proved unfounded, as over the course of its comparatively short life, the RSFSR Constitutional Court's power to review the customary application of law was used in only eight of the total of 29 decisions. In all eight cases the individual won.[23]

The RSFSR Constitutional Court also had the more orthodox jurisdiction to review the constitutionality of a range of legislation. Unlike the USSR CSC, it only considered enacted legislation, not drafts, with the one exception of international treaties. The 1991 Law forbade the Court to 'consider political issues' (Article 1(3)), but on 9 December 1992 the Constitution then in force was amended to give the Court jurisdiction over 'political parties and other social organisations' (Article 165-1). This conveniently gave the Court the necessary jurisdiction to hear the politically and socially significant case on the constitutionality of the Communist Party and the legality of Yel'tsin's ban of it and sei-

[22] W Burnham and A Trochev, 'Russia's War between the Courts: the Struggle over the Jurisdictional Boundary between the Constitutional Court and Regular Courts' (2007) 55 *American Journal of Comparative Law* 381 at 388.

[23] Figures given by Judge E Ametistov at a speech at Columbia Law School, 15 November 1993, cited in A Korkeakivi, *Justice Delayed: the Russian Constitutional Court and Human Rights* (New York, Lawyers Committee for Human Rights, 1995) 4. Judge N Vedernikov gives a different figure of 8 out of 27 in 'Problems of Constitutional Jurisprudence and the formulation of a "Rule of Law" State in Russia' (1993-94) 38 *St Louis University Law Journal* 895 at 908.

zure of its property.[24] The right to review the constitutionality of political parties, and consideration of the 'customary application of law', were two powers that were lost to the Court when it resumed sitting under the 1994 Federal Constitutional Law on the Constitutional Court.

ii. Make-up of the Court

The 1991 Law said that the Constitutional Court was to have 15 judges, each appointed for an unlimited term up to a fixed retirement age of 65 years (with a minimum age of 35). Nomination was by the Chairman of the Supreme Soviet, on the basis of recommendations from parties and factions in the Legislature. Appointment followed approval by the CPD in a secret electronic ballot by at least half of its deputies. Only 13 candidates were successfully elected, but this was sufficient to make the required two-thirds quorum so no further candidates were considered. The newly sworn-in judges elected their Court Chairman by secret ballot. They chose Valerii Zor'kin, previously a professor in the department of 'State-legal discipline' at the Higher School of Law of the USSR Ministry of Internal Affairs. He had been nominated to be a judge by the moderate faction Communists for Democracy.[25] Under his guidance the Court established itself as an important player on the Russian political and legal stage,[26] but unfortunately also became embroiled in the power struggle in 1993 between the President and the Legislature described in chapter three.[27] Zor'kin's attempts to mediate were viewed by Yel'tsin as favouring his enemies, and the Court was peremptorily suspended by Yel'tsin in September 1993. Yel'tsin justified this unlawful act by quoting Zor'kin's own declaration that the amended 1978 RSFSR Constitution had too many inconsistencies to allow for proper constitutional assessment of legislation. Yel'tsin said that the Court should therefore cease sitting until a new Constitution was in place, and in the

---

[24] See Iu Feofanov, 'The Establishment of the Constitutional Court in Russia and the Communist Party Case' (1993) 19 *Review of Central and East European Law* 623; J Henderson, 'The Russian Constitutional Court and the Communist Party Case: Watershed or Whitewash?' (2007) 40 *Communist and Post-Communist Studies* 1.

[25] J Wishnevski, 'The Constitutional Court' (1993) 2(20) *Radio Free Europe/Radio Liberty Research Report*, 14 May, 12–13.

[26] R Sharlet, 'Chief Justice As Judicial Politician' (1993) 2 *East European Constitutional Review* 32.

[27] See also Burnham and Trochev, above n 22, from 386.

meantime the judges could draft a new Constitutional Court Law. Their first draft was thought to contain excessive perquisites, but on 21 July 1994 a revised version was adopted by the new Legislature, the Federal Assembly, as the Federal Constitutional Law 'On the Constitutional Court of the Russian Federation'.

The RSFSR Constitutional Court had a difficult undertaking, to establish the first time the reality of constitutional supervision in Russia. To a large extent, it had to make up its procedure as it went along, but its members were clear-thinking academics with a strong sense of their important role and an independent approach to their task. This gave rise to some conflict with the other branches of State, but also helped to establish the Court as an important factor in Russian legal and political life.

D. The Constitutional Court of the Russian Federation – 1994 Federal Constitutional Law

i. *The Court's Jurisdiction*

The Court's powers under the 1994 Law are based on Article 125 of the 1993 Constitution. They fall under six main headings. First on the list, unsurprisingly, is abstract review, checking for conformity with the Constitution of various types of legislation, subdivided into four groups:

a) federal laws, and legislation adopted by the President, the Federation Council, Duma and Government;

b) constitutions, charters, and also laws and other legislation of federal subjects on issues within either federal or joint federal subject jurisdiction;

c) treaties between the federal Government and the governments of federal subjects, and treaties between the latter governments; and

d) international treaties of the Russian Federation which have not yet entered into force.

Of this list, the main change from the Court's powers under the 1991 Law are that only drafts of international treaties are now subject to review. The list of those with the right to appeal to the Court for abstract review has, however, been reduced. No longer can a single deputy to the Legislature initiate a case, as happened, for example, in the countersuit in the CPSU case.[28] Only the President, the Federation Council, a group of one-fifth of its members, the Duma, one-fifth of its deputies, the Government, the Supreme Court, the Highest *Arbitrazh* Court and either the legislature or government of a federal subject, have legal standing to trigger abstract review of constitutionality of legislation. The Court has, however, expanded the scope of this type of review to include federal constitutional law, which was not mentioned. Further expansion to review regulations based on federal law has exacerbated the dispute with the Supreme Court, which regards this as an illegitimate trespass into its own jurisdiction. This is discussed in section V. below.

Secondly, in keeping with the initial motivation for establishing a Constitutional Court, and in practice an important part of its work during the first phase of its existence,[29] the Court has the power to resolve separation-of-power issues between federal agencies of State power, federal agencies and federal subject agencies, and between the highest State agencies of federal subjects. Any of those agencies, or the President if he had tried conciliation, may bring a case.

Thirdly, and significant as the only means by which an individual is now able to get Constitutional Court consideration of their rights, the Court

> shall verify the constitutionality of a law being applied or subject to application in a specific case [concerning] appeals against a violation of constitutional rights and freedoms of citizens and at the requests of courts. (Article 125(4))

The final clause has been another source of dispute between the Constitutional Court and the Supreme Court, as neither the Constitution nor the Constitutional Court Law makes clear whether a court request to the Constitutional Court is mandatory or discretionary. Unsurprisingly, although unfortunately, the two leading courts have taken contrary views. This dispute is discussed further in section V. below.

---

[28] J Henderson, 'Making a Drama out of a Crisis: The Russian Constitutional Court and the Case of the Communist Party of the Soviet Union' (2008) 19 *King's Law Journal* 489.
[29] H Schwartz, *The Struggle for Constitutional Justice in Post-Communist Europe* (Chicago, University of Chicago Press, 2000) at 142 says over 40% of its rulings in its first two years were on separation of powers issues.

Fourthly, the Court may give an authoritative interpretation of the Constitution, highlighted earlier. It is made by the Court sitting in plenary session.

Fifthly, as discussed in chapter four, presidential impeachment proceedings require the Constitutional Court to give an opinion that the correct accusation procedure has been followed. So far, the Court has not been called on to exercise this power.

Lastly, the Court has the right of legislative initiative in relation to matters within its jurisdiction; effectively, its own operation and procedure. The risk that this might create separation of powers anomalies has so far been avoided by the Court not exercising its right. Nevertheless, it remains possible that it might draft legislation, which it is then asked to review. This has led some Russian academics to advocate removal of this power, although others feel that the risks are outweighed by the benefit of the Court being able to bring its expertise to relevant legislation.

In making a decision, the Court has been given a free hand as to its approach. Article 74(2) of the Constitutional Court Law specifically says it should 'evaluate both the literal meaning . . . and the meaning given to it by official or other interpretation or law-application practice that has developed'. This brings back to some extent consideration of the customary application of law. In practice the Court has used a wide range of different interpretative techniques, allowing it to be quite creative, although it is constrained by the fact that it cannot takes cases on its own initiative. Individual judges have the right to give a 'special opinion', which may support the majority or dissent. Publication of these separate opinions has been controversial in a country without a tradition of judge-made law.[30] The growth of a body of reasoned opinions is important to the Court's central position as the guardian of legality, and the inclusion of dissents emphasises the independence of the individual judges. The Court creates precedents for itself by taking a 'legal position' on an issue, which it can overturn only at a plenary meeting. The Court famously changed its 'legal position' from 1996 that regional gov-

---

[30] See A Vereshchagin, *Judicial Lawmaking in Post-Soviet Russia* (Abingdon, Routledge-Cavendish, 2007) 161; D Barry, 'Decision-making and dissent in the Russian Federation Constitutional Court' in R Clark, F Feldbrugge and S Pomorski (eds), *International and National Law in Russia and Eastern Europe* (The Hague, Kluwer, 2001) 1; A Trochev, 'Russia's constitutional spirit: judge-made principles in theory and practice' in G Smith and R Sharlet (eds), *Russia and Its Constitution: Promise and Political Reality* (Leiden, Brill, 2008) 53.

ernors should be elected, declaring in 2006 that appointment by an elected President would satisfy democratic requirements.[31]

Despite Yel'tsin's desire to limit the scope of the Court by detailing its powers in the Constitution, the list in the Constitutional Court Law is not closed. It is possible for other federal laws or federal constitutional laws to add to the Court's jurisdiction. This has already been done in three federal constitutional laws: on the referendum; on the procedure for accepting a new subject into the Russian Federation; and on the Plenipotentiary for Human Rights. All give additional rights of appeal to the Court: in the case of the first two, to the President; in the last, to the Plenipotentiary. The Federal Law on the Procuracy (Article 35(6)) also gives the Procurator-General power to appeal to the Court on behalf of an individual over the application of law in a specific case.

The Court has also broadened its range though expansive interpretation. For example, the right to appeal the constitutionality of a law being applied in a specific case is given to a 'citizen'. However, utilising the principles of fairness and equality, the Court has interpreted this to include foreign citizens, stateless persons, associations of citizens, political parties, local municipalities, and both State-owned and commercial organisations. Similarly, in relation to the same power, the Court has taken a broad view of what is meant by 'law' (*zakon*) being applied in the specific case. Normally *zakon* is the term used for primary legislation, passed by federal or subject-level legislatures. But the Court has extended the reach of its review to other local legislation and decrees of the State Duma.[32] This is despite views expressed at the Constitutional Convention in the summer of 1993 that challenge should be limited to questions of 'law', otherwise 'the Constitutional Court would have to review every "sneeze"'.[33]

The effect of a Court ruling that a law is unconstitutional is that it 'shall lose force' (Article 125(6)) and an unconstitutional draft treaty will not enter into force. The Court may also instruct the appropriate agency

---

[31] The second case was in December 2005. See Burnham and Maggs, above n 9, at 194, 233 and 240 and WE Pomeranz, 'Medvedev and the Contested Constitutional Underpinnings of Russia's Power Vertical' (2009) 17 *Democratizatsiya* 179.

[32] Trochev, above n 12, at 159, says that there was a change from the Tumanov court to the Baglai court in relation to this; the Court's jurisdiction was expanded by the latter.

[33] Burnham and Trochev, above n 22, at 404, quoting Constitutional Court Judge T Morshchakova.

to produce revised legislation. It has been a matter of increasingly acrimonious comment by successive Constitutional Court chairmen that such instructions are frequently ignored. The Constitutional Court Law was amended in December 2001 to impose time limits on recalcitrant agencies. The maximum is six months (for the legislature in a subject to the federation, non-compliance risking dissolution) and the minimum two months (for the Russian President, and for governors who could be dismissed for non-compliance). In his major study of the Russian Constitutional Court, Alexei Trochev went so far as to suggest that these amendments undermined the Court's power by implying that its rulings were not otherwise self-enforcing.[34] Continuing disquiet expressed by incoming President Medvedev in November 2008 about execution of Court decisions suggests that the amendment seven years earlier has not achieved its goal, and this remains a live issue at the time of writing in mid-2010.

ii. Make-up of the Court

Re-establishment of the Court after the 1993 suspension was not a seamless operation. The 1994 law called for 19 judges, which would allow sessions to take place in two separate chambers, doubling the Court's capacity. Unlimited tenure of the 13 existing judges until retirement at 65 continued, but six new members were required. Under the new law, they would be appointed by the Federation Council on nomination by the President, but for a once-only term of 12 years, with a minimum age of 40 and mandatory retirement at 70. Various groups could suggest candidates to the President, who was free to ignore them. Power plays between Yel'tsin and the Federation Council over his chosen nominees delayed the re-establishment of the Court until February 1995. The judges then elected a new Chairman (Zor'kin had stood down as Chair on 6 October 1993, the day before Yel'tsin suspended the Court). They chose the 68-year-old Academician and international lawyer Vladimir Tumanov, under whose charge the Court avoided controversy.

But controversy stalked the Court, on the issue of judicial tenure. Under its next Chairman, Marat Baglai,[35] the Constitutional Court faced

[34] A Trochev, 'Implementing Russian Constitutional Court Decisions' (2002) 11 *East European Constitutional Review* 95.
[35] Court Chairman from 20 February 1997 to 23 February 2003, when Zor'kin was re-elected as Chair.

a series of changes over this, at a time when judicial tenure for federal judges was also being reassessed. In 2001, President Putin set his friend and able public servant Dmitrii Kozak to review the judicial system. It was felt that hard-won judicial independence was creating too much autonomy for individual federal judges, with the risk that they would be 'independent of the law'. This development is discussed below, but Constitutional Court reforms in February 2001 improved the tenure term for judges appointed under the 1994 Law, extending it from 12 to 15 years, and eliminating the retirement age for that particular group (the original judges kept their unlimited tenure, to age 65). Ten months later a further reform reinstated a mandatory retirement age of 70, which would apply to all extant judges as from January 2005. As Trochev explains, this 'Tinkering with Tenure'[36] was deliberately timed to affect particular judges (Tamara Morshchakova and Viktor Luchin) and politicised the Court as it was caught in the machinations of Executive and Legislature competing over the tenure issue. Baglai's failure as Court Chair to protect it from divisive 'games with judicial tenure'[37] may explain Zor'kin's unexpected re-election by his fellow judges as Court Chairman in February 2003, and their confidence was reaffirmed in 2006 when he was reconfirmed as Chair, less than a month after he had been reported in *Moscow News* as espousing the need for a strong, independent Court to protect citizen's rights and rein in the Executive.[38]

Such an outspoken Chair may become a thing of the past after February 2012, when Zor'kin's current term ends. The law on the Court was amended at the beginning of June 2009 at the instigation of President Medvedev. In future the Chairman will not be elected for three-year terms by the Constitutional Court judges themselves but will be appointed for six years along with two deputies by the Federation Council on nomination by the President. The ostensible motivation is to provide uniformity, as this brings the Constitutional Court into line with the Supreme Court and Highest *Arbitrazh* Court. Cynical commentators

---

[36] A Trochev, 'Tinkering with Tenure: the Russian Constitutional Court in a Comparative Perspective' in F Feldbrugge (ed), *Russia, Europe, and the Rule of Law* (Leiden, Martinus Nijhoff Publishers, 2007) 47.

[37] KL Scheppele, 'Guardians of the Constitution: Constitutional Court Presidents and the Struggle for the Rule of Law in Post-Soviet Europe' (2006) 154 *University of Pennsylvania Law* Review 1757 at 1845.

[38] P Moore, 'Chief Judge calls for check on Kremlin's power' (2006) *Radio Free Europe/Radio Liberty Newsline*, 25 January.

suggest other motives. The next presidential elections (with the new six-year term of office) will be in 2012, so Medvedev may be preparing to have a 'friendly' Constitutional Court Chair in case of electoral law disputes – or for a comfortable career move by a former President. Retired Constitutional Court judge Morshchakova spoke out strongly that the new arrangements would significantly reduce the Court's independence, and were all the more surprising given that the year before Medvedev was considering bringing the procedure for the Chairmen of other two highest courts into line with that of the Constitutional Court, rather than the reverse.

Concern about loss of judicial independence at the Constitutional Court was heightened in early December 2009, when Anatolii Kononov, one of the longest-serving judges, resigned his tenure (which otherwise would run until 2017) as from 1 January 2010. This followed a ruling by his fellow judges at a plenary meeting that his forthright criticisms of the Russian Judiciary were in breach of judicial ethics because they could 'weaken the authority of the judicial branch'.[39] The previous day, another judge from the same court, Vladimir Yaroslavtsev, had stepped down as the Court's representative on the Council of Judges, also following criticism by the Plenum of his outspoken views, in an interview the previous August to the Spanish newspaper *El Pais*, on the parlous state of the Russian legal system. Commentators fear that the high-profile recusal of these two independent-minded judges indicates an increased level of subservience at the Constitutional Court, which is the court most appropriately placed to keep balance between the different branches of State. Court Chairman Valerii Zor'kin denied that the disciplining resulted from too many special (dissenting) opinions by the judges.[40]

Kononov's resignation, and the retirements of Sliva and Strekozov in February and July 2010 as a result of age, gave President Medvedev the opportunity to nominate three new Constitutional Court judges within five months. As a result, in February two former constitutional law

---

[39] A Pushkarskaia, '*Konstitutsionnyi sud teriaet osobye mneniia*' *Kommersant*', 2 December 2009, available online at <http://www.kommersant.ru/doc-y.aspx?DocsID=1284828>, accessed 3 December 2009.

[40] 'Russian Constitutional Court chairman comments on dissident judge's departure', report by Russian radio station *Ekho Moskvy*, 2 December, English translation (2009) *BBC Monitoring Former Soviet Union*, 3 December, available via Westlaw.

professors were appointed to the Court, Aleksandr Kokotov and Konstantin Aranovskii, and in July they were joined by criminal law specialist Aleksandr Boitsov. Both Aranovskii and Boitsov have links with the Juridical Department of St Petersburg State University where Medvedev both studied and taught. Aranovskii was a fellow graduate student and Boitsov taught there when Medvedev was a lecturer from 1991–99. Other Constitutional Court judges share the link with the University. Judges Sergei Kazantsev and Vladimir Yaroslavtsev studied there at the same time as Boitsov, and Judges Sergei Kniazev and Sergei Mavrin were St Petersburg State University graduate students who also then lectured there.[41]

A further change in the Constitutional Court's organisation will result from legislation under way in October 2010. On 22 October the Duma approved both the second and third reading of a presidential bill amending the Federal Constitutional Law on the Constitutional Court. Assuming the bill passes the other necessary hurdles, the Court will no longer sit in two chambers. Instead, decisions will be taken at plenary meetings with a two-thirds quorum. The 70-year maximum age limit for the Court Chairman is also being eliminated. Effectively, this could allow appointment for life.[42] Disciplinary procedure is also revised. Rather than dismissal requiring a two-thirds vote by the Court's other judges, the Federation Council will decide, and with increased grounds, such as repeated absence or refusal to participate.

'How does the Federation Council intend to prove a judge's absence from the session or his refusal to vote?' – [former Constitutional Court judge Tamara] Morshchakova asks, trying to understand the logic used by the draft law's authors. 'After all, there is such a concept as the secrecy of judges' conferences. Will parliament call judges onto the carpet and take evidence from them?'[43]

---

[41] A Pushkarskaya, 'They Have Brought Criminal Accountability to the Constitutional Court' (2010) *World News Connection (Newswire)*, 7 July, cited in J Henderson, 'Tenure and Discipline Developments in Russia' (2011) 17(1) *European Public Law* 1.

[42] A Samarina, 'Zorkin Will Work for 2012 Elections. Constitutional Court to be Built into Presidential Hierarchy', *Nezavisimaya Gazeta Online*, 18 October 2010, available in English translation (2010) *World News Connection (Newswire)*, 20 October, available via Westlaw under title 'Russian Experts Link Constitutional Court Reforms to 2010 Elections'.

[43] *Ibid.*

These upheavals at Russia's most powerful court could indicate a period of subservience, undermining the lead the Court has given in the establishment of a coherent legal system and an independent Judiciary in modern Russia. The Constitutional Court has also been moved away from the political centre of Moscow to Saint Petersburg, against the strongly-voiced opposition of Zor'kin. Since 2008 it has occupied the extremely prestigious former Senate building and the judges live on an island in a specially-built gated community, safe, perhaps independent, but rather remote from ordinary Russian's everyday world.

IV. THE DOMESTIC COURTS AND THE CONSTITUTION

Besides the Constitutional Court there are two separate hierarchies of courts: the domestic courts headed by the Supreme Court; and the system of *arbitrazh* courts headed by the Highest *Arbitrazh* Court.

A. The structure and scope of the domestic courts' hierarchy

The Supreme Court is the top tier of a hierarchy of courts that deal with civil, criminal, administrative 'and other cases' (Constitution, Article 126). There are three tiers. At the lower two levels there are separate domestic courts and military courts, both overseen by the Supreme Court. Military courts hear cases that involve military personnel, both permanent and conscripted. The law applied is the same as in the other domestic courts, except for military crimes and breaches of military discipline, but it is the Russian tradition that incidents arising during life in the armed forces should be heard by judges who, although legally trained and experienced (and who have passed the requisite qualification examination), are also under military service and therefore understand the particular pressures involved. The lowest tier comprises district (*raion*) courts and garrison-level military courts. These hear first-instance civil, criminal and administrative cases (both administrative offences and administrative appeals against infringement of rights), as well as having jurisdiction to rehear cases appealed from justice of the peace courts, where they exist. Since December 2009 the Procurator may also ask the Supreme Court to authorise transfer to a military court of any criminal case where the personal security of participants or those close to them is at risk.

The next level of courts consists of the supreme courts of the republics, territorial (*krai*) or regional (*oblast*) courts, the city courts of Moscow and Saint Petersburg, and the courts of the autonomous region and autonomous areas. On the military side the second tier is at a military force or naval fleet level, with analogous jurisdiction. This level of court hears first-instance serious civil and criminal cases, and appeals from the lowest tier. It is at this level that trial by jury began to be available in selected regions after reforms in 1993. Since January 2010, in all regions of Russia, defendants in serious criminal cases (except crimes against the State, after reforms in December 2008, confirmed as constitutional by the Constitutional Court on 19 April 2010) have the option of a jury trial; the alternative is trial by a panel of three judges. In general Russian judges are in favour of a jury verdict, as it bypasses the traditional informal judicial culture against acquittal and saves the judge the effort of writing a reasoned judgment.

At the top of the hierarchy, the Supreme Court itself can hear particularly important or difficult first-instance civil and criminal cases, although this is rare. The first-instance court would comprise three judges sitting as a panel. The Supreme Court hears various forms of appeal from below, and from its own first-instance hearings. Unlike courts lower in the system, the Supreme Court has separate specialist Judicial Chambers: for Civil Cases; for Criminal Cases; and the Military Chamber, as well as a Cassational Chamber to deal with appeals from the other three Chambers. (It also has a Scientific-Consultative Council.) The specialist Chambers study and generalise judicial practice and analyse judicial statistics. The Court has a Presidium, consisting of the Chairman, his deputy and judges to a total of 13, recommended by the President and confirmed by the Federation Council. It exercises supervisory review of cases that have already been subject to cassational appeal. Supervisory review, brought at the behest of a procurator, a party in a civil case, or the defendant or victim in a criminal case, considers the legality of the decision. A decision of the European Court of Human Rights in 2003 reduced the scope of supervisory review in civil cases to 'substantial and compelling' situations.[44] The Supreme Court also meets in Plenary sessions at least once a quarter. All members may attend; the quorum is two-thirds of the total of 111 judges (figure as of

---

[44] WE Pomeranz, 'Supervisory review and the finality of judgments under Russian law' (2009) 34 *Review of Central and East European Law* 15 at 19.

January 2009). The Minister of Justice and the Procurator-General also have the right to attend the Plenum, and other judges or legal academics may be invited. Guiding 'explanations' are drawn up by this Plenum. The Plenum would also exercise the Court's rarely-used right of legislative initiative.

B. The development of a commercial court system

The normal domestic courts had to adjust to a post-*perestroika* and post-soviet world, and change from nurturing new soviet man to ensuring citizen's rights. An even greater readjustment has been necessary for the *arbitrazh* courts. These courts developed from the *arbitrazh* tribunals which were tasked with ensuring that the soviet-planned economy worked smoothly. They became courts in 1991 and embedded themselves quickly as part of the commercial scheme.[45] When the *arbitrazh* courts were first created, foreign litigants were allowed to choose between them and the ordinary domestic courts. Direct foreign investment in the USSR was barely five years old and the authorities did not want to scare away potential investors lacking confidence in the new courts. By 1995 those fears had evaporated and the special dispensation was removed in the revised *arbitrazh* procedure code. Further revisions in 2001–02 brought in a system of expert lay assessors, at least two of whom sit with an *arbitrazh* judge in first-instance cases if the parties wish. Amicable settlement is encouraged.

A credible survey of business managers in November 2000 showed broad confidence in the *arbitrazh* courts, particularly for cases where the other party was not a State agency.[46] More recent in-depth interviews indicate that recourse to the court is a valuable tool in business relations, particularly as reputational trust between contractual parties is underdeveloped.[47]

[45] K Hendley, 'Remaking an institution: the transition on Russia from State *Arbitrazh* to *Arbitrazh* Courts' (1998) 46 *American Journal of Comparative Law* 93.

[46] T Frye, 'The Two Faces of Russian Courts: Evidence from a Survey of Company Managers' (2002) 11(1-2) *East European Constitutional Review* 125.

[47] K Hendley, 'Coping with Uncertainty: The Role of Contracts in Russian Industry During the Transition to the Market' (2009) 1089 *University of Wisconsin Law School Legal Studies Research Paper Series*, available at <http://ssrn.com/abstract=1458507>, accessed 22 August 2010.

There are acknowledged problems. A reform of the judicial bailiff system in 1997 (with further procedural reforms in 2008) improved enforcement of judgments in all courts, but this remains an issue, and particularly for *arbitrazh* courts serving the business community. Bankruptcy proceedings as a result of the 2009 economic downturn have overloaded the *arbitrazh* courts. Judicial independence has been compromised by interested parties, including the tax authorities; see section VI.C. below.

V. TURF WARS

It was noted in section III. above that the Supreme Court felt it was inappropriate for the RSFSR Constitutional Court to consider the constitutionality of the customary application of law. The Supreme Court's truculence translated into a refusal to re-open any cases after a Constitutional Court finding of unconstitutionality, even after a direct order. One dispute lasted from 1993 to 2000: 'Seven-and-a-half-years of defiance is truly remarkable and shows the depth of animosity between the courts.'[48]

After the 1994 Constitutional Court Law, the dispute found a fresh focus. If a judge suspects legislation applicable in a specific case to be unconstitutional, is he or she required to apply to the Constitutional Court for a ruling? This is the Constitutional Court's view. The Supreme Court disagrees. Vagueness in the wording of Article 125(4) of the Constitution was apparently a conscious decision of the drafting Constitutional Convention.[49] The subsequent Constitutional Court Law is no clearer. Article 101 on this type of referral merely says that 'a court . . . turns to the Constitutional Court with a request' for review, specifying neither a right nor an obligation. By contrast, Article 5(3) of the 1996 Federal Constitutional Law on the Judicial System says a court, 'having established . . . nonconformity . . . to the Constitution . . . adopts a decision', with no mention of referral to the Constitutional Court.[50] This formed the basis of a ruling by the Supreme Court Plenum in 1995, confirming that there is no duty to refer to the Constitutional

---

[48] Burnham and Trochev, above n 22, at 390.
[49] *Ibid* at 402.
[50] Burnham and Trochev credit the Supreme Court for this; *ibid* at 404.

Court.[51] In the following years the domestic courts dealt with thousands of such cases, including hundreds brought by procurators protesting that legislation of federal subjects contradicted federal law. The Constitutional Court had just been re-established in 1995 and did not seriously object to any of this activity until June 1998, when it issued a ruling that referral to it was mandatory when there was an issue of the constitutionality of a law being applied in a court in a specific case.

The domestic courts fought back, emphasising that they would hear procuratorial protests against subject-level legislation which conflicted with federal law, and by 2000 the Constitutional Court acceded to this, probably for pragmatic reasons as it would not be able to cope with the number of cases if it succeeded in claiming exclusive jurisdiction.

But the war was not yet over. In 2004 the Constitutional Court decided that a challenge to the constitutionality of regulations based on a law amounted to a challenge to the law itself, which therefore came within the Constitutional Court's jurisdiction. That was a significant and unjustified expansion into the Supreme Court's province. However, the following year the Constitutional Court back-tracked, realising that it would not be able to cope with the flood of cases if it persisted with this expanded power to review constitutionality. There are still unresolved issues over the extent that the Constitutional Court can review other court decisions about the legality of legislation, and whether those courts will take any notice of the result if it does. The unfortunate victim of this 'demarcation dispute' over jurisdiction is the Russian legal system as a whole, as it makes it more difficult to develop a coherent and consistent approach to legislation while the leading courts continue to squabble over which has the last word on its application.[52]

---

[51] See Burnham and Maggs, above n 9, at 102; B Bowring, 'Institutions and Change in Russian Politics: Politics, The Rule of Law and the Judiciary' in N Robinson (ed), *Institutions and Change in Russian Politics* (Basingstoke, Macmillan, 2000) 69 at 81.

[52] Burnham and Trochev, above n 22, at 427, 432, give an example of a serious difference in 2007 over whether the Supreme Court's power under the Federal Constitutional Law on Referenda to review decisions of the Central Elections Commission was constitutional.

VI. JUDICIAL INDEPENDENCE

Reforming Tsar Nicholas II's 1864 aspiration

> to establish in Russia fast, just and merciful courts, equal for all . . ., to increase judicial power, to give it the necessary independence and, in general, to strengthen . . . the respect for law without which public prosperity is impossible and which must serve as a permanent guide for the actions of all and everybody, from the highest rank to that of the lowest rank[53]

still resonates in Russia today. It requires not only practical measures (many of which are in place), but also a culture shift that may not be achieved until 'new blood' in the judicial ranks eliminates old mind-sets.[54]

A. The Soviet period – telephone law

Soviet judges were not expected to be independent from other branches of State. Marxist theory denied the validity of the bourgeois 'separation of powers', and judges were expected to play their part in transforming those they encountered in court, or in public question and answer sessions, into the ideal new socialist man or woman. Under the 1960 Criminal Procedure Code sentences for crime had the aims of reform and reeducation; 'reform through labour' justified the GULAG.[55]

The Soviet Constitution declared that judges were independent and subordinate only to law, but any candidate for judicial office would be vetted by the Communist Party under the so-called *nomenklatura* system before his or her name was put forward. It was commonly believed that in politically-sensitive cases a Soviet judge would receive instructions from the Communist Party by a phone call – 'telephone law' (*telefonnoe pravo*). Even without direct instruction, the Soviet judicial mentality included a belief that the needs of society stood above the rights of

---

[53] PH Juviler, *Revolutionary Law and Order* (London, MacMillan, 1976) 26.

[54] Opinion of Judge Olga Kudeshkina, expressed at a seminar on 8 February 2010 organised by the Bar Human Rights Committee and EU–Russia Centre: M Karp, 'The Case of Judge Kudeshkina', available at <http://www.rightsinrussia. info/home/events/the-case-of-judge-kudeshkina>, accessed 22 August 2010.

[55] GULAG is the Russian acronym for the 'Main Administration of Corrective Labour Camps and Colonies' which ran the Soviet penitentiary system.

individuals. Writing after the end of the Soviet Union, legal academic Valerii Savitskii was forthright:

> In the USSR, there never was a separate and independent judicial power. All the courts, the procuracy and the organs of investigation did in the name of the state was done on direct instruction of assorted party committees and individual members of their staff. . . . As a result, not a single constitutional provision proclaiming the independence of the courts was applied in practice. The norms of the Constitution merely served as a fig leaf covering the spineless obsequiousness and grovelling obedience of the so-called judicial power, which from day one, was under the thumb of the party apparatus.[56]

Even during *perestroika*, it was not thought inappropriate for a judge to belong to the single ruling Communist Party. When in July 1989 USSR Supreme Soviet deputies were questioning Evgenii Smolentsev, the proposed candidate for Chairman of the USSR Supreme Court, deputy Roi Medvedev[57] asked him how he would respond to the principle that a Supreme Court judge could not simultaneously be a CPSU member. Smolentsev declared that he would not work at the Court if the price was relinquishing his Party membership.[58] Even the first judges in the innovative RSFSR Constitutional Court were not immune from Party links. All but Tamara Moshchakova had been Party members, and three of the 13 were even proposed by Communist factions in the Legislature, including Zor'kin who subsequently became the Court Chair. He was nominated by the faction 'Communists for Democracy', described by Julia Wishnevsky, in a *Radio Free Europe/Radio Liberty* Research Report, as 'moderate'.[59] Two judges (Luchin and Tiunov) were nominated by the parliamentary faction 'Communists of Russia', classified by Wishnevski as 'hardline'. Some even claimed a positive benefit:

[56] V Savitskii, 'Judicial Power in Russia: First Steps' (1996) 22 *Review of Central and East European Law* 417.

[57] A Soviet Marxist historian who was expelled from the CPSU after the publication in the West in 1972 of his book criticising Stalinism, *Let History Judge*. He was reinstated in 1989 but remained a critical voice of the old establishment, supporting Gorbachev's *perestroika* reforms.

[58] *Izvestiia*, 9 June 1989, cited in J Henderson, 'The Law of the USSR: On the Status of Judges in the USSR' (1990) 16 *Review of Socialist Law* 305 at 315.

[59] Wishnevski, above n 25, at 12–13.

In unofficial communications, some . . . judges seemed to rather imply that their party past was a 'plus' in that it rooted the judges in Russian society and helped them understand what 'ordinary people' went through.[60]

Another characteristic of Soviet judges was that they were elected. Before the *perestroika* reforms, Soviet district court judges were directly elected by the local populace for five-year terms of office. Ballots were secret but, as with all Soviet elections, the number of candidates matched the number of positions. Judges of higher-level courts were elected by the Soviet of People's Deputies at the same administrative level, so the USSR Supreme Court judges were elected by the USSR Supreme Soviet. But the aspirations of *perestroika* to create a socialist rule-of-law State (*sotsialisticheskoe pravovoe gosudarstvo*) included proposals that affected judges' appointment in an effort to create a more independent Judiciary.

B. The movement towards judicial independence

In July 1988 the groundbreaking 19th All-Union Party Conference Resolution on Legal Reform implicitly acknowledged that judges did not have unconditional independence. It suggested that longer terms of office and changing who elected them would be a 'guarantee of strengthening the independence of judges'.[61] The Party's proposals were quickly taken up. Amendments to the Soviet Constitution in the autumn of 1988 preserved the principle of electivity, but the period of office before re-election was doubled to 10 years, and district court judges would be elected by the regional soviet. In December 1989 the first-ever Soviet Law on the Status of Judges came into force, which incorporated these developments and also attempted to improve life conditions for the Soviet Judiciary with various social guarantees. Importantly, the law required for the first time that a judge should have a higher legal qualification, as well as at least two years' experience of working in a legal field. Another innovation concerned the judicial oath and robes. The 1989 Soviet Law also established the Councils of Judges and Judicial

---

[60] Dr Elke Fein, personal communication to the author, 29 January 2008. Dr Fein had successfully defended her PhD thesis on the CPSU case at the University of Bremen in 2005. See Henderson, above n 24, at 494.

[61] *Pravda*, 5 July 1988; English translation in (1998) 40(38) *Current Digest of the Soviet Press* 15.

Qualifications Collegia, whose successors in Russia are an important mechanism in judicial self-regulation. The introduction of the Soviet Presidency in 1990 brought the first breach in the principle of electivity of judges. The new President would appoint judges to military tribunals.

In independent Russia, the 1993 Constitution established appointment by the President for all judges except those of the highest three courts, the Constitutional Court, the Supreme Court and the Highest *Arbitrazh* Court, where the procedure is nomination by the President and appointment by the Federation Council. The subsequent 1996 Federal Constitutional Law on the Judicial System added a wealth of detail, such as judicial examinations and the requirement for approval by the Judicial Qualifications Collegia, which should ensure that the President is not handpicking federal judges. The 1996 Law, passed at a time when Yel'tsin allowed a broad degree of autonomy in return for political support, also required approval by subject-level legislatures of the federal judges who would serve in their area. This right was removed in 2001, when Putin increased centralisation.

In Russia significant changes were made to the term of judicial office. Soviet judges all served fixed periods before possible re-election. An amendment on 9 December 1992 to Article 164 of the 1978 RSFSR Constitution introduced in Russia the principle of tenure up to a set retirement age, so that the 'Damocles sword of periodic elections (for 5 or 10 years) no longer [hung] over the head of the judges'.[62]

The 1992 Russian Law on the Status of Judges stated in its first article that 'judicial power is autonomous and operates independently of executive and legislative power'. This was an innovation pre-dating the 1993 Constitution.[63] Under the Law, federal judges are appointed to serve until the retirement age of 70 years. An initial probationary period of five years, reduced to three in December 2001, was abolished in July 2009. This eliminated a significant pathway for 'internal' pressure on new judges by their Court Chairman who could exert influence on the panel assessing suitability at the end of the probationary period.

The Judicial Department of the Supreme Court took over administration of the courts from the Ministry of Justice in 1998, as one of the reforms Russia undertook when she joined the Council of Europe in 1996 (the Ministry of Justice was given control of the penitentiary

---

[62] Savitskii, above n 56, at 418.
[63] *Ibid* at 417.

system, out of the hands of the Ministry of the Interior). The Judicial Department organises the Council of Judges of the Russian Federation (which meets at least twice a year, with more frequent meetings of its Presidium) and the Highest Judicial Qualification Collegium.[64] Both are important for the professionalisation of the Russian Judiciary. The first gives an organised forum for judges to express their opinions and is accountable to the annual All-Russian Congress of Judges, and the second heads the mechanism for judicial self-regulation, overseeing suitability of candidates for office, promotion and removal of immunity. On 9 November 2009, at the instigation of President Medvedev, legislation was amended to create a new disciplinary body to consider appeals by judges against decisions of Judicial Qualifications Collegia to strip them of immunity from prosecution in criminal cases. The law was controversial and commencement was delayed until 1 March 2010. The new Disciplinary Bench held its first hearing on 26–27 April, rejecting three appeals against early dismissal and allowing one. It is hoped that the new appeal body will be an independent check on decisions to remove judges from office, and thus undermine the opportunity for improper influence of Court Chairs, discussed below.

A funding shortage was one issue faced by courts on a daily basis, particularly during the period of economic crisis in the late 1990s. Federal courts should be funded out of the federal budget, but in practice district courts might get 'sponsorship' from local authorities and even local businessman who would expect a return of favours. In July 1998 the Supreme Court successfully petitioned the Constitutional Court over unconstitutional budget cuts.[65] The following year a Federal Law on Court Financing put this important practical issue on a more secure footing.

If the legal framework for judicial independence was more or less in place by the end of the 1990s, the new millennium and new President brought some reconsideration. There was a retrenchment as a result of fear that individual judges had become too independent. Unlimited tenure was under threat in a plan produced by economist German Gref in 2000.[66] The judges fought back, and in 2001 Dmitrii Kozak, who took

[64]   The Federal Law on Judges' Community Agencies of 14 March 2002 in Butler, above n 2, at 404.

[65]   Burnham and Maggs, above n 9, at 61.

[66]   See P Solomon, 'Putin's Judicial Reform: Making Judges Accountable as Well as Independent' (2002) 11 *East European Constitutional Review* 117 at 119.

over juridical reforms, brokered a deal which retained unlimited tenure but increased accountability by expanding membership of the Judicial Qualifications Collegia to include one-third non-judges, limiting the terms of office of Court Chairs, and simplifying the process for removal of judicial immunity. At the same time there was a major boost in court funding (affordable because of high world oil prices and more efficient tax collection) and an enhanced role for judges under a new Criminal Procedure Code. A new code of judicial ethics was confirmed by the 6th All-Russian Congress of Judges in December 2004.[67] But the progress towards a trusted and trustworthy Judiciary has not been trouble-free.

C. A new telephone law?

In recent times judicial independence has again come under question, both within and outside Russia. On 25 October 2004, Constitutional Court Chairman Zor'kin stated in an interview in *Izvestia* that

> according to research, our courts are mired in corrupt relations with business. Bribe-taking in courts has become one of the most corrupt markets in Russia . . . built on various corrupt networks operating at various levels of the power structure[68]

and that the country's judicial system is in many aspects worse than it was in the Soviet era.[69] The Supreme Court challenged Zor'kin to substantiate his allegations or withdraw them. Zor'kin countered that he was only defending the judicial system.

There has been clear evidence that courts are inappropriately pressured, for example in 'prosecutions to order' (*zakaznye dela*). The case against Mikhail Khodorkovsky and other executives of the YUKOS oil company brought a new expression to the political lexicon, named after the court where key procedural issues were (wrongly) decided: 'Basmanny justice' (*Basmannoe pravosudie*), meaning 'justice serving the needs of authorities or powerful persons'.[70] Khodorkovsky was sentenced on 31 May 2005 to nine years' deprivation of freedom for fraud and tax evasion.

---

[67] Butler, above n 2, at 447.

[68] Cited in P Solomon, 'Threats of Judicial Counterreform in Putin's Russia' (2005) *Demokratizatsiya* 325.

[69] *Izvestia*, 25 October 2004.

[70] Sakwa, above n 6, at 260.

Further prosecution is under consideration.[71] On 7 May 2009 his appeal to the European Court of Human Rights about various flaws in the prosecution process was ruled admissible. Whilst it is true that Khodorkovsky may have presided over some shady dealing in the early days of his entrepreneurship, he appears to have been singled out for politically-motivated prosecution because he made his political ambitions clear.

There are well-documented instances of judges having disciplinary action framed against them when they did not follow the wishes of the Court Chair. Court Chairs are notoriously powerful, having an important role in promotion decisions, and presiding over the court hearing an appeal by a judge against his or her dismissal by the Judicial Qualifications Collegium.[72]

In one notorious case, whistle-blower Judge Olga Kudeshkina was dismissed in May 2004 after she refused to bow to pressure to convict a senior procurator who had been investigating the Three Whales smuggling scam that implicated a number of government officials. Further, she would not condone falsification of the court record suggested by Moscow City Court Chair Judge Olga Yegorova to cover up improper prosecutorial behaviour. Kudeshkina's appeal against dismissal was allocated to a particular judge by Judge Yegorova, who was an interested party. Kudeshkina's objections were ignored. Eventually, having failed to get redress from the Judicial Complaints Commission, on 12 July 2005 she appealed to the European Court of Human Rights. The Chamber of the Court held in her favour and awarded her €10,000 for breach of Article 10 of the European Convention on Human Rights (freedom of expression). Any further appeal by Russia has been refused. Kudeshkina's case and other examples of judges being pressured from within – by their Court Chair or procurators – were highlighted in a report prepared in 2009 by former German Minster of Justice Mrs Sabine Leutheusser-Schnarrenberger for the Committee on Legal Affairs and Human Rights of the Parliamentary Assembly of the Council of Europe.[73]

---

[71] B Bowring, 'The Second Trial of Mikhail Khodorkovsky' in *Russia's Judicial System* (2009) 59 *Russian Analytical Digest* 5, available at <http://www.res.ethz.ch/analysis/rad/details.cfm?lng=en&id=99939>, accessed 22 August 2010.

[72] International Bar Association, 'Striving for Judicial Independence: A Report into Proposed Changes to the Judiciary in Russia', June 2005, available at <http://www.ibanet.org/Document/Default.aspx?DocumentUid=90A7A9FF-A0BC-44AD-A4E9-7E6CEA27655C>, accessed 22 August 2010.

[73] Document 11993 dated 7 August 2009, available at <http://assembly.coe.int/Documents/WorkingDocs/Doc09/EDOC11993.pdf>, accessed 22 August 2010.

There are other sources of illegitimate pressure. The Chairman of the Highest *Arbitrazh* Court, Ivanov, admitted in November 2006 that the tax authorities had pressurised judges after too many cases were decided in favour of taxpayers.[74] Ivanov has taken practical steps to institutionalise transparency; all communications to the Court – phone calls, letters and so on – are now published on the Court's website, which may deter outside interference in *arbitrazh* court decisions.

In May 2008 the first deputy chairwoman of the Highest *Arbitrazh* Court, Elena Valiavina, gave evidence in a defamation case brought by Valerii Boyev, an official from the Presidential Administration in charge of recommending judicial awards and promotion, against an investigative reporter who alleged that Boyev had attempted to influence judges. Judge Valiavina testified that she had been pressured by Boyev to reach a particular decision in a share-dealing case. Three other judges were also prepared to give evidence, but Boyev dropped the defamation case as soon as Valianvina had testified.[75]

In 2008 the issue of whether a case could be fairly tried in Russia was at the heart of an English Commercial Court case, *Cherney v Deripaska*.[76] Cherney had applied to pursue a claim in London rather than the venue of the events, Russia. Mr Justice Christopher Clarke held on the basis of Bill Bowring's expert evidence that there would be 'a significant risk of improper government interference if Mr Cherney would bring the present claims in Russia' (at [248]). This result was upheld by the Court of Appeal.[77]

The resignation in 2009 of Constitutional Court Judge Kononov and the retreat of Judge Yaroslavtsev (so that he would no longer act as the Court's representative), following what the other judges regarded as intemperate remarks about the state of the Russian judicial system, were noted above. Clearly, outspoken criticism is less tolerated now than it was when Zor'kin suggested in 2004 that there was widespread judicial corruption. Or perhaps the difference is the alleged source of the pressure. In 2004 Zor'kin was pointing the finger at unscrupulous *biznesmen*

---

[74] Olga Pleshanova, 'Vyshaya arbitrazhnaya sut'. Glava VAS priznalfakt davleniya' (2006) 223(3554) Kommersant', 29 November, available at <http://www.kommersant.ru/doc.aspx?DocsID=725800>, accessed 22 August 2010 (thanks to Professor B Bowring for the reference).

[75] Burnham and Maggs, above n 9, at 69, quoting *Kommersant*, 13 May 2008.

[76] [2008] EWHC 1530 (Comm).

[77] [2009] EWCA Civ 849.

with fat wallets and well-armed personal bodyguards. In 2009 Yaroslavtsev was quoted as saying that 'during the presidency of Vladimir Putin and his successor Dmitrii Medvedev the judicial branch in Russia had been turned into a instrument to serve the executive branch' and that the 'centre for decision making is in the President's staff'.[78] It may be coincidental that the two stigmatised judges 'filed blistering dissenting special opinions' in a case on presidential appointments of governors reported in 2006.[79]

One systemic factor is that many Russian judges are recruited from the ranks of court clerks, the Procuracy or police, and therefore are used to hierarchical discipline. By contrast, for example, the majority of English judges are former barristers, with a decade or more experience as self-employed advocates under a professional duty to take responsibility for their cases and, although working on clients' instructions, are autonomous in how they run them. Success at the English Bar used to be the only prerequisite for judicial appointment, so the corps of English judges was constituted by seasoned lawyers with considerable trial experience and the tradition of thinking for themselves, unlike in Russia. But there are exceptions to this generalisation about the Russian Judiciary. Independent thinkers, such as former academics, and occasionally an advocate, may attain judicial office. The redoubtable Judge Kudeshkina is a former advocate. Nevertheless, there is currently an informal rule that judges and advocates should remain separate, even to the extent that a judge should not have an advocate in his or her family. Both Kudeshkina and the 2009 Council of Europe Report call for a wider range of candidates for judicial office; a change of culture to match the important institutional changes that hoped to consign 'spineless obsequiousness and grovelling obedience'[80] to the unlamented past.

---

[78] A Pushkarskaia, 'Konstitutsionnyi sud teriaet osobye mheniia' [Constitutional Court Loses Dissenting Opinions] *Moscow Kommersant Online*, 2 December 2009, available at <http://www.kommersant.ru/doc.aspx?DocsID=1284828&stamp=634000377105470156>, accessed 22 August 2010.

[79] Pomeranz, above n 31, at 184.

[80] Savitskii, text to n 56 above.

VII. PROTECTION OF HUMAN RIGHTS

A. The development of human rights

Rights in Russia have undergone a profound change in recent decades, both in the approach to rights themselves and in the methods for their enforcement. Amongst the dramatic and far-reaching developments during the *perestroika* era, one of the most significant was the change in the theoretical basis of individual rights. In the developed Soviet system, rights were presented as something awarded to a citizen in return for the duties that the citizen performed for the State. There were no inherent 'human rights', only dependent 'individual rights' (see chapter two).

On the positive side, the Soviet approach focused on practical realisation, especially of economic rights. Each substantive constitutional article, particularly Articles 39 to 45, contained a paragraph specifying how access to the right would be ensured, for example through free professional medical care, social insurance, free education and so on. Even if these State-provided services were less than luxurious, they were universal for Soviet citizens, and in practice these measures were generally realised so that, for example, the USSR had low infant mortality and high literacy rates.

The Soviet Union did not completely ignore international legal developments in the field of rights. In 1973 it ratified the two 1966 United Nations Covenants, on Economic Social and Cultural Rights (ICESCR) and on Civil and Political Rights (ICCPR). In 1975 it signed the Helsinki Final Act at the First Conference on Security and Cooperation in Europe (CSCE) Summit of Heads of State or Government. But the 1977 USSR Constitution mentioned only the principle of 'respect for human rights' in its section on foreign policy, in regard to relations between the USSR and other States (Article 29). The USSR's decision to be one of the 35 State signatories to the Helsinki Final Act was probably taken in the expectation that it would have little internal impact. However, it resulted in human rights being monitored for the first time against an international standard, and in May 1976 the Group to Assist in the Implementation of the Helsinki Agreements in the USSR, soon known as 'the Moscow Helsinki Group', was formed to do this. This and similar grassroots pressure groups may well have had regime-changing impact.[81]

---

[81] DC Thomas, *The Helsinki Effect: International Norms, Human Rights, and the Demise of Communism* (Princeton, NJ, Princeton University Press, 2001).

The 'dependent rights' approach epitomised in the 1977 USSR Constitution was rejected during the *perestroika* era. Following a Constitutional Supervision Committee Opinion in April 1991, with impressive speed the USSR Supreme Soviet on 5 July acceded to the Optional Protocol to the ICCPR, and recognised the jurisdiction of the UN Committee for Human Rights.[82] On 5 September 1991, at the urging of renowned jurist Academician Vladimir Kudriavtsev, the USSR Congress of People's Deputies (CPD), as its last legislative act before it dissolved itself and ceded power to the new State Council, adopted the USSR Declaration of the Rights and Freedoms of Man. This watershed document declared in its Preamble that 'No group, party or State interests may be placed above the interests of the individual', and in Article 1 that

> Each person possesses natural inalienable and inviolable rights and freedoms. They are sealed in laws that must correspond to the Universal Declaration of Human Rights, international covenants on human rights and other international norms and present declaration.

The USSR Declaration enshrined the doctrine of inherent rights in Soviet law for the first time. Unfortunately, despite being passed by the CPD, the legal status of the Declaration was unclear as it did not fit within the standard Soviet hierarchy of legislation and, more importantly, clearly contradicted the Constitution then in force.[83] The practical difficulties this might have caused were precluded by the dissolution of the USSR by the end of 1991.

In the meantime, on 22 November 1991 Russia passed its own 'Declaration of the Rights and Freedoms of Man and Citizen'. In April 1992, in newly independent Russia, the provisions of this Declaration were incorporated wholesale (with the exception of one article, ironically on setting up a Plenipotentiary for Human Rights), into the Russian Constitution of 1978. Chapter 5 on Fundamental Rights, Freedoms and Duties of Citizens was replaced, giving Russia for the first time a set of constitutional rights that matched international human rights standards.

---

[82] Bowring, above n 18, at 102.

[83] GP van den Berg, in 'Human Rights in the Legislation and the Draft Constitution of the Russian Federation' (1992) 18 *Review of Central and East European Law* 197 at 202, in fn 15 looks at the legal status of the Declaration and concludes that 'declarations are deceiving documents and a serious parliament should abstain from adopting them'.

The 1993 Constitution has remained faithful to the inherent rights approach.[84] It is true that the limitation clause in Article 55(3) is rather far-reaching and does not distinguish between different types of rights, and some rights appear to be available only to citizens (for example the Article 31 right to peaceful assembly). Nevertheless, the contrast with the previous RSFSR Constitution of 1978 is striking; Russia has welcomed inherent human rights into her highest law. The first article of the chapter on rights expressly incorporates 'generally-recognised principles and norms of international law' (Article 17), and its second paragraph declares that 'the basic rights and freedoms of man shall be inalienable and shall belong to each from birth'. An earlier article, Article 15(4), includes international law within the Russian legal system; it declares that 'commonly recognised principles and norms of international law and international treaties of the Russian Federation shall be an integral part of its legal system' and treaty law shall take priority over inconsistent domestic law (see chapter three).

It is not only in the recognition of innate rights and the direct applicability of international law that the Constitution differs from its Soviet precursor. By its declaration of direct enforceability, and the fact that 'human and civil rights are secured by the judicial system' (Article 18), the Constitution also emphasises the central role of courts in the enforcement of rights. This has been an important development, although not the only one, in constitutional rights becoming enforceable in Russia by individuals rather than being policy statements, as in Soviet times.

B. Substantive rights

The content of the constitutional chapter on rights draws heavily on the *perestroika* reforms, with the result that

> the human rights section of the Constitution does not omit a single right that non-socialist countries consider essential in the civil and political rights domain.[85]

---

[84] A Korkeakivi, 'Russia on the Rights Track' (1994) 1 *Parker School Journal of East European Law* 233; A Korkeakivi, 'The Reach of Rights in the New Russian Constitution' (1995) 3 *Cardozo Journal of International and Comparative Law* 229.

[85] Korkeakivi (1995), above n 84, at 231.

As the chapter title 'Rights and Freedoms of Man and Citizen' suggests, these are individual rights. Group rights, such as rights of national-cultural minorities, are not unknown in Russia. Constitutional Article 69, in the chapter on the Federal Structure, asserts that the Russian Federation

> shall guarantee the rights of small indigenous peoples in accordance with the generally recognised principles and rules of international law and international treaties of the Russian Federation.

Currently such rights stem from the Council of Europe's 1994 Framework Convention for the Protection of National Minorities, which Russia signed on joining the Council of Europe in 1996 and ratified in 1998 without restrictions.[86]

Some articles in Chapter 2 of the Constitution give rights to 'each' and some reserve rights for citizens. (Article 62(3) specifies that foreign citizens and stateless persons enjoy equal rights and bear equal duties with citizens, except where otherwise provided by federal law or international treaty.) Both the September 1991 USSR Declaration of the Rights of Man and the November 1991 Russian Declaration of the Rights of Man and Citizen (incorporated in April 1992 into the then Constitution) made a similar distinction. It is not unknown for Constitutions to give special favours to citizens, but van den Berg's careful analysis of the Declarations and draft Russian Constitution led him to propose that a desire for stylistic variety may have influenced the draftsmen, with no legal significance necessarily intended.[87] However, the nature of the particular rights in the current Constitution suggests that the differentiation is deliberate.

i. Citizen's rights

Citizens of the Russian Federation have the right of peaceful assembly, and to hold meetings, rallies, demonstrations, marches and pickets (Article 31). The right is not qualified, but local regulations require prior notice. A movement calling itself 'Strategy 31' in honour of this constitutional article has demonstrated on the last day of each month since

---

[86] B Bowring, 'Austro-Marxism's Last Laugh? The Struggle for Recognition of National-Cultural Autonomy for Rossians and Russians' (2002) 54 *Europe-Asia Studies* 229.

[87] van den Berg, above n 83, at 235.

April 2010 to emphasise the right, and is invariably forcefully dispersed as lacking the requisite permissions.[88]

Citizens also have the right to participate in State affairs, both directly and through representatives (Article 32(1)). In the previous Constitution, as amended in April 1992, 'representatives' was qualified as being 'freely elected through universal direct and equal suffrage by secret ballot'. Those details were not included in the 1993 Constitution, and similarly Article 32(2), specifying the right to elect and be elected, does not require the ballot to be direct or secret, as previously. Article 32(3) calls for the suspension of the franchise right of those sentenced by a court to deprivation of freedom, as well as those who lack dispositive legal capacity. This is an innovation. Previously Russian prisoners could vote, even when USSR law suggested otherwise. Also new is the stated citizens' right to participate in the dispensing of justice (Article 32(5)). Article 32(4) gives citizens equal access to State service. Article 33 allows citizens the right to send individual and collective appeals to public bodies.

Although the right of private ownership is available to 'each', the right to private ownership of land is restricted to citizens and their associations (Article 36), and has the limitation that possession, use and disposition of land and other natural resources should not damage the environment or violate others' rights. The conditions and procedure for land use are set by federal law (Article 36(3)). State and local authority provision of housing, either free or for affordable payment, is available to 'indigent and other citizens' (Article 40(3)).

A number of citizens' rights were not articulated in the previous Constitution. The State now undertakes to protect the rights and freedoms of man and citizen (Article 45(1)). Article 60 allows citizens to exercise their rights autonomously from age 18. Article 61 forbids the deportation or extradition abroad of a Russian citizen. The application of this caused friction between the United Kingdom and Russia in May 2008. British prosecutors wanted to charge former KGB agent Andrei Lugovoi with the murder by the administration of radioactive polonium of Aleksandr Litvinenko in London in November 2006. Lugovoi's extradition was refused.[89] In 2007 Lugovoi was elected to the Duma,

---

[88] See L Harding, 'The Demonstrators Who Won't Give Up', *Guardian*, 30 August 2010, available online at <http://www.guardian.co.uk/world/2010/aug/30/russian-protesters-31ers>, accessed 19 October 2010.

[89] Full discussion in J Hartmann, 'The Lugovoy Extradition Case' (2008) 57 *International and Comparative Law Quarterly* 194.

and since then enjoys a deputy's immunity as well. The 1993 Constitution now allows Russian citizens to have dual nationality (Article 62(1)) 'in accordance with a federal law or international treaty'. Their Russian rights are not diminished or their duties reduced, unless federal law or international treaty provides otherwise (Article 62(2)).

ii. Unqualified rights

Most articles give unqualified rights, available to any individual, not just citizens. The first is the right to equality,

> irrespective of sex, race, nationality, language, origin, property and official position, place of residence, attitude towards religions, [personal] convictions, affiliation to social organisations, and also other circumstances. (Article 19)

It should be noted that sexual orientation is not included in this list, and despite consensual male homosexual activity being decriminalised in 1993 (by a presidential decree of Yel'tsin, which was applied to override the then Criminal Code), there is still a strong cultural prejudice against gays, fuelled by the Orthodox Church's traditional homophobia.

There is a general right to human dignity and freedom from torture (Article 21); freedom and personal inviolability (Article 22(1)); and inviolability of private life, personal and family secrecy, and defence of honour (Article 23(1)). Individuals may determine and indicate their nationality (ethnicity), and use a native language in communication, upbringing, education and creativity (Article 26). There is freedom of movement and choice of abode within Russia, and freedom for all to leave and (for citizens) freedom to return (Article 27), all of which were severely restricted in Soviet times.[90] Free choice of abode is still problematic, as some cities, notably Moscow, continue to insist on local registration, despite this '*propiska*' system having been condemned by both the USSR Constitutional Supervision Committee and the Russian Constitutional Court.[91]

---

[90] See M Matthews, *The Passport Society: Controlling Movement in Russia and USSR* (Boulder, Col, Westview Press, 1993).

[91] K Katanian, 'Freedom of Movement in the Russian Federation Today' (1998) 7 *East European Constitutional Review* 52; DS Schaible, 'Life in Russia's "Closed City": Moscow's Movement Restrictions and the Rule of Law' (2001) 76 *New York University Law Review* 344.

The freedom of conscience provision is even-handed as between believers and non-believers, allowing 'the right to profess, individually or jointly with others, any religion or none, freely to chose, have and disseminate religious and other beliefs, and to act in accordance with them' (Article 28). (See chapter three, section III.C.iv. for more on Church–State relations.)

The article on freedom of thought and speech is quite detailed.[92] A general right is given in Article 29(1), but the following paragraph prohibits hate speech 'on the basis of social, racial, national, religious, or language superiority' (Article 29(2)). There is freedom from being forced to express or renounce opinions or convictions (Article 29(3)). The right to freedom of information includes the requirement that State secrets are defined by federal law (Article 29(4)).[93] Freedom of mass media is guaranteed and censorship prohibited (Article 29(5)). Formal State censorship can be prohibited, but it is not clear what steps can be taken to control media bias in privately-owned media empires.[94] Use of 'stories to order' and less than comprehensive, free and fair representation in the media are problems which undermine informed exercise of voting rights in Russia. Attempts in electoral law to limit what was published about candidates backfired by leading to selective threats of closure of media outlets for inadvertent breaches. The Constitutional Court was asked to intervene and restored a sense of reason in the area.[95]

Article 30 gives an unqualified right of association and includes a prohibition on being forced to join, or stay in, any association. Support for the market economy is given by Article 34, with the right to use abilities and property for any entrepreneurial and economic activity not prohibited by law, whilst not exercising a monopoly or unfair competition. Article 35 protects the right to private ownership and inheritance. A judicial decision is required to deprive someone of property.

---

[92] See A Rakhmilovich, 'The Constitutional Court of the Russian Federation: Recent Cases on Protecting the Freedom of Thought and Speech and Related Matters' (1996) 22 *Review of Central and East European Law* 129.

[93] See J Henderson and H Sayadyan, 'Freedom of Information in Russia' (2011) 17(2) *European Public Law*, forthcoming.

[94] Developments in Russian media since *perestroika* are summarised in R Sakwa, *Russian Politics and Society*, 4th edn (Abingdon, Routledge, 2008) 345.

[95] J Henderson, 'The Russian Constitutional Court to the Rescue: Freedom of Political Comment Reasserted' (2005) 11 *European Public Law* 17.

Appropriation for State needs is allowed, but only with prior and fair compensation.

Article 37 deals with labour rights. Labour shall be free, and each has the right to choose his or her work activity. Forced labour is prohibited. Work conditions should be safe, and federal law sets a minimum payment and a right to protection from unemployment. There is a right to individual and collective labour disputes, federal law establishing settlement procedures. The right to strike is explicit, which is an innovation compared to the previous Constitution, even in its 1992 amended form.

Motherhood, childhood and the family are protected by the State (Article 38). Parents have the right and duty to care for and nurture their children, but adult able-bodied children must care for incapacitated parents (also an innovation). Article 39 guarantees social security for age, illness, disability and loss of breadwinner, for bringing up children and for other cases specified by law. State pensions and social benefits shall be established by law, and voluntary social insurance and additional forms of social security encouraged. Article 40 says that each shall have the right to housing. No one may be arbitrarily deprived of housing. Public bodies should encourage housing construction. The right to health care is available to each (Article 41), as is the right to a decent environment and reliable information on its condition (Article 42; an innovation). There is a right to education (Article 43(1)). General access to free pre-school, basic general and secondary vocational education is guaranteed (Article 43(2)). Free higher education in a State or municipal educational institution is available on a competitive basis (Article 43(3)). Article 44 guarantees freedom of creativity and teaching, and the right to participate in cultural life, with an associated obligation to preserve historical and cultural heritage.

iii. Judicial rights

One group of general rights concern due process. The State undertakes to protect the rights and freedoms of man and citizen (Article 45(1)), and each has the right to use any legal means to defend his or her rights and freedoms (Article 45(2)). Article 46(1) follows this by saying that judicial defence of rights and freedoms is guaranteed. Article 46(2) allows appeal to a court against unlawful actions and decisions (or omissions to act) of public bodies and social associations, and Article 46(3) gives the right of recourse to inter-State agencies on the basis of international treaty, where domestic remedies have been exhausted (see section VII.C.iv. below on the European Court of Human Rights). No one may be deprived of his or her right to have a case examined in court by a judge with appropriate jurisdiction (Article 47(1)).

Some important principles of criminal procedure are stated. In the light of the abuses of criminal process which haunt Russia's history, it was clearly felt important to secure these guarantees at constitutional level. Article 47(2) gives a right to trial by jury, 'in cases provided for by federal law'. The Concluding and Transitional Provisions, provision 6, specifically preserved existing procedure until there was a federal law on jury trial. Amendments in July 1993 to the 1960 Code of Criminal Procedure allowed the possibility of jury trials, and they were introduced for crimes which would be tried at first instance at provincial level in five pilot areas from 1 November 1993, and a further four from 1 January 1994. A new Criminal Procedure Code was passed in 2001, coming into force July 2002. It details the procedure for jury trial in serious cases when the defendant (or one of multiple defendants) so chooses at the end of the preliminary investigation. Procedure is much as it was under the reform to the old Code, that is, a panel of 12 randomly chosen from the electoral register, sitting separately from the judge.[96]

Article 48(1) guarantees the right to qualified legal assistance, free of charge in cases specified by law. Fulfilment by advocates of this pro bono duty is a serious burden.[97] Article 48(2) ensures that anyone in custody pending a criminal trial has access to an advocate (defender). The Constitutional Court has been at pains to ensure that, where possible, criminal defendants have their own choice of representative, although it supported the view that only advocates are sufficiently qualified to act in pre-trial criminal proceedings.[98] The presumption of innocence is enshrined in Article 49, and in Article 50 is found the prohibition

---

[96] See SC Thaman, 'The resurrection of trial by jury in Russia' (1995) 31 *Stanford Journal of International Law* 61; SC Thaman, 'Jury Trial and Adversary Procedure in Russia: Reform of Soviet Inquisitorial Procedure or Democratic Window-Dressing?' in Smith and Sharlet, above n 30, at 141.

[97] E Huskey, 'The Bar's Triumph or Shame? The Founding of Chambers of Advocates in Putin's Russia' in Smith and Sharlet, above n 30, at 149.

[98] Burnham and Maggs, above n 9, at 157. See also generally P Jordan, 'Criminal Defence Advocacy under the 2001 Criminal Procedure Code' (2005) 53 *American Journal of Comparative Law* 157.

against double jeopardy and use of unlawfully obtained evidence, as well as a right to appeal against conviction, and to request a pardon or mitigation. The right against incriminating oneself, one's spouse or near relatives (as defined by federal law) is in Article 51. Article 52 asserts that the 'rights of victims of crimes and abuses of power shall be protected by law'. Victims shall have access to justice and compensation, and Article 53 commits the State to compensate for harm caused by acts or omissions of State agencies or officials. Article 54 prohibits the retrospective imposition of liability or worse consequences; retrospective reduction or elimination of liability is applied.

Political asylum is offered to foreigners and stateless persons in accordance with universally recognised norms of international law, and extradition to other States of persons persecuted for political beliefs or for activities which are not criminal within Russia is prohibited (Article 63).

iv. Qualified rights

Some rights have specified limitations. The right to life includes a second paragraph (Article 20(2)) which provides that

> the death penalty may until its abolition be established by federal law as punishment for especially grave crimes against life, so long as the accused has the right to have their case considered by a count with the participation of jurors.

This justified the Constitutional Court in 1999 declaring unconstitutional the exercise of the death penalty until jury trial was available throughout Russia. Ten years later it extended the moratorium indefinitely (see below, section VII.C.iv.).

Some rights may be overridden, but only in restricted circumstances. Any limitation on secrecy of correspondence is permitted only as a result of a judicial decision (Article 23(2)). There is a prohibition on the collection, retention, use and dissemination of information about private life without consent, and a duty on public bodies to allow each person 'the opportunity to familiarise themselves with documents and materials directly affecting their rights and freedoms unless provided otherwise by law' (Article 24). A dwelling place may be entered against the inhabitant's will only where allowed under the terms of a federal law or judicial decision (Article 25).

Articles 55 and 56 deal more generally with restrictions to rights. Article 55(1) makes clear that inclusion of a right in the Constitution 'must not be interpreted as a denial or diminution of other generally recognised rights and freedoms of man and citizen', and the following paragraph forbids laws which 'abolish or diminish rights and freedoms of man and citizen', although Article 55(3) does allow rights to be limited

> by a federal law [but] only to the extent necessary to defend the foundations of the constitutional system, morality, health, rights, and legal interests of other person and ensuring the defence of the country and security of the State.

That article does not specify any non-derogable rights, unlike Article 56, which deals with limitations of rights to 'ensure the safety of citizens and defence of the constitutional system' during the imposition of a state of emergency (extraordinary situation). The procedure for this must be established by a federal constitutional law, and rights which may not be limited are listed in Article 56(1).[99] The lack of similar restriction in Article 55 could mean

> that the legislature could even restrict the range of the article prohibiting torture, if you were able to convince its audience that the measure was required, for example, for the protection of the rights of other persons.[100]

However, a study of the Constitutional Court's interpretations of Article 55(3) allays this fear and shows that the Court has developed an appropriate principle of proportionality analogous to that in the European Court of Human Rights.[101]

v. Duties

Articles 57, 58 and 59 specify duties. Article 57 obliges individuals to pay legally-established taxes, although it prohibits retrospective imposition or increase. This did not stop the Constitutional Court in 2005 from interpreting the statute of limitations in a way which allowed a court to ignore the expiry of the limitation period when a taxpayer had engaged in 'wrongful actions'.[102] This ruling was related to the tax authorities

---

[99] Those in Arts 20, 21, 23(1), 24, 28, 34(1), 40(1), 46–54.

[100] Korkeakivi (1994), above n 84, at 242.

[101] P Krug, 'Assessing Legislative Restrictions on Constitutional Rights: the Russian Constitutional Court and Article 55(3)' (2003) 56 *Oklahoma Law Review* 677.

[102] Burnham and Trochev, above n 22, at 424.

suing YUKOS for back taxes from 2001, and was part of the politically-motivated actions against its former head, Mikhail Khordorkovsky.

Article 58 imposes a duty to protect the environment, and Article 59 obliges citizens to defend the Fatherland[103] and fulfil military service in accordance with federal law, although its final paragraph gives the right to 'alternative civilian service' to those whose 'convictions or religious belief' are incompatible with military service 'and also in other instances established by federal law'. There was extensive delay before a federal law on alternative service eventually went into force on 1 January 2004. In the meantime, some judges applied the constitutional article directly to allow a conscientious objector a defence to an accusation of evading conscription. Russia still has a conscript army, although there are frequent calls for complete professionalisation. The law on alternative service was deliberately designed to minimise take-up; the period served of up to three and half years is longer than that for military conscription.[104] The procedure is also open to abuse. The pressure group Moscow Committee of Soldiers' Mothers complained that 'Moscow military commissioner's offices demand up to $800 for accepting an application'.[105]

Article 64 closes this chapter of the Constitution with a declaration that its provisions are the foundations of an individual's legal status in Russia and cannot be amended except by the special procedure provided by the Constitution (see chapter three section III.G.). However, it is not the sum total of an individual's rights in Russia, as the European Convention on Human Rights is now directly applicable (see section VII.C.iv. below).

C. Rights enforcement

Russia has an interesting patchwork of methods for enforcement of rights. In fact, the range of different remedies is so broad that one English public lawyer surveying the 'impressive array'[106] shortly after the

---

[103] '*Otechestvo*'.

[104] PD Waisberg, 'The Duty to Serve and the Right to Choose: The Contested Nature of Alternative Civilian Service in the Russian Federation' (2004) 1 *The Journal of Power Institutions in Post-Soviet Societies*, available at <http://pipss.revues.org/index224.html>, accessed 24 October 2010.

[105] J Bernstein, 'Activist Claims Officials Ask Bribes for Alternative Service' (2004) 8(11) *Radio Free Europe/Radio Liberty Newsline*, 20 January.

[106] J McGregor, 'The Law on the Plenipotentiary for Human Rights' (1998) 4 *European Public Law* 188 at 189.

adoption of the law on the Plenipotentiary for Human Rights in 1997 suggested that Russia could be in danger of breaching her requirement under the two United Nations International Covenants to provide an 'effective remedy' in the case of breach:

> It would be ironical if this rich network [of channels for challenging abuse of citizen's rights] designed to guarantee the rights of the Russian people was adjudged inadequate because of a lack of clarity about how the different strands of the network related to each other.[107]

The main enforcement strands are the Procuracy, via appeal to a court, and complaint to the more recently established Plenipotentiary for Human Rights.

i. *The Procuracy*

During the Soviet period, the Procuracy's power of general supervision over legality was the only route by which breach of rights by State agencies acting ultra vires might be remedied, so this will be considered first.

The Russian Procuracy carries out a function established for the pre-Revolutionary Procuracy and, after a hiatus between 1917 and 1922, the Soviet Procuracy, of 'supervision of legality'. This is currently defined as the oversight of compliance with the rights and freedoms of man and citizen.[108] Activity of any State agency or official, or commercial and non-commercial organisations, is subject to review. The only exceptions are the President, the Government or the Legislature at federal level, over which the Constitutional Court has jurisdiction.

Procuratorial supervision works indirectly to protect rights. The Procuracy exercises wide powers of discovery, and may then send a 'protest' querying the legal basis of a suspect act or omission. The agency targeted either has to justify its position, or modify the act or activity under review to bring it into line with legal requirements. Individuals who feel that their rights have been breached would therefore bring this to the attention of their local procurator, and hope that their cause would be taken up. If the Procuracy decides that the case is an appropriate one for action, it will be pursued at no cost to the complainant.

---

[107] *Ibid* at 190.
[108] Law on the Procuracy of 1995 in Butler, above n 2, at 773.

Such was the power and prestige of the Procuracy during Soviet times that procuratorial protests were almost invariably 'satisfied'. The system worked quite well, with some limitations. For example, there was a certain irony that the only remedy for breach of pre-trial detention limits was complaint to the Procuracy, which was the body authorising the pre-trial detention in the first place.

This is not the place to rehearse the arguments about whether the current Russian Procuracy should be reformed to focus on its role as State prosecutor, as was put forward by the prestigious academic legal reformers in their Conception of Juridical Reform, approved by the Russian Supreme Soviet in October 1991.[109] To date the Procuracy has successfully resisted attempts to reduce its power and functions, and remains proud of its activities in the field of protecting rights, particularly those of the vulnerable or elderly who may not feel competent to go to court themselves to enforce their rights, or may not have the funds to do so.[110] The Procuracy makes a particularly valuable contribution in matters such as environmental protection, where the effect of a breach might impact a large group, although for each only to a limited extent.

ii. Citizens' appeals (administrative appeal)

The development of a remedy by which individuals might take claims to court to enforce their rights has been an important step in Russia, not only because it gives individuals more autonomy, but also as part of the movement to put courts at the heart of protection of human rights. It is also epitomises the contrast between the 'empty words' of constitutional rights in Soviet times and the current self-enforcing Constitution.

The provision of a remedy for citizens was envisaged by Article 58(2) of the 1977 USSR Constitution:

> Acts of officials committed in violation of law, in excess of authority, which infringe the rights of citizens may be appealed to court in the manner established by law.

However, 10 years passed before a USSR law was enacted to provide the procedure for such appeals; and when it did appear, they were restricted

---

[109] English translation in (1994) 30 *Statutes and Decisions* 9.
[110] See M Geistlinger, 'The Function of the Russian Procuracy on Administrative Procedure', in FJM Feldbrugge (ed), *Law in Transition: Law in Eastern Europe 52* (The Hague, Nijhoff, 2002) 3.

to appeals against unlawful actions of officials. This severely limited the law's application, as few important actions were taken by individual Soviet officials. Most resulted from collegial decisions by a committee, and the legislation did not cover those. This limitation was not accidental.

As *perestroika* progressed, a less restrictive approach to individual rights enforcement led to a replacement law in 1989, which covered acts of agencies of State administration (committees) as well as officials, although some practical limitations remained.

Independent Russia adopted her own law on 27 April 1993. The 'Law of the Russian Federation on appealing to a court actions and decisions violating the rights and freedoms of citizens' was a considerable improvement on its Soviet precursor. It covered decisions not to act, as well as ultra vires activities, and also extended to citizens serving in the Armed Forces,[111] a significant group as Russia has compulsory conscription for young males and a shocking tradition of poor treatment of conscripts. Two years later the law was amended, improving the procedure. Administrative appeals are comparatively cheap – costs are awarded against a losing agency – and there are powerful discovery provisions. Not only the action or decision, but also the basis on which it was taken may be appealed. Even better, once the applicant has established a prima facie abuse of a right, the burden of proof is transferred to the official or agency concerned to show that they behaved within their powers. A successful applicant may be awarded damages for losses, including 'moral harm' (intangible damage), and a losing official may be subject to sanction, including recommendation for dismissal. Although the wording of the law restricts it to 'citizens', its scope has been extended by the courts, by including into their procedure codes provisions to allow appeals by non-citizens and, perhaps of more practical importance, legal entities. (Article 46(2) of the Constitution gives a right of appeal to a court against 'Decisions and actions (or inaction) of State agencies, agencies of local self-government, social associations and officials . . .' without qualification as to who may bring appeals.)

As a result of the developments, the number of administrative appeals has soared. On the basis of figures cited by Peter Solomon, over the decade from 1990 to 2000, the increase was well over 30-fold.[112] In

---

[111] See PH Solomon Jr, 'Judicial Power in Russia: through the Prism of Administrative Justice' (2004) 38 *Law and Society Review* 549.

[112] *Ibid*, at 560 (from just under 5,000 in 1990, to approximately 160,000 in 2000).

military courts, the initial figure when the remedy first became available in 1993 was 3,500 complaints; this would 'explode to 190,500 in 2000' – 544 times as many. Such popularity is problematic. The court system has almost been overwhelmed by the number of cases. The proposal to establish separate administrative law courts, strongly supported by the Supreme Court Chairman, Viacheslav Lebedev, has not yet been implemented. Justice of the peace courts have shouldered some of the burden, but the district courts are nevertheless overstretched. However, in the light of the long-standing ambivalence towards law and use of legal remedies in Russia, it is a positive factor that people are willing to take their grievances to court, even when opinion polls suggest that they may not be confident about the justice of the outcome. Strategic use of the court system is an improvement on active avoidance of it.

iii. The Plenipotentiary for Human Rights – Ombudsman

Dissatisfaction with a court remedy need not be the end of the story for an individual in Russia seeking redress. The 1993 Constitution provided for a new institution in Russia to oversee the implementation of human rights. This is the Plenipotentiary for Human Rights (*Upolnomochennyi po Pravam Cheloveka*), also translated as Ombudsman.[113] In November 1991, the Russian Declaration of the Rights of Man and Citizen (Article 40) proposed that there should be such a Plenipotentiary, but that article was not incorporated into the RSFSR Constitution in April 1992 with the rest of the Declaration. A year and a half later, the 1993 Constitution listed in the jurisdiction of the State Duma, 'appointing to and relieving from office the plenipotentiary for human rights acting in accordance with a federal constitutional law' (Article 103(e)). Unfortunately, it took over three years for that law eventually to be passed in December 1996, coming into force in February 1997.[114]

Despite there being no guiding law, on 17 February 1994 the Duma appointed human rights activist and former political prisoner Sergei Kovalyov to the post of Plenipotentiary. Kovalyov had been an academic biologist at Moscow State University until 1969, when he was forced to resign as a result of his activities with the 'Initiative Group for

---

[113] His LiveJournal and Twitter sites use 'Ombudsman'; see 'ombudsman_rf_ru's journal', at <http://ombudsman-rf-ru.livejournal.com/> and 'ombudsmanrf', at <http://twitter.com/ombudsmanrf>, both accessed 22 August 2010.

[114] Butler, above n 2, at 111.

the Defence of Human Rights'.[115] He subsequently edited the *Chronicle of Current Events*, which lead to his conviction in 1974 for anti-Soviet agitation and propaganda. He served seven years' deprivation of freedom, followed by three years in internal exile. In newly independent Russia, Kovalyov became involved in party politics, as a founder member of 'Russia's Choice' in 1993. This did not preclude him from being appointed by President Yel'tsin as the first chairman of the newly-created Presidential Commission on Human Rights, established on 1 November 1993. Kovalyov held that post until he resigned on 23 January 1996. Before the Duma dismissed him as Plenipotentiary on 10 March 1995, Kovalyov held both positions simultaneously; and as there was no funding for the Plenipotentiary's office (there being yet no law), Yel'tsin's Administration picked up the costs of both.

A draft law on the Plenipotentiary for Human Rights (prepared by Kovalyov and his deputy Sirotkin in the Presidential Committee of Human Rights) successfully passed its first reading in the Duma on 21 July 1994, but was thrown out seven months later when Kovalyov himself was dismissed, having antagonised the nationalistic Duma with his scathing report on human rights abuses in the Russian incursion into Chechnya in December 1994. Without Kovalyov's input, the drafting process slowed, and factionalism within the Duma impeded attainment of the necessary qualified two-thirds majority needed to pass the federal constitutional law. After protracted negotiations and the efforts of a conciliation commission, the law finally succeeded in surmounting all the necessary stages. It had been a tortuous process: the law had

> been considered at least 10 times by two different Dumas. Twice, after making it through the thornbush of the Duma, it went on to the Council of the Federation and was rejected.[116]

Now that the Plenipotentiary Law was in place, the next task was appointing a suitable office holder. This also was a protracted affair, taking much longer than the 30 days specified in the Law. The Plenipotentiary

---

[115] B Bowring, 'Sergei Kovalyov: the First Russian Human Rights Ombudsman – and the Last?' in R Mullerson, M Fitzmaurice and M Andenas (eds), *Constitutional Reform and International Law in Central and Eastern Europe* (The Hague, Kluwer, 1998) 235.

[116] J Henderson, 'The Russian Ombudsman' (1998) 4 *European Public Law* 184 at 187, citing *Kommersant-Daily*, 26 December 1996, in (1996) 48 *Current Digest* 52.

would hold office for five years, renewable but not more than once in succession. Eventually, after trading favours between Duma factions, on 22 May 1998, Oleg Mironov, a leading member of the Russian Communist Party, was appointed Plenipotentiary. Despite comment from human rights activists on the irony of a communist acting as the guardian of rights, Mironov fulfilled his office well enough. When the Duma was again deadlocked about who should be his successor when Mironov's term of office expired on 22 June 2002, it was extended until a successor could be agreed. On 13 February 2004, former Russian Ambassador to the US and former *Yabloko* Duma Deputy Vladimir Lukin was appointed, and still holds office as of August 2010. There are subject-level plenipotentiaries; addresses of 55 are listed on the federal Plenipotentiary's website,[117] and there is also a specific Plenipotentiary for Children attached to the Presidential Administration.[118]

The Plenipotentiary has powers to review administrative actions and decisions by all agencies of State power except the Legislature (federal or subject-level), and can receive appeals from dissatisfied claimants who have tried other mechanisms for complaint. He is not meant to substitute for existing enforcement methods but works to make them more effective. As is usual for ombudsmen, he issues non-binding recommendations. He relies on publicity for impact; and as well as his annual report to the Duma, and other occasions on which he is invited to address one or other of the legislative chambers, he may publish individual decisions in order to draw attention to issues of concern.

The Plenipotentiary's website stated in January 2010 that since the post was set up in May 1998, he had received over 52,000 complaints and appeals from citizens:

> Most complaints (more than 40 per cent) are connected with criminal problems. About 12 per cent of appeals concern issues of civil law and housing legislation, 9 per cent – labour relations, 6 per cent – social and pension problems, around 5 per cent – breaches in the area of constitutional procedures and administrative law. Letters from soldiers, and also members of their families comprise just over 4 per cent, complaints from refugees and

---

[117] 'UPCh v sub'ektakh RF', at <http://www.ombudsman.gov.ru/index.php?option=com_content&view=article&id=22&Itemid=25>, accessed 22 August 2010.

[118] 'Upolnomochennyi pri Prezidente Rossiiskoi Federatsii po pravam rebenka', at <http://www.rfdeti.ru/>, accessed 22 August 2010.

forced migrants – about 2 per cent, 1 per cent of appeals are devoted to questions of international law, [and] 7 per cent – to other problems.[119]

Successes include restoration of free rail travel rights for servicemen, and pensions for war widows and veteran invalids. The Plenipotentiary's website highlights his concern to be solicitous of those who might otherwise have difficulty contesting their rights themselves, such as the elderly, infirm or those serving sentences of deprivation of freedom.

Apart from such direct aid and advice, a major aspect of the Plenipotentiary's role are his reports to the Legislature on the state of human rights in Russia. This has given the office holders a well-publicised platform from which they can point a finger at rights abusers. As one example, in March 2008 Plenipotentiary Lukin highlighted to the Federation Council his concerns that the level of violence in the prison colonies was 'approaching the level of torture'.[120] Lukin has been skilled to use the opportunities his office gives to keep rights prominently on the political agenda. As he said shortly after his appointment:

> Two things are capable of influencing the situation in this country: force and authority. It is true that the human rights ombudsman has practically no force at his disposal. But if he has authority, then he can achieve a lot.[121]

iv. European Court of Human Rights

Russia's decision to apply for membership of the Council of Europe in May 1992 might in the long term be as significant as the USSR's signature on the Helsinki Final Acts in 1 August 1975, which brought for the first time the possibility of external verification of Soviet compliance with international human rights agreements.[122] In both cases, what began as a political decision has invaluable longer-term ramifications for the development and enforcement of human rights.

---

[119] Percentages do not total 100%; given in 'Osnovnye napravleniia deiatel'nosti Upolnomochennogo po pravam cheloveka v Rossiiskoi Federatsii', at <http://www.ombudsman.gov.ru/institut/naprav.shtml>, accessed 4 January 2010 (author's translation).

[120] J Bernstein, 'Lukin Says Violence in Russian Prisons Borders on Torture' (2008) 12(55) *Radio Free Europe/Radio Liberty Newsline*, 20 March.

[121] R Coalson, 'End Note: Russia's Ombudsman Speaks Out' (2004) 8(116) *Radio Free Europe/Radio Liberty Newsline*, 21 June.

[122] See DC Thomas, *The Helsinki Effect: International Norms, Human Rights, and the Demise of Communism* (Princeton, NJ, Princeton University Press, 2001).

One immediate effect of Russia's application to the Council of Europe was the inclusion in the draft 1993 Constitution of the specific provision in Article 46(3) allowing applications by individuals to extra-territorial agencies for relief when all domestic remedies have been exhausted.[123] This counteracted the traditional autarky of the Russian judicial system, for the first time acknowledging the possibility of external redress for individuals and subsequently bringing the jurisprudence of the European Court of Human Rights directly into the Russian legal system.[124] This has far-reaching repercussions for the development of a coherent set of rights in Russia.[125]

Russia was admitted to the Council of Europe on 28 February 1996. Two years later, on 30 March 1998 she ratified the 1950 European Convention on Human Rights and Fundamental Freedoms ('the ECHR'), which went into force in Russia on 1 November 1998, along with some additional protocols and the Convention for the prevention of torture. (Since then she has acceded to some other Conventions. She has still not ratified Protocol 6 abolishing the death penalty, although on 19 November 2009 the Russian Constitutional Court indefinitely extended the moratorium on its application.)

Consequentially, individuals in Russian (including non-citizens) are able to petition the European Court of Human Rights in Strasbourg, provided that, first, domestic remedies have been exhausted; secondly, the application is filed within six months of that; and thirdly, the applicant can identify a right under the ECHR that has been breached since Russian's accession to the Convention.

The decision to include Russia in the Council of Europe 'club' impacted both parties. Russia hoped to gain increased influence in Europe, but had to be prepared for 'outside interference' in many spheres. Russia's conditions of membership were listed in a 1996 opinion of the Council of Europe's Parliamentary Assembly (PACE). They

[123] See A Trochev, 'All Appeals Lead to Strasbourg? Unpacking the Impact of the European Court of Human Rights on Russia' (2009) 17(2) *Demokratizatsiya* 145, text to fn 13.
[124] The USSR accepted the jurisdiction of the International Court of Justice in The Hague during the *perestroika* era; see T Schweisfurth, 'The Acceptance by the Soviet Union of the Compulsory Jurisdiction of the ICJ for Six Human Rights Conventions' (1990) 2 *European Journal of International Law* 110, but this did not give recourse to individuals.
[125] See JD Kahn, 'Russia's "Dictatorship of Law" and the European Court of Human Rights' (2004) 29 *Review of Central and East European Law* 1.

included 12 assurances and 25 commitments.[126] The assurances ranged over a number of important areas: a revision of civil and criminal procedure, a complete change in the administration of the penitentiary system, including 'demilitarisation' by its transfer from the Ministry of Interior to the Ministry of Justice in 1998; revision of laws on the Procuracy, the Plenipotentiary for Human Rights, protection of national minorities, freedom of assembly and freedom of religion; protection of the status of the *advokatura* (advocates); undertaking to prosecute for violations of human rights in Chechnya; allowing effective freedom of movement, improving conditions in criminal detention, repatriating ethnic Russians from The Baltics, and ratifying a number of important European conventions and protocols. The PACE has been monitoring Russia's progress in these areas. There have been major improvements to legislation, but the situation in Chechnya and continuing breach of the undertaking to eliminate the death penalty cause considerable friction. The PACE's Monitoring Committee has not minced its words in criticising the dire situation in Chechnya, and in 2000 it raised such serious concerns that for a period Russia's voting rights in the Parliamentary Assembly were suspended. The death penalty issue is politically fraught, as the majority of the general population and Duma deputies wish to retain it. The new Criminal Code passed in 1996 includes five crimes for which death by shooting is an optional punishment, but only if the convict is a male between 18 and 65 years of age. A de facto moratorium from August 1996 stopped the death penalty being carried out.[127] On 2 February 1999 the Russian Constitutional Court ruled that, based on constitutional Article 20, application of the death penalty would be unconstitutional until jury trial was available throughout Russia. This had been put back to 1 January 2010. On 19 November 2009, the Constitutional Court responded to a request by the Supreme Court for clarification as to whether the death penalty would then be reinstated, and ruled that the moratorium against its use would be indefinitely

---

[126] See PA Jordan, 'Russia's Accession to the Council of Europe and Compliance with European Human Rights Norms' (2003) 11 *Demokratizatsiya* 281; B Bowring, 'Russia's Accession to the Council of Europe and Human Rights: Compliance or Cross-Purposes?' (1997) 6 *European Human Rights Law Review* 628; B Bowring, 'Russia's Accession to the Council of Europe and Human Rights: Four Years On' (2000) 4 *European Human Rights Law Review* 362.

[127] See DD Barry and EJ Williams, 'Russia's Death Penalty Dilemmas' (1997) 8 *Criminal Law Forum* 231.

extended. This more or less fulfils Russia's promise to the Council of Europe without (yet) the much-delayed formal ratification by the Duma of Protocol 6 of the ECHR to abolish the death penalty in peacetime.

For the Council of Europe, the decision to admit Russia (and other Eastern European States) was fraught with risk. Some feared that the inclusion of countries with poor human rights records would dilute the effect of the Council, whose powers are largely advisory and whose decisions are made by consensus. However, rather than rejecting Russia's application, the Council of Europe decided it was better to have her within the fold subject to improving influences and monitoring, such as the Report highlighted above in section VI.C. which publicised pressure on judges. What may not have been fully appreciated at the time was the enormous impact on the caseload of the Court in Strasbourg which Russia would bring.

Slowness in procedure at Strasbourg, and its unfamiliarity to Russians and their lawyers, meant that the deluge began as a trickle. Before June 2001, no case from Russia passed the initial admissibility test. But the numbers of applications grew, and increasingly they surmounted the admissibility hurdle. The first substantive decision was given on 7 May 2002, when Russia lost in a case brought by a pensioner denied compensation for injuries suffered whilst cleaning up after the Chernobyl nuclear disaster. Alexei Trochev calculates that

> Since then, the number of judgments has increased exponentially, from just 2 judgments in 2002 to 244 in 2008. By May 1, 2009, there were a total of 745 judgments involving Russia as a defendant.[128]

The number of applications continued to grow. Bill Bowring noted that 'By November 2004 there were more than 70,000 cases pending',[129] although by February 2009 Anatoly Kovner, the Russian judge at the European Court of Human Rights, could report to Russian Constitutional Court judges that

> the number of complaints from Russians has been decreasing. 'The highest number of complaints, or 12,200, came in 2006. In 2007, 11,700 complaints came from Russia. In 2008, some 10,500 complaints came from Russia' . . .

---

[128] Trochev, above n 122, at text to fn 25.
[129] B Bowring, 'Russia in a Common European Legal Space. Developing Effective Remedies for the Violations of Rights by Public Bodies: Compliance with the European Convention on Human Rights' in K Hober (ed), *The Uppsala Yearbook of East European Law 2004* (London, Wildy, Simmonds & Hill, 2005) 89.

which accounted for 26% of the total number. Of these, Russia won nine cases against complaints, partially won five cases, and 30 cases were dropped due to amicable agreements.[130]

The impact on the Court of the deluge of applications has been little short of catastrophic, and it was exacerbated by Russia's longstanding refusal up until February 2010 to ratify of Protocol 14, which allows an expedited procedure for assessing admissibility. The backlog of cases to be assessed – 100,000 in 2008 – led to unconscionable delays, although, as Kahn pointed out, increasingly applications are referred to the Russian Government for comment before the admissibility hearing, and this 'frequently' leads to measures to ameliorate the potential applicant's situation.[131] In any event, applications will speed up now that President Medvedev has signed the law (on 4 February 2010) which will allow Protocol 14 to be implemented.

One major advantage of the European Court of Human Rights, compared with the Russian domestic courts, is its ability to enforce its judgments when they are eventually given. Indeed, almost half of the cases to the Court from Russia involve complaints about failure to implement Russian domestic court decisions. The net result is, as Trochev wryly observes, that the Strasbourg Court 'is the most popular court in Russia today'.[132] He tracks the impressively speedy growth in Russia of public recognition of the right to take a case to Strasbourg. In 2001, a reputable public opinion survey

> reported that only 2–3 per cent of Russians recognized the possibility of protecting their rights in the [European Court of Human Rights]. Only a year and a half later, the same agency reported that 19 per cent of Russians reported that they were prepared to complain to the Strasbourg court.[133]

By August 2008, a nationwide poll by the Public Opinion Foundation showed that 61 per cent of its respondents knew about the possibility, and 29 per cent said they would take a case to the European Court of Human Rights; this is 'despite the fact that very few Russians actually know anything about the functioning of the Strasbourg-based court'.[134]

---

[130] 'Russian Citizens Send Greatest Number of Complaints to Strasbourg Court', Interfax-AVN report, 27 February 2009, available via Westlaw.
[131] Kahn, above n 124, at 5.
[132] Trochev, above n 122, at 145.
[133] *Ibid*, text to fn 17.
[134] *Ibid*.

The significance of Russia's dealings with the Strasbourg Court go beyond satisfaction for a small though increasing number of litigants. Russia's accession to the Convention has brought the full panoply of the Court's jurisprudence directly into the Russian courts. Judges are supplied with Russian translations of the Court's findings, and increasingly citation is made of Convention rights by Russian courts, even if as yet in a sporadic and unsophisticated manner.[135] It is to the Russian Government's credit that it has paid any damages awarded against it by the European Court of Human Rights and 'the most powerful human rights system currently in existence in the world today'[136] is beginning to impact Russian behaviour in the legal sphere.

VIII. CONCLUSION

The content of this chapter gives cause for both optimism and pessimism about Russian courts. Clearly they are incomparably more effective in protecting rights than Soviet courts, and the law they enforce compares well by international standards. Court procedures can be timely and effective. Constitutionality and legality have assumed such importance that courts even battle over which has jurisdiction.

But some traditional elements remain. Reliance on 'contacts' and informal networks undermine the ideal of impartiality: 'The first question a client asks is "Do you know the judge? Do you have access to the judge?"'[137] Nevertheless, despite strong expressions of mistrust in opinion polls, in reality Russians (individuals and companies) make use of courts as one of their strategies for dealing with neighbours or business partners. And familiarity with courts (prior use) tends to encourage further use, rather than to discourage it.[138] Kathryn Hendley discusses this paradox and concludes that may be inappropriate to expect rule of law from a 'Western' perspective in Russia, when 'for decades, if not centuries'

---

[135] See A Burkov, *The Impact of the European Convention on Human Rights on Russian Law* (Stuttgart, ibidem-Verlag, 2007).

[136] Kahn, above n 124, at 2.

[137] D Holiner, barrister and *advokat*, at the Bar Human Rights Committee and the EU-Russia Centre meeting, London, 8 February 2010; see report, Karp, above n 54, at 3.

[138] K Hendley, 'Telephone Law and the Rule of Law: the Russian Case' (2009) *Hague Journal on the Rule of Law* 241.

Russians have coexisted with telephone law and have a strategic awareness of which cases might be subject to influence and which not. As she puts it, 'Russians are actually savvy consumers. They know when to bring a case and when to stay away'.[139] Their legally-trained President is not content with this; he wants uniformly respected courts as a requirement for economic investment and growth, and takes a personal interest in improving transparency and accessibility.[140] If he has his way, and as a new generation of lawyers becomes familiar with the jurisprudence of the Strasbourg Court, Russia will no longer be a State isolated from Europe by geography (as in pre-Revolutionary times) or ideology (as during the Soviet era), and she may attain the aspiration to be a rule-of-law State, claimed in the first article of her Constitution.

FURTHER READING

B Bowring, 'Russia and Human Rights: Incompatible Opposites?' (2009) 1 *Göttingen Journal of International Law* 257.

W Burnham and A Trochev, 'Russia's war between the courts: the struggle over the jurisdictional boundary between the Constitutional Court and regular courts' (2007) 55 *American Journal of Comparative Law* 381.

J Henderson, 'The Constitutional Court of the Russian Federation: the Establishment and Evolution of Constitutional Supervision in Russia' (2008) 3 *Journal of Comparative Law* 138.

K Hendley, 'Remaking an institution: the transition on Russia from State *Arbitrazh* to *Arbitrazh* Courts' (1998) 46 *American Journal of Comparative Law* 93.

P Jordan, 'Russia's accession to the Council of Europe and compliance with European human rights norms' (2003) 11(2) *Demokratizatsiya* 281.

A Ledeneva, 'Telephone Justice in Russia' (2008) 24 *Post-Soviet Affairs* 324.

O Schwartz, 'The creation of an independent judiciary and the changing nature of courts and the courtroom' in WA Pridemore (ed), *Ruling Russia: law, crime and justice in a changing society* (Lanham MD, Rowman & Littlefield, 2005).

P Solomon, 'The new Justices of the Peace in the Russian Federation' (2003) 11 *Demokratizatsiya* 381.

---

[139] *Ibid* at 261.
[140] P Solomon, 'Can President Medvedev Fix the Courts in Russia? The First Year' in *Russian Analytical Digest*, above n 71, at 3.

——, 'Judicial Power in Russia: through the prism of administrative justice' (2004) 38 *Law and Society Review* 549.

——, 'Informal practices in Russian justice: probing the limits of post-Soviet reform' in F Feldbrugge (ed), *Russia, Europe, and the Rule of Law* (Leiden, Nijhoff, 2007) 79.

A Trochev, *Judging Russia: Constitutional Court in Russian Politics, 1990–2006* (Cambridge, Cambridge University Press, 2008).

——, 'All Appeals Lead to Strasbourg? Unpacking the Impact of the European Court of Human Rights on Russia' (2009) 17 *Democratizatsiya* 145.

7

Conclusion

❧✦❧

N OW IS THE time to take a step back and consider the Russian Constitution in the bigger context of Russia's development. Overall, the exploration in this book has revealed positive and negative features of the constitutional framework in practice.

Taking first the negative – some would say realistic – view, powers assigned to the branches of State by the Constitution are not well balanced, and the formal trappings of a constitutional structure have not obliterated cultural practices which undermine it. The Executive wields extensive powers and there are insufficient effective mechanisms for holding it to account. Neither does the Russian media 'perform a "watchdog" role, so essential to the working of markets and democracy'.[1] The Federal Assembly does not work well as either a legislative or a representative agency. It seems that a significant number of its members give more attention to furthering their own business ends than proper scrutiny of draft legislation.[2] Democratic representation is sabotaged by the lack of a functioning multi-party system and by widespread use of dirty tricks during elections. Perhaps most worryingly, surveys of public opinion indicate that the majority of people are content to be led by a strong ruler and do not see any point to the Federal Assembly's existence in its current form.[3] There is also a widespread belief that justice can be bought or that judges are subject to inappropriate pressure – from

[1] AV Ledeneva, *How Russia Really Works: The Informal Practices that Shaped Post-Soviet Politics and Business* (Ithaca, NY, Cornell University Press, 2006) 74.
[2] S Whitmore, 'Parliamentary Oversight in Putin's Neo-patrimonial State. Watchdogs or Show-dogs?' (2010) 62(6) *Europe-Asia Studies* 99 at 1018.
[3] See A Zakharov, 'The Russian Parliament and Vladimir Putin's Presidency' in K Malfleit and R Laenen (eds), *Elusive Russia. Current Developments in Russian State Identity under President Putin* (Leuven, Leuven University Press, 2007) 73 at 82.

litigants with deep purses, members of the Executive or Presidential Administration, or from higher in the judicial hierarchy itself.

Almost as soon as the Constitution was adopted, it began to be undermined:

> During the nineties, President Yeltsin tried to build his relations with the regions via a system of exclusivity, the development of political favouritism and personal bargaining. Informal institutions and rules of the game began to either replace the new formal institutions or to fill the existing institutional vacuum.[4]

Yel'tsin's successor Putin carried on this trend with the development of a number of institutions, discussed in chapter four, which were not directly contemplated in the Constitution (labelled, accordingly, 'para-constitutional' by Richard Sakwa).[5] The federal balance, already imprecisely defined in the Constitution, has been shifted towards central control through the Presidential Federal Representatives and other para-constitutional innovations, marginalising the Constitution.

However, it would be inappropriate to judge the development of Russia's constitutionalism by North-American or northern European standards. Political scientists writing about Russia categorise it as a transition State, although they do not always agree on exactly from what or to what it is transiting.[6] Certainly the Soviet era has been analysed as almost the ultimate in a totalitarian State,[7] and the current Constitution undoubtedly takes Russia a long way from that. Sarah Whitmore cogently argues that conceptualising the Russian State as neopatrimonial, 'where formal liberal democratic institutions are infused with informal, patrimonial practices such as clientelism, patronage and rent-seeking',[8] is helpful to an understanding of the complex cross-currents that impact Russian State behaviour, although

---

[4] I Busygina, 'Federalism in Russia: outcomes of the decade 1993-2003 and the newest developments' in K Malfleit and R Laenen (eds), *Elusive Russia. Current Developments in Russian State Identity under President Putin* (Leuven, Leuven University Press, 2007) 52 at 55.

[5] R Sakwa, *Russian Politics and Society*, 4th edn (Abingdon, Routledge, 2008) 341.

[6] *Ibid* at 451.

[7] FJM Feldbrugge, *Russian Law: the End of the Soviet System* (Dordrecht, Nijhoff, 1993) at 3.

[8] Whitmore, above n 2, at 99.

empirical work in the post-Soviet space suggests that the relationship [between formal institutions and informal practices] is a complex one that will not easily lend itself to elegant theorising.[9]

Russia's legal nihilism is legendary and her folk proverbs disparaging courts and judges well-known.[10] However, care must be taken to separate rhetoric from current reality. In her case study on use of law, or otherwise, in contemporary Russia, Kathryn Hendley found evidence that despite expressing distrust of courts, her informants felt that their cases would be too trivial to evoke corruption, and consequently they did contemplate litigation, even if as a last resort. Further, Hendley found that 'Prior experience with the courts seemed to embolden my respondents to go down that road again'.[11] A similar dissonance between expressed negative opinion and actual usage (in this case of the *arbitrazh* courts by small businesses) was recorded by Timothy Frye.[12] There is clear inconsistency. People say that they avoid courts – 'the media drumbeat about difficulties of using the courts in Russia has taken its toll'[13] – but in fact they increasingly make use of them in their personal or business strategies.

Even the subversion of law, which Ledeneva so eloquently catalogues, brings its use to the fore:

> Somewhat paradoxically, the manipulative use of the law (both in terms of violating its spirit and its letter) in the organisation of election campaigns makes the law central to the activities of PR firms and results in a special role for lawyers.[14]

This is not quite the rule of law advocated by so-called mature democracies, but neither is it absolute legal nihilism. Ironically, law and legal knowledge become valuable, even when used transgressively.

---

[9] *Ibid* at 1003.

[10] Some examples in M Suhara, 'Corruption in Russia: A Historical Perspective' in T Hayashi (ed), *Democracy and Market Economics in Central and Eastern Europe: Are New Institutions Being Consolidated?* (Hokkaido, Slavic Research Centre, 2004) 383 at 388, available at <src-h.slav.hokudai.ac.jp/sympo/03september/pdf/M_Suhara. pdf>, accessed 28 August 2010.

[11] K Hendley, 'Resolving Problems Among Neighbors in Post-Soviet Russia: Uncovering the Law of the *Pod''ezd*' (2009) 1097 *University of Wisconsin Legal Studies Research Paper Series* 1 at 28.

[12] T Frye, 'The Two Faces of Russian Courts: Evidence from a Survey of Company Managers' (2002) 11(1-2) *East European Constitutional Review* 125.

[13] Hendley, above n 11, at 29.

[14] Ledeneva, above n 1, at 51.

Taking a more straightforwardly positive perspective, the Constitution, although not flawless as a legal document, has shown itself to be work-able and sufficiently effective. As the first 'real' Constitution in post-Imperial Russia, it has encouraged the formal development of the accoutrements necessary for the modern democratic, rule-of-law State that Russia claims to be. The Constitutional Court in particular has, over its couple of decades' existence, become an influential factor in Russia's legal and political life. Its interpretations and applications of the Constitution have strengthened the Constitution's role; in contrast to Soviet Constitutions, the 1993 Constitution has become a valuable ref-erence point, utilised both by figures in public life and members of the general population. Even if one might cynically conclude that some public figures treat respect for the Constitution as something of a game, they at least seem impelled to pay lip service to that game's rules.

Practical application of the Constitution has gone hand-in-hand with an enhanced roles for courts, for example in overseeing pre-trial crimi-nal process and resolving appeals against abuses of rights. In respect to this, the impact of Russia's membership of the Council of Europe and accession to the ECHR cannot be over-emphasised. As with the USSR signing the Helsinki Final Act in 1975, what may have started off as political vanity triggered profound changes. In the case of the Helsinki Final Act, this was monitoring of human rights; in the case of the ECHR, it is that Convention jurisprudence is now an integral part of the Russian legal system and international standards are being increas-ingly internalised (see chapter six).

There are very positive side-effects of these developments. Across Russia, a new generation of bright law students is growing up with excellent knowledge of Public International Law, International Human Rights Law and the ECHR. Their interest and expertise in rights law is evidenced by an increase in both the number and quality of teams tak-ing part in prestigious international mooting competitions, such as the Philip C Jessup International Law Moot Court Competition. Professor Bill Bowing has now marked Memorials and acted as a judge in the Competition's quarter and semi-finals in Moscow on five occasions. He comes away each year a renewed optimist as regards the future of the rule of law in Russia.[15]

---

[15] Personal correspondence from B Bowing, 23 August 2010. He has observed that the number of Russian university law school teams taking part in the Russian

Looking back on Russia's history, there is a strong tradition of the rulers feeling themselves above the law, and very little tradition of the State working under law. For individual citizens, interpersonal relationships are valued more highly than conformity to imposed legal rules. However, Russia is no longer the isolated State that she has been for much of her history, and there is cause to hope that the generational change (that is even seen in Medvedev as President) will allow the Constitution to embed as a respected framework for democratic Russia, upholding rule of law and respect for human rights in the largest State on Earth.

FURTHER READING

B Bowring, 'Human Rights in Russia: Discourse on Emancipation or Only a Mirage?' in I Pogany (ed), *Human Rights in Eastern* (Aldershot, Edward Elgar, 1995) 87.

K Hendley, 'Telephone Law and the Rule of Law: the Russian Case' (2009) *Hague Journal on the Rule of Law* 241.

———, 'Resolving Problems Among Neighbors in Post-Soviet Russia: Uncovering the Law of the *Pod"ezd*' (2009) 1097 *University of Wisconsin Legal Studies Research Paper Series*, available at <http://ssrn.com/abstract=1479558>, accessed 26 August 2010.

J Kahn, 'Vladimir Putin and the Rule of Law in Russia' (2008) 36(3) *Georgia Journal of International and Comparative Law* 511.

AV Ledeneva, *How Russia Really Works: The Informal Practices that Shaped Post-Soviet Politics and Business* (Ithaca, NY, Cornell University Press, 2006).

R Sakwa, *Russian Politics and Society*, 4th edn (Abingdon, Routledge, 2008).

round has grown in six years from 12 to 54, from Kaliningrad to Vladivostock. In April 2010, seven Russian teams travelled to Washington DC for the finals. Russian teams are some of the best of 500 law school teams in 80 competing countries, and the quality of their legal drafting and oral argument, all in English, is impressive.

Index